# Writing Through Reading

Stephen C. Lewis  /  M. Cecile Forte
*Suffolk County Community College*

Prentice-Hall, Inc./Englewood Cliffs, New Jersey 07632

*Library of Congress Cataloging in Publication Data*

LEWIS, STEPHEN C.
  Writing through reading.

  1. English language—Rhetoric.  2. College
readers.  I. Forte, M. Cecile, joint author.  II. Title.
PE1417.L49    808'.0427        82-7599
ISBN  0-13-971630-0             AACR2

© 1983 by Prentice-Hall, Inc., Englewood Cliffs, N.J. 07632

All rights reserved. No part of this book
may be reproduced in any form or
by any means without permission in writing
from the publisher.

Printed in the United States of America

10  9  8  7  6  5  4  3  2  1

ISBN 0-13-971630-0

Manufacturing buyer: *Harry P. Baisley*
Interior design: *Marybeth Brande*
Cover design: *Wanda Lubelska*

PRENTICE-HALL INTERNATIONAL, INC., *London*
PRENTICE-HALL OF AUSTRALIA PTY. LIMITED, *Sydney*
PRENTICE-HALL CANADA INC., *Toronto*
PRENTICE-HALL OF INDIA PRIVATE LIMITED, *New Delhi*
PRENTICE-HALL OF JAPAN, INC., *Tokyo*
PRENTICE-HALL OF SOUTHEAST ASIA PTE. LTD., *Singapore*
WHITEHALL BOOKS LIMITED, WELLINGTON, *New Zealand*

# Acknowledgments

PAGE 6: *Up from Slavery*, Booker T. Washington, Doubleday & Company Inc.
PAGE 6: *Grapes of Wrath*, John Steinbeck, 1939, The Viking Press
PAGE 7: From *Two Weeks in Another Town*, Irwin Shaw, Random House, Inc.
PAGE 7: *Patterns of Culture*, Ruth Benedict. Copyright © 1934 by Ruth Benedict. Copyright renewed 1962 by Ruth Valentine. Reprinted by permission of the publisher, Houghton Mifflin Company.
PAGE 30: Houghton Mifflin Company. Reprinted by permission from the *American Heritage Dictionary of the English Language, New College Edition.*
PAGE 61: *Interpretation of Reading Materials in the Social Studies* (GED), 1973, Richard Miner, M.A., reprinted by permission of Cambridge Book Company.
PAGES 61–62: Reprinted with the permission of the publisher from *Gates-Peardon Reading Exercises, Advanced Level SA.* (New York: Teachers College Press, copyright © 1963 by Teachers College, Columbia University.) All rights reserved.
PAGES 63–64: From *nigger* by Dick Gregory, with Robert Lipsyte. Copyright, ©, 1964 by Dick Gregory Enterprises, Inc. Reprinted by permission of the publisher, E. P. Dutton.

*Acknowledgments continue on pages 277–278, which constitutes an extension of the copyright page.*

For Mrs. Myrtle Gordon Forte

# Contents

Preface  ix

## 1  Thinking Skills  1
PREVIEW  1     DISTINGUISHING FACT FROM OPINION  2     MAKING INFERENCES AND DRAWING CONCLUSIONS  5     EXERCISE  9     DETECTING PERSUASIVE LANGUAGE  10     EXERCISE  12     INDUCTIVE AND DEDUCTIVE REASONING  14     EXERCISE  17     RECOGNIZING PURPOSE  19     THINKING SKILLS CHECKLIST  21

## 2  Vocabulary Building  23
PREVIEW  23     IMPROVING READING VOCABULARY  25     READING EXERCISE  32     IMPROVING WRITTEN VOCABULARY  33     WRITING EXERCISE  37

## 3  Words in Context  43
PREVIEW  43     USING CONTEXT  44     CONTEXT CLUES  46     READING EXERCISE  48     WRITING WORDS IN CONTEXT  51     WRITING EXERCISE  55

v

## 4 Denotation and Connotation  59
PREVIEW  59     READING FOR DENOTATIVE AND CONNOTATIVE MEANING  60     READING EXERCISE  64     WRITING FOR DENOTATIVE AND CONNOTATIVE MEANING  66
    WRITING EXERCISE  70

## 5 Sentence Sense  76
PREVIEW  76     READING FOR SENSE  77
    READING EXERCISE  82     WRITING FOR SENSE  84
    WRITING EXERCISE  92

## 6 The Simple Sentence  99
PREVIEW  99     READING SENTENCES  100
    READING EXERCISE  106     WRITING YOUR OWN SENTENCES  109
    WRITING EXERCISE  112

## 7 The More Complicated Sentence  116
PREVIEW  116     READING MORE COMPLICATED SENTENCES  117
    READING EXERCISE  123     COMPOSING MORE COMPLICATED SENTENCES  126     WRITING EXERCISE  131

## 8 Main Idea and Topic Sentences  135
PREVIEW  135     DETERMINING MAIN IDEAS  136
    READING EXERCISE  141     COMPOSING TOPIC SENTENCES  145
    WRITING EXERCISE  149

## 9 Paragraph Patterns  152
PREVIEW  152     IDENTIFYING PARAGRAPH PATTERNS  153
    READING EXERCISE  161     ARRANGING DETAILS IN YOUR PARAGRAPHS  165     WRITING EXERCISE  169

## 10 Paragraph Development  173
PREVIEW  173     METHODS OF DEVELOPMENT  174
    READING EXERCISE  182     DEVELOPING YOUR PARAGRAPHS  185
    WRITING EXERCISE  197

## 11 Paragraph Coherence 204
PREVIEW 204   READING FOR COHERENCE 205   READING EXERCISE 209   WRITING COHERENT PARAGRAPHS 212   WRITING EXERCISE 217

## 12 The Essay 220
PREVIEW 220   READING ESSAYS 221   READING EXERCISE 225   WRITING ESSAYS 229   WRITING EXERCISE 235

## Appendix A: Study Skills 241
PREVIEW 241   A METHOD FOR READING AND STUDYING TEXTBOOKS 242   A METHOD FOR TAKING NOTES 244   PREPARING FOR AND TAKING TESTS 245

## Appendix B: Punctuation and Usage 249
PREVIEW 249   PUNCTUATION 250   CAPITALIZATION 254   SUBJECT-VERB AGREEMENT 255   PROBLEM AREAS 256   PRONOUN REFERENCE 261   SENTENCE ERRORS 263   MODIFIERS 265   PUNCTUATION AND USAGE EXERCISE 268

## Index 273

# Preface

*Writing Through Reading* reflects the growing awareness that writing and reading are closely related cognitive processes. Language acquisition and use feed each other through the cumulative experiences each individual has with his or her language, so it makes sense to teach writing skills by demonstrating how they relate to reading.

The more proficient an individual becomes as a reader, the better able he or she will be to write. This book identifies language elements that must be recognized to comprehend reading material and then demonstrates how these elements can be used in effective writing.

The organization of *Writing Through Reading* proceeds from the smaller to the larger, from words to essays. This organization parallels language acquisition, from the awareness that certain spoken cues indicate particular words, to the understanding that these words can be patterned into meaningful statements in sentences, paragraphs, and essays. Each of these levels of communication is presented first as a reading experience and then as a writing opportunity.

Each chapter introduces a reading skill, such as identification of the main idea in paragraphs, and then through a series of exercises reinforces mastery of that skill. The chapter continues by using the reading skill as a basis for introducing a similar writing skill. For example, identification of the main idea in reading leads to formulation of a topic sentence in writing. The chapters conclude with writing exercises that have the student produce his or her own versions of the model reading materials, with particular emphasis upon the skill highlighted in the chapter.

It is not sufficient, however, to show that writing is an imitation or reversal of reading. It is equally important to underscore the importance of reasoning skills in the communication process and to emphasize the patterns that underlie both reading and writing. Therefore, *Writing Through Reading* focuses on the necessary analytical skills of good reading and, consequently, of effective writing. Reading comprehension is tied to these analytical skills, and quite clearly it is impossible to write well without knowing what one wants to say as well as how one wants to say it.

Although this text is designed for writing courses, it can be used in teaching situations in which either reading or writing is the main subject. Current research indicates that instruction in one skill improves performance in the other. Moreover, the instructor need not have special preparation in both areas to use the text successfully.

We are indebted to many people without whose help, encouragement, and cooperation this book would not have been possible. Among our colleagues, we would like to thank those who offered suggestions and additions to our material at such professional conferences as the Northeast Regional Conference on English in the Two-Year College, the International Reading Association, New York State Reading Association, Nassau Reading Council, NCTE, CCCC; Lawrence Epstein, Lowell Kleiman, Millie Murphy, and Louise D. Robbins at Suffolk Community College; Norwell Therien and William Oliver, whose initial enthusiasm for the idea brought us together with Prentice-Hall; Joyce Perkins, our production editor whose good judgment and good humor smoothed the final stages of preparation; Frank W. Smith, Executive Director, Project NOAH, Hofstra University, who gave us the opportunity to develop the manuscript in a real teaching situation; most particularly, Sharon Marshall, Katherine Morrisette, and Louise Schmitt, who worked tirelessly typing the manuscript and who endured countless changes, corrections, and requests; and Linda Spotkov, whose additional secretarial help was invaluable.

S.C.L.

M.C.F.

# 1
# Thinking Skills

PREVIEW

Your ability to think is important to your general survival and to your academic success. In developing good reading and writing skills, you need to develop an active, questioning mind. The decisions you make about the things you read and write are always directly related to how you think. More precisely, what you read and write are expressions of others' thoughts (reading) and your own (writing).

This chapter presents some of the thinking skills you can sharpen to improve your ability to read and to express your thoughts in writing. It provides examples of each skill for improved reading and writing, and should help you master the other reading and writing skills discussed in this book.

**Key Terms**

**Fact.**  Something known to exist or to have happened.
**Opinion.**  Something believed to be true.
**Inference/conclusion.**  That which is concluded on the basis of information known, observed, or suggested.
**Persuasive language.**  Language used to influence or sway someone's thinking.
**Inductive reasoning.**  A thinking pattern that goes from specific information to a general conclusion.
**Deductive reasoning.**  A thinking pattern that goes from a general conclusion to specific information.

**Author's purpose.** The reason for, and the intended effect of, a piece of written communication.

Every day of your life, you use your ability to think and to reason. An active, questioning mind enables you to make decisions which affect every part of your life. These decisions involve distinguishing between safety and danger, choosing a job or career, selecting friends and associates, purchasing goods and services, determining your life style, and a host of other judgments that touch you personally.

The ability to think and reason is well developed in most people because it is exercised every day, many times each day. Whether a decision is simple or complex, we use the same skill in making a choice. Whether we are learning to avoid hot objects or to work mathematical equations, we use our reason. Reasoning is a process made up of distinct skills: distinguishing fact from opinion, making inferences and drawing conclusions, detecting persuasive language, and using inductive and deductive processes. Strengthening these skills improves our general reasoning ability. It also improves our ability to analyze and understand what we read and to express ourselves verbally and in writing. So we will look first at thinking, and then at reading and writing as expressions of thought in the form of written language. Both, as we will see, depend upon thinking skills.

## DISTINGUISHING FACT FROM OPINION

One important thinking skill is the ability to distinguish between fact and opinion. A *fact* is something known to exist or to have happened. A fact is something that can be proved, verified, or tested. An *opinion* is something that is believed to be true. Because opinions are beliefs, they cannot be proved, verified, or tested. Opinions can vary from one person to another; facts cannot. Here are some examples of each.

**Facts**

There are thirty days in the month of September.
Martin Luther King, Jr. was a civil rights leader who believed in nonviolence.
Presidential inaugurations in the United States always occur on January 20.
Physicians, dentists, surgeons, veterinarians, osteopaths, and chiropractors are all doctors.
Thomas Edison invented the lightbulb.
Water boils at 212°F and 100°C.

**Opinions**

September is the most beautiful month of the year.
Martin Luther King, Jr., was the best civil rights leader of his time.

Presidential inaugurations are costly and boring.
Chiropractors are better doctors than osteopaths.
Thomas Edison was a great man.
A watched pot never boils.

All the fact statements above can be proved with such sources as calendars, history books, and dictionaries. The opinion statements cannot be verified by appealing to authoritative sources. Instead, such statements can only be characterized as the beliefs or judgments of some people. Words like "most," "best," "costly," and "great," which appear in the opinion sentences, are judgmental, not factual. Even though many people may believe these statements to be true, they remain opinions, since they cannot be proved or tested.

Read the following two paragraphs. For each numbered sentence, indicate whether it is a statement of fact or opinion by placing F or O on the numbered lines following each paragraph.

The name telephone was adopted by the inventor Alexander Graham Bell in 1876.(1) The name literally means sound at a distance.(2) This communications instrument has improved the lives of everyone who uses it.(3) Verbal communication has become more convenient.(4) It has also become so automated that the caller need not contact a central operator when making every call.(5) Instead the person making certain calls can be placed in direct communication with the party dialed.(6) In addition to being a general means of communication, the telephone can be used for specific services like banking and paying bills.(7) The invention of the telephone is one example of the superiority of machine over man.(8)

1._____   5._____
2._____   6._____
3._____   7._____
4._____   8._____

Sentences 1, 2, 5, 6, and 7 are all statements of fact. They can be verified in an unabridged dictionary, an encyclopedia, or a book on the history of the telephone. Sentences 3, 4, and 8 are opinion statements. It is not certain, nor can it be proved, that the telephone changes the life of every person who uses it. Nor can we verify the idea that verbal communication is made more convenient by using the telephone. Most people might believe this is so, but it cannot be verified. Similarly, the word "superiority" can be interpreted in a number of ways; therefore, the sentence is an opinion.

"Disco," a term used to describe both a particular type of club and the music played there, became popular in the 1970's.(1) Coined from the French word *discothèque,* discos usually feature DJs who play the latest records and dancers who perform disco dance steps.(2) These intricate dances are difficult to learn.(3) All the dancers spend hours perfecting their steps and compete in contests for recognition as the best.(4) The music is loud in clubs like these, but because dancing is the focus, no one cares.(5) If all this sounds appealing, you may be catching "disco fever."(6)

1._____  4._____

2._____  5._____

3._____  6._____

Sentences 1 and 2 are statements of fact. Periodical articles or books written about social customs of the 1970s provide information to verify these statements. Sentences 3, 4, 5, and 6 are opinion statements. Words like "difficult" and "loud" and generalities like "all" and "no one" are judgmental, not factual. They provide no basis for proof and are therefore opinions.

Although it is important to differentiate between statements of fact and of opinion, you should not favor one over the other. Facts are necessary in those instances where, as reader or writer, you want to verify or test information. But opinions can also be useful. After all, we rely on the opinions of doctors about our health, those of lawyers about our legal affairs, those of accountants about our taxes, those of economists about our financial future, and those of clergy about our spiritual concerns. Still, we must take care to be sure that our opinions or the opinions of others are sound. In other words, the reader or writer must ask: Are these opinions reasonable and well grounded?

Suppose you meet an individual who expresses strong opinions. It is not necessary for you to immediately accept or disregard them. Instead, you should ask questions to decide whether the opinion is sound and then decide to accept or reject the opinions:

Who is the person expressing the opinions?

Why is she or he talking about this subject?

Is she or he biased?

Does she or he support these opinions with facts or other opinions?

Does she or he foresee and consider the questions these opinions might raise and answer them?

The answers will help you decide whether or not the individual is qualified to hold the opinions she or he expresses.

For example, a banker may not be qualified to discuss the teaching of business courses on college campuses. Even if the individual's opinions are published, his or her qualifications to write about a certain subject should be carefully examined. Ask yourself what the individual stands to gain or lose by expressing the opinions. Motives are important because they can color or change the expression of a person's ideas. Do you detect any unfairness or partiality in the opinions? If so, the individual is probably not reporting the opinions in an objective way. Be careful to look for the way in which the individual supports the opinions. You should be cautious in accepting opinions supported only with other opinions. Generally speaking, well-grounded opinions are developed from a knowledge of facts. Finally, ask yourself whether the individual has taken the time to consider other people's questions and answer those that may arise. An individual who does so will probably hold opinions you will want to accept. And whether you are reading the opinions of others or writing your own, be sure to report them with as much care as you take when reporting facts.

## MAKING INFERENCES AND DRAWING CONCLUSIONS

In addition to distinguishing between fact and opinion, we need to be able to draw conclusions from what we see or hear. Consider the following statement:

> The pale, sweating child sat stiffly gripping the armrests of the chair as he waited to see the doctor.

After reading this statement, you might *infer* that the child was fearful about seeing the doctor, although you do not know for sure that this is the case. The evidence presented about the child's physical appearance leads you to draw a certain conclusion.

Now suppose you encountered the following situation:

> As you are about to enter a store, a man runs into you and almost knocks you down. He does not stop, but keeps running. When you get inside the store, you find the storekeeper bound and gagged, and the cash register open and empty.

Here are some of the inferences you might make:
1. The running man tied up the storekeeper and robbed the store.
2. The running man was going for help.
3. The running man was a customer frightened by what he had found when he went into the store.
4. The running man was trying to get out of the store quickly so he would not be caught robbing it.

You use the evidence—what you know or, in this case, observe—to draw these conclusions.

We do this type of thinking often and almost automatically. However, we must be careful to make inferences, or draw conclusions, which are directly related to what we know or observe. For example, if you concluded or inferred that the running man had robbed another store down the street, or that because he was running he was guilty, you would not be using the evidence correctly. In this example, any of the four inferences above might be correct. Further evidence would be necessary to determine which one in fact described the situation.

When making inferences from written material, you form opinions based on what is stated, and also on the way it is stated—on what the writer suggests. "Reading between the lines" is a skill that helps us understand more than just what the individual words say. The author supplies the "evidence" from which the reader can get both a *stated* meaning as well as an *implied* or *suggested* meaning. We get the implied meaning through careful attention to the clues or hints provided by the author. Read the following paragraph:

> During the time that I was a student at Hampton my older brother, John, not only assisted me all that he could, but worked all of the time in the coal-mines in order to support the family. He willingly neglected his own education that he might help me. It was my earnest wish to help him to prepare to enter Hampton, and to save enough money to assist him in his expenses there.

Although the author states what his brother did to help him, he also implies or suggests his appreciation. Words like "willingly neglected" and "earnest" provide clues to the author's feelings. From the evidence in the paragraph, the reader can infer that the writer had very positive feelings about his brother.

This next paragraph also provides clues to the author's implied meaning:

> And it came about that owners no longer worked on their farms. They farmed on paper; and they forgot the land, the smell, the feel of it, and remembered only that they owned it, remembered only what they gained and lost by it. And some of the farms grew so large that one man could not even conceive of them any more, so large that it took bookkeepers to keep track of interest and gain and loss; chemists to test the soil, to replenish;* straw bosses** to see that the stooping men were moving along the rows swiftly as the material of their bodies could stand.

The writer here emphasizes the growth and change in farming; most of the details in the paragraph concern the operation of a large farm. The reader

---

*Renew.
**Foremen.

can infer that these changes in farming have caused the farm owners to lose contact with the land. But although the owners are now wealthy enough to hire bookkeepers, foremen, and workers, the writer implies that they have given up a more important thing: contact with the soil.

Several inferences can be drawn from the next passage:

> "Mrs. Weller," Archer said.
> "Fourth floor," the elevator man said. "Does she expect you?"
> "Yes." Archer sniffed the mingled odors of oil, dust and age, and it brought back the memory of the pleasant evenings he had spent a long time ago in this house, when Alice's husband, who had been Archer's friend, was alive. Since his death, Archer had visited Alice less and less frequently, salving* his conscience with the knowledge that he had found work for her more or less steadily ever since he had become a director, even though there had been times when he had to fight the producers of his shows to do it.

Inferences:

1. Archer feels obligated to Alice.
2. His friendship with her dead husband may be the reason.
3. Archer feels guilty about visiting less frequently.
4. Alice needs to work.
5. It isn't easy to get work for Alice.

These conclusions are based on the description of Archer's thoughts as he rides the elevator to Alice's apartment, although none of the five statements is made directly.

In the following paragraph, the author clearly implies that an Indian boy's initiation is an ordeal:

> In American Indian tribes so much time is not usually given to boys' initiation, but the ideas are often the same. The Apache, with whom the Suni have many relations, say that breaking a boy is like breaking a young colt. They force him to make holes in the ice and bathe, run with water in his mouth, humiliate him on his trial war parties, and generally bully him. The Indians of Southern California bury him in hills of stinging ants.

Again, the conclusion that an initiation is an ordeal can be inferred. Such details as describing the boy as a young colt and forcing him to bathe in ice cold water provide the evidence to call the initiation an "ordeal," although that word is not used in the paragraph.

These examples show how inferences can be made from material we read. When we write, we provide the evidence from which a reader will make inferences. So how we express ideas can add to a reader's com-

*Easing.

prehension and appreciation of what we have to say. For example, if you choose words that imply rather than state directly, you leave room for the reader's imagination to become more involved. Consider the following pairs of sentences:

> Sara is beautiful.
> Sara looks like a fashion model.
> The girl sneaked down the hall.
> The girl kept looking over her shoulder as she tiptoed down the hall.
> Don doesn't talk much.
> Don's mouth requires a key to open it.

Each pair of sentences conveys the same idea, but with different words. The second sentence in each pair provides the reader with a suggestion of what is more directly stated in the first sentence. The second sentence allows the reader more use of his or her imagination to produce individual mental images.

Another way to provide hints or clues is to emphasize certain ideas. The following paragraph provides a basis for inference through emphasis:

> Beverly is special. It isn't her beauty, but her warmth that makes you notice her. It isn't her wealth, but her generosity that impresses. It isn't her wit, but her open good humor that causes you to want to be near her. And it isn't her handicap, but her courage in coping with it that forces you to admire and respect her.

Without saying so directly, the writer demonstrates that it is Beverly's character rather than her outward appearance or actions which are so attractive. All the details in the paragraph stress that her personal qualities of warmth, generosity, good humor, and courage are remarkable. This emphasis on her character leads to the inference that hers is an inner rather than an outer beauty.

Providing details that lead the reader to a conclusion is an effective writing technique because the reader will be convinced by his or her own reasoning processes. For example, you might want to demonstrate that egoism, when pushed to an extreme, is self-destructive. In order to write about egoism, you could think of details that show it as a cause leading to a certain effect:

Egoism causes an individual to

- value his or her freedom above everything else;
- resist taking advice;
- avoid relationships;
- refuse to take orders.

These characteristics of egoism can create a personality type that is so self-centered it is destructive. Using the details listed above, we could write a paragraph which implies that egoism is self-destructive without making this statement directly:

> More than anything, Phillip valued his freedom. He took every possible precaution to preserve and defend it. Advice from friends and relatives notwithstanding, he claimed independence and held on to it stubbornly. No opportunity great or small was more important than his freedom. No sacrifice of Number One to be part of two could ever seem worthwhile. Even though a promotion would mean more prestige and money, he would take orders from no one. And so every day, Phillip was free to be bored by dull routine, and every evening, he was free to be alone.

This paragraph describes Phillip's concern for his freedom. Such a concern is usually positive, but in Phillip's case it led to his being alone and isolated. The paragraph *implies*, that is, it provides details without stating directly, that extreme self-centeredness is harmful. The reader would *infer* that Phillip's egoism was destructive: He cherished his freedom so much that "he was free to be alone."

### EXERCISE

Try writing a paragraph that implies a conclusion without stating it. Choose one of the following topics:

Pride
Ambition
Concern for others
Assertiveness

Each of these characteristics can lead to a positive or negative personality type. For example, a certain level of pride in what you do is positive, but too much pride can make you unwilling to learn from others. Write a sentence that summarizes your conclusion. Use the following sentence as a model:

Too much pride can make you unwilling to learn from others.

_____

_____

Now list details that demonstrate this conclusion. Use the details on the left as a model:

| *Too much pride* | *Your details* |
|---|---|
| Has to do a job his or her own way | _____ |

Thinks other people do not
   know anything    _____

Considers his or her work the
   best    _____

Now, write a paragraph using these details. State the details in such a way as to *imply* your conclusion. After you are finished writing the paragraph, give it to another person in your class to read. See if your reader can *infer* your conclusion.

_____

_____

_____

_____

_____

_____

_____

_____

_____

## DETECTING PERSUASIVE LANGUAGE

Closely related to the skills of distinguishing fact from opinion and making inferences is the ability to detect *persuasive language*. Developing this skill enables you to make decisions about whether to accept or reject what is expressed when it is clear that the intent is to influence or sway your thinking. The intention need not be judged good or bad, but it should cause you to look carefully at the information presented.

Persuasive language can be used for honest or deceptive reasons: an individual may want to persuade others to fight against air pollution just as she or he may want to persuade people to buy a defective product. We are bombarded with examples of the art of persuasion in everyday life. The actor who endorses a certain car on television, the advertisements that ask us to buy this deodorant or that detergent, the politician who campaigns on an ethnic platform, and the public figure who comes out against homosexuality are all attempting to sway the attitudes and opinions of the public.

## Persuasive Techniques

Attempts at persuasion can be detected in the following types of language:

*Name Calling.* The persuader uses a label that is considered negative to describe an individual. Examples include "revolutionary," "warmonger," "Nazi," "Communist," "Fascist," "junkie," "stool pigeon," "pothead."

*Glittering Generalities.* The persuader uses words that are generally considered positive but that have little real meaning. Examples include "God-fearing," "all-American," "professional," "patriotic," "loyal," "sportsmanlike," "heroic".

*Testimonials.* Here the claims of others, generally celebrities or other well-known people, are employed to convince you that a certain attitude or opinion is the one you should have. An example would be using Jane Fonda's name and activities against nuclear energy to persuade you that you too should share her point of view.

*Card Stacking.* The persuader deliberately leaves out all that is negative and includes only that which is positive, or leaves out all that is positive and includes only that which is negative in order to convince. A presentation that reports only the positive aspects of hitchhiking and none of the negative has been produced by someone who is card stacking.

*The Just Plain Folks Approach.* Communication that attempts to make a person "just like everyone else," "one of the crowd," illustrates this method. To describe someone as a "good ole boy" is an example of the just plain folks approach.

*The Bandwagon Approach.* This technique emphasizes what most people say, do, find, need, prefer in order to convince you to accept something because everyone else does. An advertisement that suggests you should buy a small car because that is what most people are doing is using this approach to persuade you.

## Propaganda

All these techniques are often lumped together as types of *propaganda*. Propaganda is defined as "information or ideas deliberately spread in order to influence public opinion."* As you can see, all these varieties of

---

*\*Random House Dictionary of the English Language, 1973.*

persuasive language do indeed attempt to influence opinion. Should your task be to write sentences, paragraphs, or passages that are persuasive in nature, you can use any of these approaches. And as the following exercise shows, you can use these techniques for different purposes and results.

EXERCISE

I. Read each of the following statements or paragraphs and see if you can detect the type of persuasive language used. Write your answers in the spaces provided.

1. He's a real miser. How can he tell us how to spend money?

2. Gorgeous Gloria, stage and screen star, uses Sexy Brite toothpaste.

3. These people are true Americans.

4. You should play tennis. Everyone's doing it!

5. Tracy is rich, but you'd never know it. She's just one of the girls.

6. You must try the food at Burger Heaven. Everyone I've talked to loves it. The atmosphere is cozy and all your friends will be there. In no time at all people will stop eating at the Lieutenant's Chicken Palace and at McDavid's Burger Barn and eat here. Don't miss out on the fun and the food. Stop in today.

7. Walking the tightrope is the most thrilling experience a circus performer can have. The hushed voices of the crowd below watching with pounding hearts as you leave the platform and take the first step speak their concern. With grace and skill you stride the rope time and again. The cheers and obvious admiration of those who see you perform is your reward. And that reward is all that counts.

8. Tom Daniels is an ordinary guy. He works for the people he represents as if he were working for himself. As senator, he finds time to talk to the corner merchant and to shoot marbles with the kids in

the street. When his limousine pulls up at his office, especially during an election year, he jumps out and into the crowd, kissing babies and wringing hands as he goes. He's never lost the common touch.

Answers:

1. Name calling.
2. Testimonial.
3. Glittering generality.
4. Bandwagon.
5. Just plain folks.
6. Bandwagon.
7. Card stacking.
8. Just plain folks.

II. Imagine you are trying to convince somebody to vote for a certain person, to buy a particular product, or see a popular movie. Use one of the types of persuasive language described in this section in a short paragraph:

_____
_____
_____
_____
_____
_____
_____
_____
_____
_____

Now, try negative persuasion on the same topic. Use one of the persuasive language types to convince somebody *not* to vote for the person, *not* to buy the product, or *not* to see the movie:

_____
_____

_____

_____

_____

_____

Give your paragraphs to a friend, and see if he or she can detect the persuasive language.

## INDUCTIVE AND DEDUCTIVE REASONING

Thinking involves making decisions, and these decisions help us make choices. Decision making enables us to arrive at conclusions, and then to apply these conclusions to particular situations. Without being able to make decisions, we would be unable to function for even one day.

You can reach these conclusions by observing your own experiences or by studying those of other people. Your own experience regularly guides your behavior. Suppose that every time you study for a test, you earn a higher grade than on those occasions when you do not study that hard. Let's say that in a given year you took ten tests. For seven of these you were well prepared and scored a high grade. For the other three, however, you were not so well prepared, and your grades were lower. You could then reach a conclusion:

> When I am well prepared for a test, I get higher grades than when I am not as well prepared.

This conclusion results from your own experience. If you want it to, it can guide your behavior. If you decide you want to do well on a particular test, you know you will have to study for it.

Such reasoning is called *inductive*. It leads from individual situations to a conclusion. In the example above, the individual situations were all the tests you took during a year. The conclusion was the general statement that showed a relationship between grades and preparation for tests.

Inductive conclusions do not have to be based on personal experience. By observing the experiences of others, you can also arrive at an inductive conclusion. For example, you could study the results of football games over a period of time and check to see how often the home team won. Based on this study, you might conclude that the home team won more often than not. Or, suppose you observed people in supermarkets and noticed that most of the shoppers were women. An inductive conclusion from this evidence would be that shopping for food is a job usually done by women.

These examples illustrate how inductive reasoning works. But inductive reasoning only points to a conclusion when you have some idea what you are looking for. You could read football scores for years, but unless you were checking for a home team advantage, that pattern would not have been obvious. And you could shop every week without noticing the male-female ratio in the store. In order to reason inductively, you must have an idea of what factor, or variable, you are studying. This variable was home team success in the first example, and number of women shoppers compared to men in the second.

As useful as inductive reasoning is, you should observe certain cautions. The most important of these is to be sure that you have enough information to draw a conclusion. If, for example, you checked the football scores for a couple of weekends instead of a full season, you might not get a true picture of the home team success ratio. If you paid attention to the number of women and men shoppers on just a couple of occasions, your conclusion might not be accurate. You must also be aware that other factors might influence the situation. Maybe women outnumber men during morning or afternoon hours, but the ratio might be more balanced in the evening or afternoon hours. And perhaps the home team advantage would be of little use to a very poor team, and not so important to a very good team that wins most of its games no matter where they are played. Inductive reasoning, then, demands that you look for a particular factor, that you gather enough evidence, and that you take into account other factors which might influence the situation you are studying.

*Deductive* reasoning is the opposite of inductive: it moves from a generalization to a specific situation. The classic example of this type of reasoning demonstrates how we all come to the realization that we are mortal—that we will, at some point, die. The deductive reasoning that leads to this conclusion begins with this generalization: "All living things die." It then fits a particular example into the generalization: "I am a living thing." The conclusion shows a relationship between the first and the second statements, and produces the statement "I will die."

Deductive reasoning, then, moves from a generalization to a specific example and finally to a conclusion that shows a relationship between the generalization and the example. Just like inductive reasoning, the conclusions reached through deduction also guide our lives. Of course, the realization that we all must die is probably the most important conclusion any person must face. But in many other situations, deductive reasoning enables you to function from day to day. For example, if you have a job that begins at 10 A.M. on Saturday mornings, deductive reasoning helps you arrive at work on time. In this situation, the general statement would be something like this: "I must leave for work at 9:30 A.M. every Saturday."

The specific statement would be "It is now 9:30 A.M." And the conclusion, which shows the relationship between these two statements, would be "I must leave for work now."

You would not recite these statements to yourself every Saturday morning before leaving for work. But as you glanced at your watch to check the time, your mind would be running through these deductive steps, and you would prepare to leave for work. Countless day to day activities are determined in this way by a deductive process. Every obligation or responsibility you have becomes a general statement that applies at certain times to specific situations or points in your life.

Inductive and deductive reasoning are not completely separate processes. Often they come together as you think through problems or try to make decisions. For example, inductive reasoning can often provide the general statement that is the first step of a deductive process. Suppose you have decided to buy store brands instead of name brands at your local supermarket because they are cheaper. After buying a number of such products, you might discover that nonfood products such as trash can liners or aluminum foil are as good as name brand versions of similar products. But you might also find that you do not like the taste or quality of the food products as much as those of the name brands. Your inductive process would result from individual experiences that lead to conclusions, as the example below shows.

| | **Nonfood Products** | **Conclusion** |
|---|---|---|
| Experience 1 | Aluminum foil | As good as name brands. |
| Experience 2 | Trash can liners | As good as name brands. |
| Experience 3 | Paper towels | As good as name brands. |
| Experience 4 | Detergent | As good as name brands. |
| Experience 5 | Napkins | As good as name brands. |

*Conclusion:* Store brand nonfood products are as good as name brands for these items.

| | **Food Products** | **Conclusion** |
|---|---|---|
| Experience 1 | Canned peas | Not as good as name brands. |
| Experience 2 | Frozen french fries | Not as good as name brands. |
| Experience 3 | Potato chips | Not as good as name brands. |
| Experience 4 | Ice cream | Not as good as name brands. |
| Experience 5 | Soda | Not as good as name brands. |

*Conclusion:* Store brand food products are not as good as name brands for these items.

These conclusions, in turn, could lead to new *deductive* conclusions. One day you might be walking down the aisle of the supermarket and discover a new store brand product. Your decision to buy or not to buy this product could be determined deductively, using the inductive conclusions as starting points:

| | |
|---|---|
| General statement | Store brand nonfood products are as good as name brands. |
| Specific statement | "Spring Soap" is a new nonfood store brand product. |
| Deductive conclusion | "Spring Soap" is as good as name brand soap. |
| General statement | Store brand food products are not as good as name brands. |
| Specific statement | "Wheatfield Grain Cereal" is a new store brand food product. |
| Deductive conclusion | "Wheatfield Grain Cereal" is not as good as a name brand cereal. |

Based on these conclusions, you might decide to buy the soap because it will probably get you just as clean for less money than the name brand. On the other hand, you might choose not to buy the cereal because, although it is cheaper than the name brand, it might taste like the cardboard box in which it is packaged.

These conclusions are not guaranteed to be accurate. It is possible that the soap might disintegrate the first time you use it and turn your bathtub green, and that the cereal might taste good, much better than you thought possible. The only way to know for certain would be to try the particular product. But the reasoning process is still useful. It will either confirm your beliefs or lead you to change them. Or it will be a fairly good guide if you choose not to experiment with the new products.

Besides helping you to make decisions that guide your life, these reasoning processes are important to good reading and writing. They are the foundation of all thought processes because thought processes attempt to make relationships. Language expresses idea relationships in sentences, paragraphs, and essays. Knowing how these relationships are established will help you to read with greater understanding and to write with greater accuracy.


EXERCISE

Try doing your own inductive study on the relationship between the number of hours students work and the number of hours they are able to study each week. Ask at least twenty students for this information, and fill in the following form:

| Student | Number of Hours Worked | Number of Hours Studied |
|---|---|---|
| 1. | | |
| 2. | | |
| 3. | | |
| 4. | | |
| 5. | | |
| 6. | | |
| 7. | | |
| 8. | | |
| 9. | | |
| 10. | | |
| 11. | | |
| 12. | | |
| 13. | | |
| 14. | | |
| 15. | | |
| 16. | | |
| 17. | | |
| 18. | | |
| 19. | | |
| 20. | | |

Review the numbers you have recorded. Try to state a conclusion that summarizes these figures:

Conclusion: _____

_____

Now, see if you can develop a *deductive* application of this conclusion. Begin with your *inductive* conclusion as stated above:

General statement     _____
                     _____

Specific statement    _____
                     _____

Deductive conclusion  _____
                     _____

(Use pp. 16–17 above to help you complete the deductive thinking process.)

## RECOGNIZING PURPOSE

People communicate for a variety of reasons, but always for *some* reason. When we have nothing to say, we are generally silent. Therefore, besides recognizing techniques of communication, it is also useful to try to understand why, or to what purpose, these techniques are employed.

For a reader, recognizing purpose will aid in understanding; for a writer, determining purpose will help in choosing the best approach to a topic. We can recognize and determine the purpose of a piece of communication by answering the following questions:

1. Does it entertain or move me emotionally?
2. Does it provide information?
3. Does it persuade?
4. Does it lead to an action?

These purposes can be served by the following parts of the communication:

1. Organization
2. Language
3. Tone

Quite often purposes are combined, but most communications have one central purpose. This purpose is served by the techniques discussed earlier in this chapter. Let us look at some examples.

Being able to distinguish between fact and opinion in the paragraph about the telephone leads you to a better understanding of the purpose of the paragraph:

The name telephone was adopted by the inventor Alexander Graham Bell in 1876. The name literally means sound at a distance.

> This communications instrument has improved the lives of everyone who uses it. Verbal communication has become more convenient. It has also become so automated that the caller need not contact a central operator when making every call. Instead the person making certain calls can be placed in direct communication with the party dialed. In addition to being a general means of communication, the telephone can be used for specific services like banking and paying bills. The invention of the telephone is one example of the superiority of machine over man.

This paragraph presents certain facts about the invention and expanding uses of the telephone. These facts serve the purpose of communicating information, which is the primary goal of the paragraph. However, the opinion sentences attempt to persuade that the telephone is a major, positive force in making modern life more convenient. Notice that the language of the opinion sentences contains value judgment words like "improved" and "superiority," while the language of the fact sentences is neutral.

The following paragraph led to certain inferences:

> More than anything, Phillip valued his freedom. He took every possible precaution to preserve and defend it. Advice from friends and relatives notwithstanding, Phillip claimed independence and held on to it stubbornly. No opportunity great or small was more important than his freedom. No sacrifice of Number One to be part of two could ever seem worthwhile. Even though a promotion would mean more prestige and money, he would take orders from no one. And so every day, Phillip was free to be bored by dull routine, and every evening he was free to be alone.

In this paragraph, organization and tone help communicate purpose. The paragraph is organized into two sections. From the first to the next to the last sentences, all the details show how Phillip cherishes his freedom. The last sentence turns this usually positive trait into a negative one by demonstrating that Phillip's concern for his personal freedom has become self-destructive. The tone of the paragraph supports this purpose by being cold and lacking in emotion.

Similarly, persuasive language is employed to convince the reader or listener that he or she should accept a certain belief or perhaps take a certain action. For example, name calling is designed to cause the reader or listener to lose respect for an individual or group. In an election, the purpose would also be to persuade the voter not to vote for an individual or party.

The section on inductive and deductive reasoning described a comparison between store brand and name brand products. If this comparison were developed in a formal study, the purpose of that study would be to obtain information, and a report based on it would have as its purpose the communication of that information. In addition, the purpose of the study would also determine the method of investigation. Since the study would attempt to discover whether consumers liked store brands as well as name brands, the method would start with the individual experiences of a number of consumers. It would then work toward a general conclusion that would represent a summary statement based on all these individual situations. In other words, the inductive method would be used.

Mastering the thinking skills discussed here will improve your ability to make decisions about what you read and write. It will also increase your academic success and the success with which you make choices in every area of life. The key is to develop an active, questioning attitude as you approach anything you wish to learn.


## THINKING SKILLS CHECKLIST

Use this checklist whenever you make use of the reasoning skills discussed here.

1. *Distinguishing Fact from Opinion*

    Is the information factual? Does it concern someone or something known to exist or to have happened?

    Is the information an opinion? Does it concern someone or something that is believed to be true?

2. *Making Inferences and Drawing Conclusions*

    What information or evidence is known, observed, or suggested?

    Are implied meanings a part of the information given?

    Are any clues or hints provided? Choice of words? Choice of emphasis? Intended response from reader?

    Who is the author? Why is he or she writing about this subject? Is he or she biased? Does he or she foresee and consider the questions these opinions might raise and answer them?

3. *Detecting Persuasive Language*

    Are techniques designed to influence or sway the reader employed?

    Name calling?
    Glittering generalities?
    Testimonials?
    Card stacking?
    Just plain folks approach?
    The bandwagon approach?

4. *Types of Reasoning*
   Deductive reasoning. Does the information reflect a thinking pattern that goes from a general conclusion to specific statements?
   Inductive reasoning. Does the information reflect a thinking pattern that goes from specific statements to a general conclusion?
5. *Recognizing Purpose*
   A. Why did the author write about this?
      1. To entertain or move the reader emotionally?
      2. To provide information?
      3. To persuade?
      4. To lead to an action?
   B. Are there hints to help the reader understand the purpose?
      1. Organization?
      2. Language?
      3. Tone?

# 2
# Vocabulary Building

PREVIEW

Communication commonly takes four forms: listening, reading, speaking, and writing. Listening and reading enable you to receive information; speaking and writing permit you to express your ideas and feelings to others. Words (vocabulary) are the basis for all these activities. Vocabulary building is the process of learning new words to increase your ability to listen, read, speak, and write.

Your total vocabulary includes all the words you can recognize and use. Most people recognize more words as listeners than they do as readers, and use more as writers than as speakers. Building your total vocabulary means increasing your knowledge of words and your ability to use them effectively.

Vocabulary building requires real effort. English contains about half a million words, and most people do not know much more than 10 or 20 percent of that number. Everyone, therefore, can profitably spend a lifetime learning new words.

Approaches to learning new words include expanding your reading; learning prefixes, roots, and suffixes; using context clues along with a dictionary; recording new words on index cards and reviewing them periodically; and practicing using these new words in speaking and writing. These methods, combined with an attitude that makes vocabulary building an important daily activity, will help you increase your skill.

**Key Terms**

**Total vocabulary.** All the words you know as a listener, speaker, reader, and writer.
**Listening vocabulary.** Words you recognize when you hear them.
**Reading vocabulary.** Words you recognize when you read.
**Speaking vocabulary.** Words you can use comfortably as a speaker.
**Writing vocabulary.** Words you can use comfortably as a writer.
**Prefix.** A word element placed at the beginning of a word to add meaning or change grammatical form.
**Suffix.** A word element placed at the end of a word to add meaning or change grammatical form.
**Root.** A basic word part.
**Context.** The words that surround a particular word and add to its meaning.

Verbal communication includes receiving information as listeners and speakers, and presenting ideas as speakers or writers. The basis for all these activities is words. Whether we wish to express thoughts and ideas orally or in written form, or to understand the thoughts of others when we read or listen, words make such expression possible. Combinations of words form sentences, paragraphs, and passages of verbal communication. The more words we know, the greater our ability to combine words to express ourselves effectively and to understand the communications of others. *Vocabulary building* is the process of increasing the number of words we know and understand. It is an active, ongoing process that continues throughout our lives.

Four types or levels of vocabulary parallel the four communication activities: reading, listening, speaking, and writing. Your *reading vocabulary* consists of the words you understand when you read. Your *listening vocabulary* consists of the words you understand when they are stated orally. Your listening vocabulary may be larger than your reading vocabulary because you may know a word when you hear it but not when you see or read it. Your *speaking vocabulary* consists of the words you are able to use to express your thoughts and ideas orally. If you have difficulty pronouncing some words that you may read or listen to and understand, your speaking vocabulary may be smaller than your reading and listening vocabularies. Your *writing vocabulary* consists of the words you can use to express yourself in written form. It is usually larger than your speaking vocabulary because most people write in a more formal way than they speak. *Reading and listening vocabularies are the words you know when others express themselves; speaking and writing vocabularies are the words you can use to make yourself understood.*

All these vocabularies include the words we understand and/or use correctly, and they constitute our *total* vocabulary. It has been estimated that the average total vocabulary of a twelfth-grade student ranges from 50,000 to 80,000 words. Although these numbers may seem high, remember than an unabridged dictionary contains close to 400,000 words!

This chapter provides suggestions to help improve total vocabulary through techniques to increase reading vocabulary and include these words in writing vocabulary. Making these techniques part of your daily study routine will pay dividends in many different ways. The more words you know and can use, the greater your range of understanding and the easier it is for you to grasp new ideas and make choices.

## IMPROVING READING VOCABULARY

Here are six methods that will improve reading vocabulary.

### Study Common Prefixes, Suffixes, and Roots

These word parts are often helpful in discovering the meanings of new words. A *prefix* is a syllable found at the beginning of a word; a *suffix* is a syllable found at the end of a word; a *root* is a basic word. If a prefix and/or suffix is added to a root, a new word results. For example, "cover" is the root of these words: "discover," "uncover," "covering," and "coverage." The prefixes *dis-* and *un-* and the suffixes *-ing* and *-age* have been added to the root, and we now have four additional words. Prefixes and suffixes themselves have meanings. Knowing these meanings allows you to more easily figure out what a word in which they are used means.

The following list contains frequently used prefixes and suffixes:

| Prefix | Meaning |
|---|---|
| a- | on, in, to, of, from, not, without (amoral, atypical, akimbo) |
| anti- | against, opposite (antiwar, anticoagulant, antihero) |
| be- | about, around, upon, over, completely, greatly, to make, to cause to be (bedevil, bedew, believe) |
| com- | with, together (compatriot, companion, commit) |
| de- | down, away, reversal of an action, remove (descend, deliver, debase) |
| en- | in, into, on, upon, to make or cause to be, to provide with (encase, enclave, endure) |

| Prefix | Meaning |
|---|---|
| e-, ex- | out, from, former (emit, ex-wife, exhibit) |
| in- | not, lack of, in, into, on, upon, toward (inward, ingest, inimitable) |
| pre- | before, in front, ahead of, above, over (prepare, present, prelude) |
| pro- | before, taking the place of, favor, support (propose, proponent, profess) |
| re- | again, anew, back, backward (reverse, redress, redeem) |
| sub- | under, underneath, nearly, less than, subordinate (subhuman, submarine, subject) |
| un- | without, reversal of an action, removal, completely (uneven, unfasten, unexceptional |

| Suffix | Meaning |
|---|---|
| -able | forms *adjectives* meaning tending to, able to be (teachable, readable, tractable) |
| -age | forms *nouns* meaning action, progress, state, condition, number of, group, cost of (stoppage, coverage, nonage) |
| -al | forms *adjectives* meaning like, relating to; forms *nouns* meaning act of, amount or cost of (referral, developmental, peripheral) |
| -ate | forms *adjectives* meaning like, having quality of; forms *verbs* meaning make or cause to be, to perform the process of, to take the form of; forms *nouns* meaning resulting from an action, an office or function, a group (moderate, liberate, doctorate) |
| -ence | forms *nouns* meaning an action or process, state, condition (divergence, emergence, pre-eminence) |

| Suffix | Meaning |
|---|---|
| -ful | forms *adjectives* meaning full of, having the quality of, tendency to, having the ability or capacity of; forms *nouns* meaning amount contained in (wonderful, playful, roomful) |
| -ics | forms *nouns* meaning field of knowledge or study, system or practice, actions of a certain kind (economics, histrionics, mechanics) |
| -ity | forms *nouns* meaning state, condition, quality, or characteristic (parity, ability, viability) |
| -logy | forms *nouns* meaning a field of knowledge or study (theology, sociology, anthropology) |
| -ly | forms *adjectives* and *adverbs* meaning once in a period of time, toward, from a certain direction, like, resembling (daily, crisply, approximately) |
| -ment | forms *nouns* meaning an action, result of an action, means or instrument (establishment, fulfillment, entertainment) |
| -ness | forms *nouns* meaning a state or quality (largeness, business, astuteness) |

Prefixes and suffixes, like words, have several meanings. Notice that in addition to meanings, a suffix provides the reader with information about the grammatical form the word takes when the suffix is added to the root.

The meanings of common prefixes and suffixes can help you define unknown words. However, you should be careful not to rely upon them too much. Many of our words come from different language families. Although they may have word parts spelled in the same way as other common prefixes or suffixes, their meanings may be entirely different. The way to be sure is to check the dictionary.

## Read Widely

Read different kinds of materials in large quantities. Doing this will increase your exposure to words and your opportunity to meet new words, or familiar ones in new settings. Wide reading should include recreational reading (books, magazines, articles, essays that appeal to your interests), study reading (informational or technical materials required for school or career), and survival reading (materials that contain information to help you to live a better, richer life). Wide reading provides two benefits: first, it keeps you well informed by broadening your knowledge and experience; second, it enables you to see language used to express ideas in a variety of ways. Wide reading provides the opportunity for vocabulary development. To make it worthwhile, you should work with context clues, develop a card file, and use a dictionary and/or a thesaurus as reading aids.

**Use Context Clues**

One of the best ways to build vocabulary is to read words in context. *Context* refers to the other words that surround a particular word in a sentence, paragraph, or passage. Context often helps you figure out meaning without using a dictionary. It is particularly useful because it focuses your attention on the multiple meanings nearly all words have. Learning words in this way allows you to see that words can have different meanings according to the way in which they are used.

**Notice New Words**

As you read, take notice of words and how they are used. Sometimes a word will appeal to you because of its sound, its spelling, or because you decide it fits your personality. When new words have such appeal, underline them, circle them, make note of them in some way. Use context to help you define the word or to choose the best definition from the dictionary. Once you have learned their meanings, practice using the words as you speak or write. The practice will help you to make these words part of your own vocabulary.

When you are required to notice new words as part of study reading, the same suggestions apply. However, you may need to be more systematic in keeping track of these words. The next technique can be helpful when you must learn new terminology or jargon for school or career.

**Keep a Card File of New Words**

An efficient way to keep track of new words or multiple word meanings is to record spelling, grammatical form, origin, definition(s), and example(s) of their use on $3 \times 5$ cards. Use a separate card for each word. Write the word on one side of the card and then record its spelling by

**Figure 2.1**

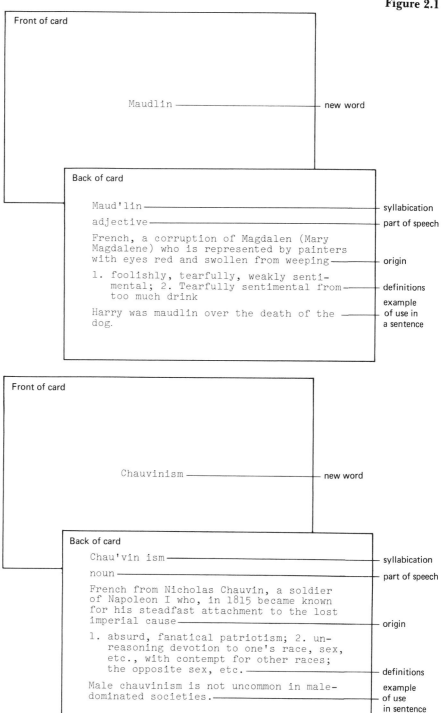

syllables, grammatical form, origin, definition(s), and example(s) of use on the other, as the samples in Figure 2.1 show.

As you record the words on cards, keep them in order alphabetically or according to subject. Study these cards frequently. A few minutes spent in review each day will help you remember the words. Have someone quiz you every so often. As you learn the words, concentrate on the ones that give you trouble, and just review those that come to you easily.

**Use a Dictionary**

The best source of precise word meanings is the dictionary. Using the dictionary is generally helpful once words have been read in context and you need a specific meaning. If there are no context clues, or if context does not help pinpoint the meaning, the dictionary is necessary. All the information about the sample words given on the 3 × 5 cards came from a dictionary. The dictionary provides much more than just definitions, as the sample here shows.

        a  b  c  d

**group** (grōōp) *n. Abbr.* **gr.** **1.** An assemblage of persons or objects; aggregation: *a group of dinner guests; a group of Chinese porcelains.* **2.** Two or more figures that make up a unit or a design, as in sculpture or painting. **3.** A number of individuals or things considered together because of certain similarities.  —e

f — **4.** *Linguistics.* A subdivision of a linguistic family, less inclusive than a branch. **5.** A military unit consisting of two or more
f — ~~battalions and a headquarters.~~ **6.** *U.S. Air Force.* A unit of two or more squadrons, smaller than a wing. **7.** Any class or collection of related objects or entities, as: **a.** Two or more atoms behaving or regarded as behaving as a single chemical unit. **b.** A vertical column in the periodic table of elements. **c.** A geological stratigraphic unit, especially a unit consisting of
f — ~~two or more formations.~~ **8.** *Mathematics.* A set together with a binary operation under which the set is closed and associative, and for which the set contains an identity element and an inverse for every element in the set. —*v.* ~~grouped~~, grouping, —g
groups. —*tr.* ~~To place~~ or arrange in a group or groups. —*intr.*
h — ~~To form or be part of a group.~~ [French *groupe,* from Italian *gruppo,* "knot," from Germanic. See ger-³ in Appendix.*]
i — **Usage:** *Group,* as a collective noun, can be construed as singular or plural in determining the number of the verb it governs. A singular verb occurs when the persons or things in question are considered as one or as acting as one, or when they are related by membership in a class or category. A plural verb is possible when *group* refers to persons thought of as acting individually. The grammatical number of related pronouns and pronominal adjectives in turn agrees with that of the verb: *The group* (of persons) *is determined to retain its identity despite the merger. The group* (of persons) *were divided in their sympathies. This group* (of plants) *shows variation in coloring.*

*The American Heritage Dictionary of the English Language,* New College Edition. Boston: Houghton Mifflin Co., 1976.

Vocabulary Building

The word entry reprinted here is keyed to the explanation below. Remember that dictionaries differ and that as a result the form will change from dictionary to dictionary.

a. *The entry.* This word is usually identified by a different kind of typeface. Check the spelling; often, there are two (or more) accepted ways to spell a word, as in "ax" and "axe." In these cases, the spelling that appears first is usually the one used more commonly. If an entry has more than one syllable, the syllables are identified by dots or dashes, as in al·low·ance. A capital letter for an entry indicates that it is a proper noun.

b. *Pronunciation.* Immediately after the entry, dictionaries give you an explanation of how to pronounce the word. Keys to the symbols used often appear at the bottom of each page. In the case of "group," you would look to the key to find "oo." This means that the "ou" sound in "group" is pronounced like the "oo" sound in "boot." In the cases of words with more than one syllable, dictionaries indicate which syllables are accented or stressed, as in "col·lege (kŏl′ĭj)." The first syllable of this word is accented, as indicated by the stress mark (′). When there are two accepted pronunciations, they appear in the order of most commonly used, as in colleen (kŏl′·ēn, kŏ·lēn′) or Byzantine (bĭz′·sn·tēn, ·tīn′, bĭ·zăn′·tīn).

c. *Grammatical form.* This abbreviation indicates the grammatical name of the word. In this case, "group" is listed as *n.* and defined as a noun. (The other abbreviations are *v.* for verb, *adv.* for adverb, *adj.* for adjective.) Notice that the definition part of the entry is broken in two parts, noun and verb. The definitions are significantly different, for the word serves different functions as its grammatical function changes.

d. *Abbreviation.* When there is an accepted abbreviation for a word, it is indicated in the entry.

e. *Definition.* In most dictionaries, definitions are listed in order of use, from most common to least common. Although there may be considerable disagreement about the order of the definitions, all are considered acceptable. The more definitions you know for an individual word, the more precise you can be.

f. *Specific definitions.* Specific definitions apply to the field, profession, or activity indicated. In addition to *linguistics, U.S. Air Force,* and *mathematics,* the definitions in this entry include *general military use* (5) and *general scientific use* (7a, 7b, 7c).

g. *Other grammatical functions.* One of the properties of modern English is that often the same word can be used for a different grammatical function. You will find it helpful when you are looking up a word, to know what its grammatical function is. If you do not know, the dictionary can help you find out. Here, "group" is defined as a verb as well as a noun. Notice that this particular dictionary helps you by providing the principal parts of the verb—"grouped" (the past participle) and "grouping" (the present participle). The dictionary may give more forms of the verb should they present spelling or grammatical problems, as in "lie: lay, lain, lying, lies."

h. *Derivation.* Words have origins—family trees. This section of a dictionary entry tells you where the English word originated.

i. *Usage.* This part of a dictionary entry includes information on the use of the word. In the case of "group," it can be used with a singular or a plural verb or pronoun. At the end of this part of the entry, there are examples of both uses of the word.

Another useful source for developing vocabulary is a *thesaurus.* A thesaurus, like a dictionary, contains lists of words in alphabetical order. Its special feature is that it provides *synonyms,* words similar in meaning, and *antonyms,* words opposite in meaning, for each word listed. The thesaurus is a good companion to the dictionary.

Improving reading vocabulary through these six techniques will help to improve total vocabulary. The more you use these techniques, the more successful you will be in achieving a broader vocabulary.

## READING EXERCISE

1. Make a list of 10 basic words (roots). Add prefixes and/or suffixes to each word and indicate how meaning or grammatical function change.

| | Root | Prefixes and/or Suffixes | Word Change |
|---|---|---|---|
| 1. | _____ | _____ | _____ |
| 2. | _____ | _____ | _____ |
| 3. | _____ | _____ | _____ |
| 4. | _____ | _____ | _____ |
| 5. | _____ | _____ | _____ |
| 6. | _____ | _____ | _____ |
| 7. | _____ | _____ | _____ |
| 8. | _____ | _____ | _____ |
| 9. | _____ | _____ | _____ |
| 10. | _____ | _____ | _____ |

2. Make a list of the materials you read for recreation, study, and survival. Create a card file of new words from this reading. Be sure to use a dictionary for the pronunciation, origin, and definition of each word.

3. Use a thesaurus to locate synonyms and antonyms for the words in your card file. Add these to the information on the back of the card for each word.

## IMPROVING WRITTEN VOCABULARY

To write well, you need to be able to use words that say what you want to say. You draw these words from your stored knowledge of the meanings of words you have heard or read. To improve written vocabulary, you must first increase the number of words stored in your mind by ways such as those described in the first section of this chapter. Then, with practice, you can begin to work new words into your spoken and written vocabularies. This practice requires conscious effort.

Most people can use more words comfortably when they write than when they speak. Writing gives you time to pause and consider which words you want to use; speaking demands an almost instant recall of available words. Skill in one area strengthens the other. The more words you can use when speaking, the more you will be able to use when writing, and vice versa.

This section of the chapter presents an approach to expanding your spoken and written vocabularies. To begin to add new words to your written and spoken vocabularies, you first have to break bad habits and discover how to use verbs, nouns, and modifiers more precisely. In other words, you need to learn how to choose the words that say what you mean most clearly and directly.

### Breaking Bad Habits

Knowing what you want to say is as important as knowing the words you want to use to express your ideas. Knowing what you want to communicate will help you find the right words. For example:

I want something to eat.
I want a piece of fruit.
I want a peach.

The third sentence communicates more clearly than the second, and the second is clearer than the first. What separates the first from the third is not vocabulary, it is the thought behind the sentence. When you think carefully as you speak or write, you decide exactly what thought you want to express, and you then seek the words that best fit that thought.

Often, spoken or written vocabularies are limited more by laziness than by lack of words. We often make do with the approximate word or expression rather than the exact one, or we use a general, catchall word instead of one with a more limited and specific meaning:

George wanted to *make up* with Susan.
George wanted to *appease* Susan's anger.
George wanted to *reconcile* his differences with Susan.
George wanted to *make amends* for what he had said to Susan.
George wanted to *rejuvenate* his relationship with Susan.

The first sentence expresses George's desire to patch things up with Susan in a general and vague way. Each of the following sentences narrows George's feelings to a definite area of concern. Both the thought behind the sentences and the vocabulary are more clearly defined:

| | |
|---|---|
| appease | To soften or reduce (Susan's anger) |
| reconcile | To bring different points of view together |
| make amends | Compensation or payment for a wrong done |
| rejuvenate | To return to an earlier state of youthful energy and feeling |

To use such words, of course, you must know them. But more important, your thinking must be clear enough to provide a need for such words. If you know *exactly* what you want to say, you will be able to use all the words in your vocabulary. If you only have a vague idea of what you want to say, you will probably use a vague word or phrase to express it.

**Finding the Exact Word or Expression**

Once you know what you want to say, you can seek the word that most exactly expresses your thought. A dictionary or thesaurus can help, but you must first make the decision not to be satisfied with anything less than the best word for your idea—the best action word (verb), the best category word (noun), and the best descriptive words (modifiers).

*Verbs.* Verbs generally express an action. There are many verbs with similar meanings that range from general to more specific. For example:

Joe *ate* his supper.
Joe *gobbled* his supper.
Joe *nibbled* at his supper.

Susan *walked* into the room.

Susan *strode* into the room.

Susan *marched* into the room.

Shirley *thought about* the problem.

Shirley *wrestled* with the problem.

Shirley *agonized* over the problem.

In each series, the first sentence expresses an idea in a general way. The following sentences express the idea in more specific terms because the verbs are more precise:

| | |
|---|---|
| eat | Ingest food |
| gobble | Eat with enthusiasm |
| nibble | Eat slowly with little appetite |
| walk | To move one's legs |
| stroll | To move at a slow, casual pace |
| march | To move with purpose and energy |
| think about | To use one's brain |
| wrestle | To think about something without being able to find an answer |
| agonize | To think slowly and carefully about a difficult problem |

Finding the right verb requires knowing exactly what action you want to describe. The verbs in the lists above are similar in meaning, but the differences are more important than the similarities. They do not give the same impression. As you write and speak, try to find the verb that best conveys the action you have in mind. By doing this, you will be able to transfer verbs you know from your listening and reading vocabularies to speaking and writing situations.

*Nouns.* Nouns describe categories of persons, places, or things. Like verbs, some nouns are more specific than others. For example, we generally refer to the place where we were born and raised as our "home town." The expression thus can mean anything from a city to a village. If we want to be accurate in terms of size, we might choose another word: hamlet, village, city, metropolis. These nouns describe categories from smallest to largest, from hamlet (a small village) to metropolis (a large city).

Choosing a noun usually means deciding between a general and a more specific word:

| | |
|---|---|
| Rags is my *pet*. | General |
| Rags is my *dog*. | |
| Rags is my *cocker spaniel*. | Specific |

I like *fruit*.          General
I like *apples*.
I like *Cortlands*.      Specific

Tom is an *athlete*.     General
Tom is a *baseball player*.
Tom is a *centerfielder*.  Specific

Sometimes, though, the choice involves level of formality or social standing:

She dreamed of someday becoming a *garbageman*.
She dreamed of someday becoming a *sanitation engineer*.

His father is a *teacher*.
His father is a *professor*.

All the stray dogs in the neighborhood ran from the *dog catcher*.
All the stray dogs in the neighborhood ran from the *dog warden*.

The second noun in each pair describes essentially the same category as the first, but it is more formal and communicates a higher social standing. Since nouns identify categories, and not individual persons, places, or things, it is important to choose the noun that best describes the person, place, or thing you have in mind.

*Modifiers.* Modifiers are words that describe other words. They refine and limit meaning.

| Modifier | Noun |
|---|---|
| sweet | dessert |
| tasty | dessert |
| long | assignment |
| hard | assignment |
| burdensome | assignment |

| Verb | Modifier |
|---|---|
| work | slowly |
| work | carefully |
| work | painstakingly |
| speak | confidently |
| speak | boldly |
| speak | arrogantly |

The lists above illustrate the most common positions for one-word modifiers: right before a noun, or right after a verb. Sometimes, one modifier is used in combination with another as in "a bitterly cold day" and "a ridiculously long distance"; "walked very slowly" and "spoke extremely carefully."

English is rich in modifier words, and they add clarity and color to our communication. Although they are always less important than verbs and nouns because they change rather than establish meaning, they add precision and interest to whatever we say or write.

## WRITING EXERCISES

I. Find at least three other verbs for each of the following sentences. Be prepared to explain the differences among them.

1. He *read* the book.

    _____

    _____

    _____

2. She *thought about* the future.

    _____

    _____

    _____

3. Joe *walked out of* the house.

    _____

    _____

    _____

4. Mary nervously *wrote* her name on the form.

    _____

    _____

    _____

5. Aunt Milly *put up* the money for the house.

    _____

    _____

    _____

6. The singer *sang* the song.

    _____

    _____

    _____

7. In his nervousness, he watched the hands of the clock *move* around the dial.

8. The dog *barked* at the stranger.

9. After an unpleasant meeting, she *closed* the door and left the room.

10. Rain *came down* all morning.

II. Find at least three other nouns for those shown in italics in the following sentences. Be prepared to explain the differences among them.

1. For dessert, she ordered a *pastry*.

2. Reginald invited Georgia to go sailing on his *boat*.

3. He thought smoking was a *habit*.

Vocabulary Building

_____

_____

4. The *thief* snatched the woman's pocketbook.

_____

_____

5. The singing dog act was the *highlight* of the show.

_____

_____

6. Her *lack of effort* concerned her teacher.

_____

_____

7. She got up early each day and approached her work with *enthusiasm*.

_____

_____

8. He wanted to win so badly that his friends called him a *wild man*.

_____

_____

9. Pat figured the only way out of the situation was to tell an *untruth*.

_____

_____

10. For Trisha, painting was a *preoccupation*.

_____

_____

_____

III. Find at least three other modifiers for each of those shown in italics in the following sentences. Be prepared to explain the differences among them.

1. After the meeting she walked *quickly* out of the room.
   _____
   _____
   _____

2. His new job paid a *good* salary.
   _____
   _____
   _____

3. Rising prices have caused gasoline to become *difficult* to afford.
   _____
   _____
   _____

4. Cindy's mother thought her daughter's new outfit was *inappropriate*.
   _____
   _____
   _____

5. George turned on the stereo and looked for a station playing *quiet* music.
   _____
   _____
   _____

6. The ads described the new science fiction film as *very interesting*.
   _____
   _____
   _____

Vocabulary Building

7. Paula read the assigned book *carefully*.

   _____

   _____

8. Zeke was *unusually* afraid of going to the dentist.

   _____

   _____

9. The passenger thought the taxi driver's conversation was *uninteresting*.

   _____

   _____

10. Phil looked at his wrecked car *philosophically*.

    _____

    _____

IV. Write a description of a house you want to sell. Use as many positive, descriptive words as you can. Underline these words.

_____
_____
_____
_____
_____
_____
_____
_____
_____
_____
_____

V. Write copy for an advertisement for a new cleanser. Describe its qualities using as many verbs as you can (*attacks* dirt, *eliminates* odor). Underline these words.

VI. Describe yourself for a dating service using combinations of nouns and modifiers (*extraordinary dancer, concerned environmentalist*). Underline these words.

# 3
# Words in Context

PREVIEW

Individual words can often mean several different things. It is the context or setting of a word that usually determines what that word means in a particular sentence or passage. The context of a word includes both its grammatical structure and the ideas established by the surrounding words. The grammatical structure makes a particular word perform a certain function, and this function can change meaning: "a dash of salt" is very different in meaning from "I dash to school every day." The ideas established by context also establish the meanings of individual words, even when the grammatical structure is the same: compare "fresh vegetables" to "a fresh remark."

As a reader, you use context clues to help you identify the meanings of unfamiliar words. As a writer, you create a context that shapes the meanings of individual words. Studying context, then, is becoming aware of how the part relates to the whole, how an individual word works in relationship to the words around it.

**Key Terms**

**Context.** The grammatical and meaning environment of an individual word.
**Synonym.** A word that is similar in meaning to another.
**Antonym.** A word that is opposite in meaning to another.
**Definition.** The explanation of the meaning of a word.

**Example or Illustration.** The explanation of a word in terms of a familiar situation or circumstance.
**Grammatical unit.** The grammatical structure—phrase, clause, or sentence—in which an individual word occurs.
**Jargon context.** A kind of context that requires use of specialized vocabulary.
**Concept context.** A kind of context that defines a type of idea.
**Descriptive context.** A kind of context that establishes meaning according to physical or emotional factors.

Generally speaking, the smallest unit of communication is the word. When a child learns to speak, the first level of communication is the single word. As ability to communicate increases, the child's vocabulary expands, as does his or her ability to use simple grammar. In an amazingly short time, the child is able to produce fairly complicated sentences to express ideas, desires, and needs. In school, the child learns to read in much the same way. Single words are learned first, then simple sentences. Eventually, the child learns to read longer sentences with ease. The more words the child knows, and the more aware he or she is of grammatical structures, the better his or her understanding of reading material.

Every good reader, regardless of age or level of reading, continues to learn new words. Quite often these words occur in new material. The word is part of a sentence, paragraph, or passage—what we call the *context* of the word. Context can help the reader determine the meaning of an unknown word because it communicates part of the message the word completes.

## USING CONTEXT

The following sentences show how context determines the meaning of a word:

Maria has a beautiful *face*.
The baby made a *face* when he tasted the broccoli.
On the *face* of it, she appeared to be an honest person.
You must decide to *face* the consequences.
The builder decided to *face* the house with brick.

As you can see, each sentence uses the word "face," and the context of each sentence determines which meaning of the word is being employed—"front part of the head from forehead to chin," "look or expression," "outward appearance," "to deal with," "to cover." Notice that the context also has a grammatical form. The first three sentences use "face" as a noun, and the last two use it as a verb form called an infinitive ("to face"). Context, then, provides both a meaning and a grammatical environment for a word.

Words in Context

Read the following sentences. See if you can supply the appropriate meaning of the word "center" as it is used in each sentence:

Donald agreed to meet his friends at the shopping *center*.
Rosalie loved being the *center* of attention.
Harold played *center* for the Falmouth Falcons.
*Center* your attention on the young man in the crowd.
The children tried to *center* the painting on the wall.

The context, and perhaps a dictionary, should have helped you understand that Donald agreed to meet his friends at a place; that Rosalie loved being the source of interest; that Harold played a middle position on a team; that you should concentrate your attention on the young man; and that the children tried to place or position the painting at the midpoint of the wall. The dictionary would have given you all these possible meanings for "center," and it would also have distinguished between the noun forms in the first three sentences and the verb forms in the last two.

See if you can use the context of the following sentences to help you select the correct word from the list to fill in the blanks:

| | |
|---|---|
| dramatic | advice |
| criticism | classical |
| prick | amateur |
| fledgling | sting |
| operatic | predators |

1. An intern is a _____ doctor.

2. Salt will _____ raw flesh.

3. The tiger and the lion are both _____ because they eat the flesh of other animals.

4. You can _____ your finger with the sharp point of a pin if you are not careful.

5. Her first _____ performance was in the play, "Children of a Lesser God."

6. _____ music was played by the symphony orchestra, while jazz was played by the band.

7. Harold dislikes _____ of any kind, even if it is constructive.

8. Only the _____ is allowed to compete in the Olympics.

9. Leontyne Price, a well known American singer, has an _____ voice.

10. A counselor's _____ can be helpful when choosing the college you would like to attend.

Although it seems possible, at first, to use the same word in more than one sentence, careful attention to the context of each will help you to decide which word best completes the sentence.

## CONTEXT CLUES

Sometimes the context itself will provide hints or clues that give you an idea of what a particular word means. In other words, the reader can use context to figure out meaning without using a dictionary. Sometimes the reader has to rely on context clues to discover meaning. For example when taking an exam, the reader might not be able to determine the meaning of an unfamiliar word. Therefore, context clues might help you to make an "educated" guess as to the word's meaning.

There are four basic types of context clues: synonym, antonym, definition, and example or illustration.

### Synonym Clues

A synonym clue is a word or words in the sentence, paragraph, or passage which is (are) the same or similar in meaning to the unfamiliar word. In the following examples, the synonym clues for the italicized words are enclosed in parentheses.

The teacher asked us to provide a brief *synopsis* or (summary) of the book.

His wife's argument was *fallacious*, (misleading)—just plain wrong!

*Pertinacity* was the cause of most of his problems. (Stubbornness) can get you into trouble.

A (baby carriage) or *perambulator* is very useful to parents of infants.

### Antonym Clues

An antonym clue is a word or words in the sentence, paragraph, or passage that is (are) opposite in meaning to the unfamiliar word:

Gregarious rather than diffident people love the company of others.

The words "rather than" suggest that what follows is the opposite of "gregarious"; therefore, gregarious means to love the company of others.

Some people are quite loquacious, but others hardly talk at all.

"But" nearly always signals a change in meaning. In this sentence, it suggests that people who "hardly talk at all" are different from those who are "loquacious." In fact, "loquacious" does mean very talkative.

>To avoid being involved in <u>clandestine</u> activities, they did things quite openly.

The sentence says "they did things quite openly" so as not to be involved in "clandestine" activities. So "clandestine," which means secret, is opposite in meaning to doing things in the open.

Sentences containing antonym clues often have words like "rather," "but," "instead," and "or," which indicate changes in, or opposite, meaning.

## Definition Clues

A definition clue contains a group of words that actually explains a particular word in a sentence, paragraph, or passage. In the following sentences, definition clues for the italicized words are enclosed in parentheses.

> An *ascetic* is (one who lives a life of self-denial and believes that it leads to spiritual perfection.)
> The meeting took place at the *Pentagon*, (a five-sided building named for its shape.)
> Earl is an *optimist*. (He is a person who sees everything in a positive way.)

Definition context clues almost always follow the same pattern: the word being explained is followed by "is" (or "are") and then a phrase that gives the word's meaning.

## Example or Illustration Clues

An example or illustration clue uses a situation or circumstance to clarify the meaning of a particular word in a sentence, paragraph, or passage.

> <u>Mammalian</u> creatures, including humans, seals and whales, are all members of a group of related animals.

Humans, seals, and whales are all mammals. Therefore, you can conclude that "mammalian" is used to describe a group of similar creatures and means "having the qualities of a mammal."

Theologians, such as pastors, rabbis, ministers and priests, help people with their spiritual concerns.

Pastors, rabbis, ministers, and priests are provided as examples; therefore, the word "theologians" means members of the clergy.

As the pressure increased, they became more belligerent. They were like two boxers waiting for the bell; they stood ready to challenge all comers.

The meaning of the word "belligerent" is suggested by the descriptions of attitudes and behavior. As it is used here, "belligerent" means eager to fight.

The small boy was recalcitrant. He would not answer when the teacher called on him, he was always out of his seat, and no matter how many times he was punished, he refused to change.

Examples of the boy's behavior suggest that "recalcitrant" means stubborn and disobedient.

Knowing the basic types of context clues enables you to discover the meanings of unfamiliar words in a variety of ways. Remember, however, that context clues only help you *guess* what a word means, and you may not always guess correctly. The dictionary should always be your primary source for word meaning.

## READING EXERCISE

Read each of the following sentences. In the space provided indicate (1) the meaning of the underlined word and where possible (2) the type of context clue(s) given in the sentence.

1. Donna and David are twins. Donna is outgoing, but David is diffident.

    Meaning _____

    _____

    _____

    Context clue _____

Words in Context 49

2. The girl's largesse became apparent when she gave her friend a $50 gift certificate.

   Meaning _____

   Context clue _____

3. The teacher showed no compunction in failing the students; there was no regret in his voice or his manner as he gave out the grades.

   Meaning _____

   Context clue _____

4. Under constant tension, James soon became a dyspeptic, a person bothered with indigestion.

   Meaning _____

   Context clue _____

5. The club was under John's aegis; therefore, no one else could claim sponsorship.

   Meaning _____

Context clue _____

_____

_____

6. Rather than create a scene, Deborah controlled her anger and <u>seethed</u> in silence.

   Meaning _____

   _____

   _____

   Context clue _____

   _____

   _____

7. Dominic is a <u>stoic</u>. His expression never reveals his true feelings.

   Meaning _____

   _____

   _____

   Context clue _____

   _____

   _____

8. The <u>conflagration</u> was the most destructive in the town's history. Almost every building burned to the ground.

   Meaning _____

   _____

   _____

   Context clue _____

   _____

   _____

9. The honest person hates <u>duplicity</u>.

   Meaning _____

   _____

   _____

   Context word _____

## WRITING WORDS IN CONTEXT

What enables a word to communicate a specific meaning is the context in which it occurs. The context, which includes both the surrounding words and the grammatical form of those words, shapes and refines an individual word's meaning. A writer's task, then, is to find not only the right word, but also to place it in the right context.

Every time you put some words together, you create a context for the words that will follow. Writing is, in a very real sense, the creation of context. For example, look at this sentence:

The farmer decided to _____ the pig.

The context created by "the farmer" doing something to "the pig" demands a word appropriate to that situation:

The farmer decided to <u>butcher</u> the pig.

Other words, such as "kill," "exterminate," or "murder," would describe the same action. But farmers "butcher" animals for market; they do not "kill," "exterminate," or "murder" them.

In other contexts, "butcher" can mean to kill brutally and callously:

The murderer *butchered* his defenseless victim.

The battle resulted in the *butchering* of the defending troops.

In these sentences, the word is shaped by its context to describe violence aimed at people, not the death of animals for profit.

Context, then, develops as you write. It often demands that you choose a certain word and keeps you from using another. As a writer, you should recognize that composing sentences involves the whole unit. You cannot write efficiently if you write word-by-word. In particular, notice that grammatical units form contexts which can influence your choice of words. In addition, the meanings of surrounding words limit the number of words which can complete a sentence. It is a good idea to be aware of the context you are creating as you write.

### Grammatical Unit

The grammatical unit within which a particular word occurs can change the meaning of that word:

The pigs rolled in the mud in their *pen*.
She *penned* a letter to her friend.
They had been *pen* pals for years.

In the first sentence, "pen" is a noun indicating an enclosure; in the second, "penned" is a verb meaning to write; and in the third, "pen" is an adjective describing a friendship held together by letters. Each of these different grammatical forms helps to shape the meaning of the word. Consider the following:

She asked him to *light* the candle.
The *light* package blew away in the wind.
He was the *light* of her life.

Again, the grammatical unit in which the word "light" occurs shapes its meaning. In the first sentence, "light" is an infinitive (a verb form) and it means to ignite or cause to burst into flame; in the second, it is an adjective that means of little weight; and in the third, it is a noun that means a very positive influence.

## Surrounding Words

The words you place next to an individual word also shape its meaning by providing a particular context:

I like to drink my coffee in a *mug*.
Betty's mother thought her daughter's friend John was a *mug*.

In both sentences "mug" is a noun, but the meanings are very different. The first "mug" refers to a container for liquids and the second suggests a person of bad character.

Different meanings can also be communicated by the word "mug" as a verb:

The actor *mugged* while reading his lines.
The criminal *mugged* the old man in the park.

"Mug" is a verb in both sentences, but the meanings are different: "made faces" in the first, and "attacked" in the second.

## Jargon Context

Every special area of expertise or interest has its own vocabulary. This vocabulary, which is called *jargon,* establishes a particular word environment:

| Sports: | The quarterback threw a *bomb*. |
| Arts: | The famous playwright's new work was a *bomb*. |
| Student: | The student thought he had *bombed* the final examination. |

The same word—"bomb"—takes on very different meanings because of the particular jargon context in which it occurs. These sentences can be rewritten using nonjargon words:

> The quarterback threw a long touchdown pass.
>
> The famous playwright's new work was a financial and artistic failure.
>
> The student thought he had failed the final examination.

Jargon words demonstrate your knowledge of a particular field or area. In formal writing, however, jargon words may be unacceptable. It is practically impossible to create a list of situations in which jargon is, or for that matter is not, appropriate. The best rule is to avoid jargon unless you are certain your readers will be able to understand it easily and will gain more from the jargon words than from less colorful substitutes.

The vocabularies used in the professions of medicine and law include generally acceptable jargon:

> According to the *ophthalmologist,* George was *myopic.*
>
> The heirs of the millionaire faced a long struggle to divide up his estate because he died *intestate.*

These sentences can be rewritten with standard vocabulary that any reader will understand:

> According to the eye doctor, George was nearsighted.
>
> The heirs of the millionaire faced a long struggle to divide up his estate because he died without leaving a will.

"Ophthalmologist" and "myopic," however, are more specific than "eye doctor" and "nearsighted," and "intestate" conveys in one word what "died without leaving a will" says in five words.

## Concept Context

Often you will want to express a general idea rather than state a specific fact. In these instances, your context is determined by the idea. For example, if you want to say something about rising prices, your context will be an economic one, and the words you choose will be understood as having an economic meaning.

> The economy has been suffering from *inflation* over the past few years.

In other contexts, "inflation" can refer to things as widely separated as rafts or balloons filled with air, or a person's ego being boosted by praise. The fact that the sentence concerns an economic fact shapes the word's meaning to indicate steadily rising wages and prices.

Perhaps you want to state a philosophical idea:

> Clem's lack of concern about death results from his *fatalistic* attitude toward life.

Here the word "fatalistic" captures the idea that life is determined by some unknown force, and that it is foolish to worry about things beyond our control.

Political concepts are communicated through particular contexts:

> The governor's *liberal* policies caused his defeat in the election.
>
> Voter registration drives in the South in the 1960s were aimed at ensuring that nobody would be *disenfranchised* because of race.
>
> Senators will sometimes attempt a *filibuster* to stop the passage of a bill they oppose.

The italicized words all specify particular political concepts.

**Descriptive Context**

Describing a particular place, or person, or thing also creates a special context:

> Weather conditions on the Texas *panhandle* range from one extreme to the other.

"Panhandle" literally is the handle of a pan, but it is widely used to describe certain kinds of geographical areas. These areas jut out from a larger area in a shape that roughly resembles a handle.

Similarly, certain words are generally applied in describing people.

> The old man had a *craggy* face, and a *sharp* temper.

"Craggy" describes a face which has the look and texture of a steep rock formation, or mountain "crag." Context is a subtle but important influence on our choice of words. "Sharp" is an ordinary word which in this context identifies a type of emotional condition. Somebody who has a "sharp" temper is one who easily loses control. "Keen" means much the same thing as "sharp," but we do not say "She has a *keen* temper." Similarly, police reports say that a victim was killed with a "blunt" instrument, not a "dull" or "flat" instrument.

As you write, try to identify the particular context you are establishing. Then you will be able to choose the words which best fit that context. Correctly matching words and context will strengthen your writing.

# WRITING EXERCISE

I. Fill in the blanks with appropriate words. For each word you have filled in, determine the context that shaped your choice—jargon, concept, or descriptive.

1. The land jutted out into the ocean for many miles, forming a _____. Context type _____
2. The recent election showed that politicians who held _____ positions seemed most popular. Context type _____
3. The popular singer hit a _____ note, much to her embarrassment. Context type _____
4. After years of working in the sun, his face has a _____ texture. Context type _____
5. The race car driver _____ his engine before the starting flag was waved. Context type _____
6. The doctor declared that John was suffering from _____ which made it difficult for him to breathe. Context type _____
7. Her psychiatrist said Jeanette needed to understand that her _____ behavior was a symptom and not a cause. Context type _____
8. The teacher informed his class that he believed in _____ exams which tested students' knowledge of facts. Context type _____
9. The child's _____ face suggested she was incapable of doing anything wrong. Context type _____
10. He believed that social _____ must be understood before individual exceptions could be identified. Context type _____

II. Provide two different grammatical contexts for each of the following:

1. run
   a. _____
   b. _____
2. place
   a. _____
   b. _____
3. fire
   a. _____
   b. _____
4. oil
   a. _____
   b. _____
5. frost
   a. _____
   b. _____
6. finger
   a. _____
   b. _____
7. jerk
   a. _____
   b. _____
8. store
   a. _____
   b. _____
9. motel
   a. _____
   b. _____
10. flash
    a. _____
    b. _____

III. Provide two different meaning contexts for the following words, but use the same grammatical form.

1. fit
   a. _____
   b. _____
2. waste
   a. _____
   b. _____
3. hit
   a. _____
   b. _____
4. file
   a. _____
   b. _____
5. strike
   a. _____
   b. _____
6. tube
   a. _____
   b. _____
7. roll
   a. _____
   b. _____
8. tip
   a. _____
   b. _____
9. fuzzy
   a. _____
   b. _____
10. crash
    a. _____
    b. _____

IV. A. Write five sentences that establish a context of specialized knowledge or expertise, and use at least five jargon words. Underline the jargon words.

IV. B. Write five sentences that explore a certain type of concept area (politics, economics, philosophy). Use a word related to this area in each sentence. Underline these words.

IV. C. Write five sentences that describe a place, person, or thing. Use descriptive words for contexts. Underline these words.

# 4

# Denotation and Connotation

PREVIEW

Words communicate both a literal, or *denotative*, and attitudinal, or *connotative*, meaning. The denotative meaning of a word indicates that something belongs to a group of things, actions, or qualities. For example, the word "dog" describes a four-legged domestic animal that belongs to the canine family. The connotative meaning of a word communicates an attitude toward something. This attitude can be negative, neutral, or positive. "Dog," for example, has a generally positive connotative value. "Rat," on the other hand, would have a generally negative connotative value.

But as we have seen, words can never be fully understood either denotatively or connotatively without a context. Different contexts can change both meanings. For example, the denotative meaning of stamp changes with different contexts:

I put the *stamp* on the envelope.
My boss gave me a *stamp* of approval.
*Stamp* out poverty!

Connotation, too, depends on context:

Hungrily, I eyed the *fat*, juicy peach.
I filed the *fat* folder of papers.
The dog was *fat* and old.

The first sentence suggests a positive quality of the peach; the second a more or less neutral physical description of the folder; and the third a somewhat negative attitude toward the condition of the dog.

Denotative and connotative meanings are extremely important in both reading and writing. Sensitivity to the denotative and connotative meanings of the words you read will provide you with a fuller understanding of the material. And the skillful use of words denotatively and connotatively will add precision and emphasis to your writing.

**Key Terms**

> **Denotation.**  Characteristic of language that indicates a group of things, actions, or qualities.
> **Connotation.**  Characteristic of language that communicates an attitude toward a group of things, actions, or qualities.
> **Abstract.**  Level of meaning that cannot be experienced by the senses.
> **Positive.**  Favorable connotation.
> **Negative.**  Unfavorable connotation.
> **Neutral.**  Neither a favorable nor an unfavorable connotative attitude.

As you are probably aware, almost all words have more than one meaning. A simple word like "run" has, according to *Webster's New Twentieth Century Unabridged Dictionary,* more than a hundred different meanings! How many times have you looked up a word in the dictionary, only to face the difficulty of choosing the correct meaning from those listed?

In order to choose the correct meaning, you must consider the context, the words that surround the word you are attempting to define. Examining the context enables you to select the appropriate meaning because only a certain meaning of a given word will make good sense in a particular situation.

## READING FOR DENOTATIVE AND CONNOTATIVE MEANING

Your work as a reader involves determining the *type* of meaning the word communicates—denotative or connotative.

### Denotative Meaning

When a word *denotes,* it stands for, indicates, points to, signifies, or names something. A word can denote an object like a lamp, an event like an election, an idea like freedom, or a quality like kindness. In other words, denotation can refer to something concrete like a lamp, or something abstract like freedom.

Usually the denotative meaning of a word is clear. The denotation is the literal, dictionary definition of a word which refers to an object, idea, event, or quality. As a reader, you identify the author's words by knowing or learning their denotative meaning. The words in italics in the following sentences are used denotatively—that is, to communicate their literal meaning.

>José, unaccustomed to using English, was shy and *taciturn*.
>The baby's disappearance was *inexplicable*.
>*Diligence* is a necessary quality of the good student.
>The smile on the girl's face seemed *disingenuous*.

With the help of a dictionary if necessary, the reader understands that José was not fond of talking; that the baby's disappearance could not be explained; that the good student constantly works hard; and that the girl's smile seemed false or calculating.

Words that communicate most clearly on the denotative level are generally used in materials that are informative, factual, and objective. The following paragraphs depend upon denotation to communicate their information. (Use a dictionary when necessary to check for definitions of unfamiliar words, and keep a written record of the words and their meanings.)

>President Abraham Lincoln on May 15, 1862, signed a bill that established the Department of Agriculture. The bill was one of three designed to serve the interests of the family farmer. The other two were the Homestead Act, May 20, and the Land-Grant College Act, July 2. Isaac Newton took the oath of office as first commissioner of agriculture on July 1. He inherited the staff of nine employees and facilities of the Agricultural Division of the Patent Office. The new department a year later had a horticulturist, a chemist, an entomologist, a statistician, an editor, and 24 others.

>Cloning was a word that used to be used only in connection with nonsexual reproduction of simple animals and plants. In recent years, however, it is used in relation to higher level animals. Biologists are finding ways to induce the individual cell of a mature animal to multiply so as to create another copy exactly the same as the original.

>"Rings on her fingers and bells on her toes...." So goes one of the old Mother Goose rhymes. The wearing of rings is one of the oldest customs of mankind; no one knows when or where it started. A ring on the finger is of course still a very popular form of personal

adornment. (Certain tribes in Africa and the South Sea Islands also adorn themselves with rings in the nose, in the ears, on the toes, and around the arms and ankles. And until sometime in the fourteenth century Europeans often wore thumb rings.) Most rings worn as ornaments are made of gold or other valuable metals, and their variety—from the simple band to massive creations elaborately carved and set with precious stones—is practically infinite. A ring may have initials engraved on it, or some other seal, in which case it is called a "signet ring."

If we used only denotative meanings for words, there would be little confusion and little trouble with oral and written communication. Language would be straightforward and precise, and the dictionary would answer all our questions. Communication would be simple, but also not very interesting. But people and life are not always clear and straightforward; and words reflect this complexity in their connotative meanings.

**Connotative Meaning**

When a word *connotes,* it suggests or implies an attitude to which the reader will react with certain feelings. The reaction of the reader is usually an emotional response to these words because the reader already has either a *positive* or *negative* attitude toward them. Words like "fat," "skinny," "love," "hate," "sex," "death," "drugs," "sneak," "hypocrite," "Democrat," "Republican" all have connotative as well as denotative meanings. These words can cause the reader to react negatively or positively to the material in which they occur.

The reactions will be determined by the reader's feelings toward the idea being communicated. The reader's feelings, in turn, are shaped by his or her experiences. Although connotative meanings can produce different reactions, and therefore different interpretations of the same material by different readers, this can be a special advantage. Connotative meanings enrich our language and broaden our interpretations. When two or more readers discuss their different reactions to the same material, the discussion challenges each reader and encourages critical thinking.

Writers often use connotative meanings to stimulate the reader's thinking; moreover, the writer usually has a specific reaction in mind. To produce this reaction in the reader, the writer chooses words carefully for their connotative value. The writer can use connotative meanings to persuade, to dissuade, to convince, to "sell," to antagonize, to propagandize. All these purposes can be accomplished, in large part, by words whose connotations work on the reader's likes, dislikes, and prejudices. Your goal as a reader is to understand what the author is saying not only denotatively but connotatively, so that you will be aware of both the factual and the suggestive message of the material.

The following sets of sentences convey the same denotative idea, but the connotative meanings of the words cause positive or negative reactions in readers:

> Alan is *fat*. (negative)
>
> Alan is *plump* and *round*. (positive)
>
> Louise is *skinny*. (negative)
>
> Louise is *slender*. (positive)
>
> Florence is a *sneak*. (negative)
>
> Florence is *discreet*. (positive)

The next group of sentences also contains connotative meanings, but in these the context determines the reader's emotional reaction:

> Nancy's *childlike* behavior seemed unsuitable for a woman her age. (negative)
>
> Incidents like Watergate give the *presidency* a bad image. (negative)
>
> *Love* is a useless, wasted emotion. (negative)
>
> Larry was *sneaking* around behind Karen's back to plan her surprise birthday party. (positive)
>
> John *hated* to witness an injustice of any kind. (positive)

Although the word "childlike" usually refers to the positive qualities of childhood, words like "unsuitable" and "woman of her age" make its connotation negative in this sentence; the reference to Watergate and the word "bad" change the usually positive connotation of "presidency" to a negative reaction; when called "useless" and "wasted," "love" becomes negative rather than positive; Larry's "sneaking" becomes positive in the context of planning a surprise party; and John's "hate" is positive in terms of the object of his hatred.

Read the following paragraphs. Notice that in each a particular word is used very effectively because of its connotation.

> The teacher thought I was stupid. Couldn't spell, couldn't read, couldn't do arithmetic. Just stupid. Teachers were never interested in finding out that you couldn't concentrate because you were so hungry because you hadn't had any breakfast. All you could think about was noontime, would it ever come? Maybe you could sneak into the cloakroom and steal a bite of some kid's lunch out of a coat pocket. A bite of something. Paste. You can't really make a meal out of paste, or put it on bread for a sandwich, but sometimes I'd scoop a few spoonfuls out of the paste jar in the back of the room. Pregnant people get strange tastes. I was pregnant with poverty. Pregnant with dirt and pregnant with cold and pregnant with shoes that were never bought for me, pregnant with five other people in my bed and no Daddy in the next

room, and pregnant with hunger. Paste doesn't taste too bad when you're hungry.

I say to you today, my friends, even though we face the difficulties of today and tomorrow, I still have a dream. It is a dream deeply rooted in the American dream. I have a dream that one day this nation will rise up and live out the true meaning of its creed: "We hold these truths to be self-evident, that all men are created equal." I have a dream that one day, on the red hills of Georgia, sons of former slaves and the sons of former slave owners will be able to sit down together at the table of brotherhood.

The word "pregnant" usually carries a positive connotation, but here it is used in a negative way to produce strong emotional response in the reader toward the hunger and poverty of the child; the word "dream" here carries a positive connotation and is repeated effectively in that way to convey the hope its author has for the future.

Connotation appears in prose as well as poetry, and in fiction as well as nonfiction. Connotation enhances and improves written communication because it enables a writer to express himself or herself with many shades and shifts of meaning that reveal the many ways of looking at facts, ideas, or events.

## READING EXERCISE

Read the following paragraphs and define the words listed at the end of each denotatively; also describe any connotative meaning the word carries. Use the context and your reaction to what you have read to help you define words that have connotative meanings. Not all the words have connotative meanings as they are used here.

If smoking is so bad for you, then why do people begin smoking? There are many reasons. Some young people begin smoking because their parents or their friends do. Some smoke because it makes them feel adult. Others start smoking because it's the "in" thing to do. They don't want their friends to think they are "uncool." Still others begin to smoke because they are curious.

adult _____

in _____

uncool _____

Denotation and Connotation

A listener must adjust to the pace of the person talking, but a reader can set his own pace. If the material spoken is difficult to understand and comes at a fast pace, the listener usually cannot slow it down. A reader, however, has the opportunity to slow down, to study and ponder over what is before him. The listener usually hears the words once and they are gone, sometimes for good. The reader can go back to reread until he understands what is written.

pace _____

ponder _____

A traveler, returned from an ancient land, tells the narrator of a ruin he observed in the desert. It was once the statue of a mighty king. All that remains, however, are the statue's broken legs and fallen head. The cold and arrogant expression of the ruler, placed there by the sculptor to mock the king, is still evident. On the broken base of the statue is carved the boast: "My name is Ozymandias, king of kings: Look on my works the things I have built, ye Mighty, and despair!" But Ozymandias is long dead, and his kingdom and power have long since vanished. Only the ruined statue with its boastful inscription remains to mock the foolish pride of tyrants.

ruin _____

cold _____

arrogant _____

mock _____

boastful _____

tyrant _____

Female roles, in general, receive less money, prestige, and power. The role of the housewife is an unpaid one that involves no real political power outside the household and that is increasingly held in low esteem. Other female roles—teacher, librarian, social worker, cashier, and secretary—are similarly undervalued. Such a situation places women in a position of inequality: They are more likely to receive less money, power, and prestige for performance of their roles.

prestige _____

political _____

esteem _____

undervalued _____

The Beaux Arts Ball is famous for the dazzling spectacle of the costumes people turn up in and, at every ball, the most spectacularly dressed person of all is its chairman. She appears in glittering headpieces of towering tinsel, furs, feathers, jewels, and gowns bedizened with sequins and gold paillettes. At a recent ball, the glamorous chairman was presented to the audience stepping out of a huge mock-up of a champagne bottle, wearing a gown of silver lamé, a jeweled breastplate and a crown of white ostrich plumes.

dazzling _____

spectacle _____

tinsel _____

bedizened _____

paillette _____

mock-up _____

lamé _____

breastplate _____

## WRITING FOR DENOTATIVE AND CONNOTATIVE MEANING

Since words communicate on both denotative and connotative levels, you should be sensitive to both types of meanings when you write. Each word you choose should clearly identify the group of things, actions, or qualities you want to describe. Further, each word should suggest the attitudinal value appropriate to your purpose.

### Denotation

Denotation serves as a means by which the writer can communicate precise, factual information. English has a word for any idea you might want to express. In fact, quite often several words with closely related meanings are available to you. For example, if a parent is unhappy with a child's behavior, he or she could be described as doing any of the following:

*correcting* the child
*scolding* the child
*chastising* the child
*berating* the child

All these words denote that the parent is showing the child the error of his or her ways:

| | |
|---|---|
| *correct* | A mild statement |
| *scold* | A stronger, more angry statement |
| *chastise* | Even stronger |
| *berate* | A very angry attack |

In turn, the child can become any of the following:

| | |
|---|---|
| *ashamed* | Child admits wrongdoing. |
| *sullen* | Child resents correction. |
| *stubborn* | Child refuses to change behavior. |
| *intransigent* | Child refuses to budge. |

These examples suggest the range of possibilities available. With some thought, and with the aid of a good dictionary, you can work to make your writing more precise and accurate on the denotative level.

Words also denote things, actions, and qualities that are less obvious, less precise, because they do not relate as directly to the physical world:

I *love* you.
*Love* blooms in the spring.
She is a *lovable* person.
He looked at her *lovingly*.

In these four instances, "love" is used denotatively as a verb (action), thing (noun), and quality (adjective and adverb). But the denotative communication is less clear than with "dog," "walk," or "fat." "Love" cannot be experienced in the same way as "dog," for example.

Because *abstract* words such as "love" communicate less clearly on the denotative level, they need to be placed in a sharply defined context:

> While I was walking through the park, I saw a young couple sitting together on a bench, just staring into each other's eyes as if to hold the moment between them. For a full five minutes, they seemed hardly to breathe. They did not talk. Then, suddenly and unexpectedly, their faces burst into smiles, and they got up from the bench and walked away. It's not that love is speechless, but it speaks most clearly in silence.

Since "love" is a state of mind rather than a physical object, its denotative value is weak. You cannot see "love" walking down the street, but you can observe two people "in love." By providing a setting for the word, a context in which it occurs, the denotation can be strengthened. In the paragraph above, the scene between the two people who are in love provides a more specific denotative meaning for the word. The actions of silent staring into each other's eyes, and then the sudden smile, suggest that one denotative meaning of "love" is the quiet sharing of a moment. Another denotative meaning suggested by the paragraph is that "love" involves the ability to communicate feeling without words.

Denotation, then, is clearest in words that refer to a thing, action, or quality which can be experienced physically. Words that do not have an exact physical basis are less clear in their denotative meanings. Quite often, moreover, words that are vague in their denotative quality are the very words that carry the strongest connotative value.

## Connotation

Besides identifying things, actions, or qualities, language also communicates an attitude toward what is being described. Connotation tells us how we should feel about something rather than what that something is. For example, if you were to describe a particular building as a "factory," you would be using a word that denotes a place where goods are manufactured. "Factory" does not have a particularly strong connotative level of meaning. It probably does not arouse strong emotions. If you were to describe the same building as a "sweatshop," you could be using a word with the same denotative meaning, but with a strongly negative connotation as well. "Sweatshop," although it too denotes a place where goods are manufactured, *connotes* a business in which the owners are interested only in profit and callously disregard the welfare of those who work for them.

Let's return to the child whose behavior upset his or her parents. The word "child" denotes a young human being. It carries a mildly positive connotative value. However, consider the following words, which could also be used to refer to this individual:

brat
imp
urchin

All of these describe a child whose behavior might be troublesome. However, the words differ sharply in their connotative values:

| | |
|---|---|
| brat | Suggests a negative attitude; the child's behavior is unacceptable and disturbing. |

| | |
|---|---|
| imp | Suggests a positive attitude; the child's behavior is cute. |
| urchin | Suggests a negative attitude, but not as negative as "brat;" the child's behavior is still unacceptable, but there is something attractive about it. |

Connotative values of words describing the same thing can be very different. In addition, connotation, much more than denotation, is influenced by context. Since connotation reflects an attitude, that attitude is usually present throughout the material.

Because connotation appeals to our emotions rather than our reason, it is a powerful tool for the writer. It adds interest and persuasion to any kind of writing. As a writer, you should be aware of connotation and use it carefully. You should remember, for example, that if you want to present a factual, objective message, you should try to use words with strong and clear denotative meanings. If you want to arouse a strong emotional reaction in your reader, you should search for words with strong connotations.

Consider writing two descriptions of a fire. The first is objective and denotative, as would be appropriate to a news story, police report, or legal brief. The second is emotional and heavily connotative, as might appear in a newspaper editorial or political speech.

### The Facts

*Event:* Fire
*Time:* Cold winter night
*Place:* One-family frame house in old section of town
*Cause:* Defective kerosene heater
*Background:* Couple had lived in house fifty years; they had shut off heat to save money; they were trying to keep warm in the bedroom with the kerosene heater.
*Result:* Complete destruction of house; death of couple

### Denotative Report

A fire destroyed an old frame house last night. Mr. and Mrs. Smith, who had lived in the house for fifty years, died in the fire. The fire was caused by a faulty kerosene heater which Mr. and Mrs. Smith were using to heat their small bedroom after they had shut off their oil burner in an attempt to save money. The house, located in the oldest section of town, burned to the ground before the fire department could bring the fire under control.

### Connotative Description

A roaring blaze consumed a decrepit frame house last night. Mr. and Mrs. Smith, who had made their home in the house for fifty years, fell victim to the inferno. The holocaust was started by an illegal kerosene heater with which Mr. and Mrs. Smith had tried in vain to heat their tiny bedroom after they had shut off the oil burner in a desperate attempt to save a few pennies. Their home, located in this once fashionable neighborhood, crumbled to the ground before the fire department could bring the fire under control.

The information contained in the two paragraphs is exactly the same. In fact, much of the language is the same. However, a number of words in the denotative paragraph have been replaced by more strongly connotative words:

| **Denotative** | **Connotative** |
| --- | --- |
| fire | roaring blaze |
| destroyed | consumed |
| lived | made their home |
| die | fell victim |
| fire | inferno |
| fire | holocaust |
| faulty | illegal |
| used | tried in vain |
| small | tiny |
| attempt | desperate attempt |
| money | few pennies |
| house | home |
| oldest | once fashionable |
| burned to the ground | crumbled |

The words in the denotative list do not create much of an emotional response. They present the story in a matter-of-fact, objective way that minimizes the strong feelings this story could easily arouse. The connotative words work in just the opposite way: they intensify the emotional possibilities of the story by encouraging sympathy for the couple. The key word "fire" is replaced in the connotative description by words with strongly negative values: "roaring blaze," "inferno," "holocaust."

Neither denotation nor connotation is "more correct." Both are necessary to express the full range of human experience. The key factor in choosing between denotative and connotative language is purpose. Certain occasions and audiences demand a factual presentation, and in those instances the writer chooses a denotative approach. In those circumstances and for those audiences that invite an emotional treatment, the writer selects a connotative approach.

WRITING EXERCISE

I. Fill in the blanks in the following sentences with words you

Denotation and Connotation

think complete the messages of each. Then consult a dictionary or a thesaurus to discover three closely related words that can also be used. List them and their definitions.

1. After the party, the man _____ home.
       Other choice                        Definition

   a. _____
   b. _____
   c. _____

2. The playful puppy gave my hand a _____ bite.
       Other choice                        Definition

   a. _____
   b. _____
   c. _____

3. My friend _____ refused to go with me.
       Other choice                        Definition

   a. _____
   b. _____
   c. _____

4. The _____ student thought the course would be easy.
       Other choice                        Definition

   a. _____
   b. _____
   c. _____

5. The bestselling novel appealed to its readers' _____ interests.
       Other choice                        Definition

   a. _____
   b. _____
   c. _____

II. For each of the italicized words or phrases, list ten connotative choices—five positive, and five negative. One word has been provided to start you off in each category.

1. an *overweight* person

       Negative                                               Positive

fat                                                                   plump

_____      _____

_____      _____

_____      _____

_____      _____

2. a *stubborn* person

       Negative                                               Positive

pigheaded                                           persistent

_____      _____

_____      _____

_____      _____

_____      _____

3. an *optimistic* person

       Negative                                               Positive

unrealistic                                          idealistic

_____      _____

_____      _____

_____      _____

_____      _____

4. *careful about money*

       Negative                                               Positive

miser                                                        frugal

_____      _____

_____      _____

_____      _____

_____      _____

5. *having a good appetite*

| Negative | Positive |
|---|---|
| piggish | healthy |
| _____ | _____ |
| _____ | _____ |
| _____ | _____ |
| _____ | _____ |

III. Write a description that attempts to define denotatively by providing a physical context for one of the following abstract words: (1) pride, (2) freedom, (3) happiness, (4) friendship, (5) competition.

IV. Rewrite the description you composed for III and add as many strongly connotative words as you can.

V. Write an objective, denotative description for one of the following lists of facts.

1. A touchdown in the last five seconds of a championship game.
   Come from behind victory for home team.
   Touchdown scored on deflected pass.
   First championship for home team.
   Pass thrown by rookie quarterback.
   Pass caught by veteran playing last game.
2. Prolonged drought in wheat-growing state.
   Temperatures averaging over 100°.
   Farmers fail to keep crops alive with irrigation.
   Many small farmers cannot pay bills.
   Some farmers face foreclosure.
   Governor asks federal government for special loans to farmer.
   Congress is reluctant to set a precedent.
3. Movie star signs multimillion-dollar contract for new film.
   Film will be about star's love affair with a pet dolphin.
   Star used to be an Olympic champion swimmer.
   Star swims better than he or she acts.
   Movie is expected to be a smash hit.
   Star is extraordinarily good looking.

VI. Rewrite your choice for V and attempt to arouse an emotional reaction through connotative language.

# 5
# Sentence Sense

PREVIEW

The sentence is the basic unit of communication because it is the form we use to make statements. These statements can express facts or opinions. The statements are more or less clear depending upon the words we use, and they are more or less believable depending upon the reasoning behind them.

A definite or *absolute* statement says that something is true at all times and in all circumstances. A qualified or *conditional* statement says that something is generally, but not always, true. Facts are usually stated in absolute language; opinions are usually presented in conditional terms. Both readers and writers need to distinguish between absolute and conditional statements as well as between facts and opinions.

The working together of individual words in a sentence conveys the meaning of the statement. The reasoning behind the statements adds believability to what you read and write. The purpose of reasoning is to shape logical conclusions that can be expressed in language.

**Key Terms**

    **Fact.**  Something that can be shown to be true.
    **Opinion.**  A belief that something is true.
    **Absolute language.**  A way of saying something is true at all times and in all circumstances.
    **Conditional language.**  A way of saying something is generally, but not always, true.

**Vocabulary.** The words that carry the meaning of a sentence.
**Logic.** Thinking that draws connections between ideas.

A sentence conveys a complete thought. Whether it consists of one or one hundred words, it is the basic unit of verbal and written communication. Sentences express ideas the speaker or author wishes to communicate to the listener or reader. Sentences show various relationships among grammatical forms and among ideas. Certain sentence *types* (Chapters 6, 7) are chosen by a writer to communicate relationships among ideas. But every sentence, no matter what its form or purpose, must make sense if we are to understand what it means. Three elements make a sentence "make sense": language, vocabulary, and logic.

# READING FOR SENSE

## Absolute and Conditional Language

Language, as it is used here, means the author's choice of words: restricted, inflexible, and limited, or less restricted, more flexible, and less limited. Language that falls into the first category is called *absolute,* and language that fits the second is *conditional.*

*Absolute Language.* How many times have you heard, or used, sentences like these?

Larry is always late.
Anna never remembers to take her keys.
He must be crazy.
I'll never speak to her again!

Often, perhaps. However, how many times did you or the speaker actually *mean* what was said? These sentences mean that Larry, at all times and in all situations, is late; Anna, at all times, and in every situation, forgets her keys; "he," at all times, and in all situations, is insane; and, no matter what happens, "I" will not speak to "her" ever again.

Chances are the users of sentences like these do not *mean* what they say. They have overstated the degree to which these ideas are true. When we use absolute words like "always," "never," and "must," their meanings must be considered; otherwise, communication can become confused. Consider the following sentences:

All dogs are canines.
Only females give birth.

Every month of the calendar year has at least twenty-eight days.

Humans must breathe to stay alive.

In each sentence, an absolute word has been used. But these sentences do not overstate. Instead, they are carefully constructed with absolute language to express a particular idea. Notice that each of these sentences can be checked for truth. The same thing cannot be done with the first series above.

Words that may be used as absolutes include the following:

| | |
|---|---|
| always | must |
| never | ever |
| all | only |
| am | will |
| is | necessarily |
| are | |

The reader should look for absolute words in sentences and consider the ways in which these words may affect understanding of the author's message:

1. Do these words overstate the author's ideas?
2. Are these ideas, expressed in absolute words, always true?
3. Should this information be remembered as fact?

*Conditional Language.* Most things in life are not absolute; they depend upon circumstances, situations, possibilities, and exceptions. Conditional words like "frequently," "maybe," "might," and "can" allow greater flexibility in expressing ideas:

Nurses are *frequently* women.

*Maybe* we will go to the movies tomorrow.

It *might* be the best time to go on vacation.

Smoking *can* cause cancer.

These sentences use conditional words to convey ideas. They allow for the possibility of an exception. No exceptions are allowed when sentences are phrased in absolute terms:

Nurses are women.

We will go to the movies tomorrow.

It is the best time to go on vacation.

Smoking causes cancer.

These sentences have less chance of being true because the absolute language does not leave room for exceptions or error. Conditional words, on the other hand, do provide for other possibilities. The careful reader identifies sentences as absolute or conditional. "Nurses are frequently women" says something quite different from "Nurses are women." The conditional word "frequently" increases the degree of truth of the sentence, since it allows for the fact that many nurses are, in fact, men.

Words that may be used in conditional expressions include the following:

| | |
|---|---|
| maybe | might |
| frequently | seems |
| sometimes | generally |
| not necessarily | appear |
| some | could |
| usually | can |
| often | should |
| may | |

Consider how these words affect your understanding of the author's message:

1. What other conditions, possibilities, exceptions are allowed for in this sentence?
2. Are these ideas, expressed in conditional terms, true?
3. Should this information be remembered as fact?

## Vocabulary

Vocabulary, as an element of understanding, means understanding the meaning of words as they are used in particular sentences. You can read a sentence over and over again, but if you do not know the meaning of the words, you will not understand the sentence. For example, knowing that the statement "All dogs are canines" is expressed in absolute language (because of the word "all") will not be enough unless you recognize the word "canine." If you know that "canine" is defined as "belonging to the dog family," the sentence will be clear. If you do not know the definition of that word, the absolute language will only tell you that "all dogs" are something or other. And without knowing that key word, you will not be able to judge whether the statement is true.

Each of the following sentences uses words you may not know:

The club is under John's *aegis*.
The senator's remarks were *superfluous*.
Jack's *largesse* is well known.
The witness's *credibility* was questioned by some members of the jury.

In order to understand the author's message in each of these sentences, you need to know that "aegis" means supervision; that "superfluous" means excessive; that "largesse" means generosity; and that "credibility" means believability.

Sometimes authors use familiar words in unfamiliar ways:

*Parents* must be people.
Alfred holds a *chair* at Columbia University.
Farmers *corn* some animals at least once a day.
Ruth was known to *pepper* her comments with humor.

To understand these sentences, you need to know that "parents" refers to anyone or anything that produces offspring; that "chair" means to hold a position of dignity for distinguished service or achievement; that "corn" means to feed with corn or grain; and that "pepper" means to sprinkle. If your understanding of the definitions of these words does not fit these particular contexts, you will not understand the author's message.

**Logic**

The logic of a sentence means whether or not it makes sense. In other words, is the idea expressed in the sentence reasonable? Consider the following sentences:

Elephants are canines.
The word "comfortable" has five syllables.
Airplanes travel great distances by water.
Cars made during the present decade are now more than ten years old.
Nursery schools probably give high school diplomas to their graduates.
If we travel across country and drive approximately 200 miles per day, we will cover 1200 miles in five days.

Even after you have decided what type of language was used and discovered the meanings of unfamiliar words, you will find that these sentences are illogical—they just do not make sense. Elephants do not belong to the dog family; there are four syllables in the word "comfortable;" cars made during the present decade are less than ten years old; nursery schools do not give high school diplomas; and at 200 miles per day, the distance traveled will be 1000 miles in five days. The language and vocabulary of illogical sentences offer clues as to why the ideas they contain are nonsense.

Although authors do not usually write illogical sentences on purpose, you as a reader must be certain that the ideas are reasonable, especially when you read a series of sentences that all relate to the same idea, like those contained in a paragraph:

In an age when few people could read, places of business were known by such signs as "The Green Goose," "The Piper," "The Red

Lion." Stores in colonial America were often named in this fashion with such colorful titles as "The Copper Kettle," or "The Spinning Wheel," or "The Airport Cafe."

    Arteries may be defined as blood vessels that carry blood away from the heart. Most arteries lie hidden under thick layers of muscles or bones and therefore can be easily seen and felt. The blood that they bring to the heart is rich in oxygen.

    A new trend in home building is the widespread use of perimeter heating. Warm air is carried into a room at or near the floor level along the outside walls, preferably near the windows. The warm air, which comes from a radiator in the center of the room, rises and returns itself to the furnace through a return air grill.

The illogical or unreasonable ideas expressed in sentences in these paragraphs are fairly obvious and easily identifiable by the careful reader.

    Less obvious instances of illogical sentences can be found, for example, in advertisements designed to persuade consumers to buy certain products. Many advertising slogans employ a subtle form of illogical reasoning:

>  Gentlemen prefer Hanovers.
>  If you're a woman, Zebra is you.
>  When Barton speaks, people listen.
>  Choke adds life.
>  With Amor, you never looked so good.

In their effort to sell such products and services, advertisers suggest that women who wear a certain brand of pantyhose will attract a certain kind of man; that wearing a certain brand of jeans will make you a woman; that the advice given by a certain investment house will be heeded by everyone; that a certain soft drink will give more life; and that a certain brand of cosmetic makes you look better than ever before. The reasoning in these statements is faulty because they assume the general conclusion applies to everyone, when in fact it does not. Such statements are really only opinions, but the language suggests that they are facts. They are illogical because they suggest that if the consumer buys these products, he or she will experience the outcomes stated. In fact, the consumer may or may not have such an experience.

    The type of language, the meaning of unfamiliar words, and the sense, or nonsense, of the ideas are important elements in understanding all types of sentences. With practice, you can learn to recognize each of these elements, and your understanding of the ideas in written material will increase.

## READING EXERCISE

Read each of the following sentences or paragraphs. Indicate in the spaces provided (1) which sentence element(s) are significant and (2) whether those elements make the sentence or paragraph true or false by placing a T or F on the line at the right. Rewrite all false statements to make them true.

1. August is always a summer month.   T/F _____

    Elements: _____

    _____

    Rewritten: _____

    _____

2. Brenda, the Jones's daughter, and Gary, Brenda's brother-in-law, are sisters.   T/F _____

    Elements: _____

    _____

    Rewritten: _____

    _____

3. Children are always younger than their uncles and aunts.   T/F _____

    Elements: _____

    _____

    Rewritten: _____

    _____

4. There are twelve months in every calendar year.   T/F _____

    Elements: _____

    _____

    Rewritten: _____

    _____

5. "Compartmentalize" has six syllables.   T/F _____

    Elements: _____

    _____

Sentence Sense 83

    Rewritten: _____
    _____

 6. Societies are formed only by humans.          T/F ____
    Elements: _____
    _____

    Rewritten: _____
    _____

 7. Plants are not necessarily green in color.    T/F ____
    Elements: _____
    _____

    Rewritten: _____
    _____

 8. A benediction is tantamount to a malediction. T/F ____
    Elements: _____
    _____

    Rewritten: _____
    _____

 9. Lexicons provide valuable information about words and their
    meanings.                                     T/F ____
    Elements: _____
    _____

    Rewritten: _____
    _____

10. Felix is fastidious while Oscar is slovenly.  T/F ____
    Elements: _____
    _____

    Rewritten: _____
    _____

11. In 1692 the town of Salem, Massachusetts, was beset by the fear of witchcraft. Old and deformed women were accused of being witches and the governor set up a court in downtown San Francisco for their trial. Before the terror was dispelled, twenty innocent victims had been put to death.          T/F ____

Elements: _____

_____

Rewritten: _____

_____

_____

_____

_____

_____

12. Language is constantly changing. Yet it changes so gradually that it may be regarded as fixed with adhesive tape for the lifetime of any one writer. The usage to which we must conform, therefore, is that of our own time. Our standard must be the practice of good writers of the present day.     T/F _____

Elements: _____

_____

Rewritten: _____

_____

_____

_____

_____

_____

_____

## WRITING FOR SENSE

The purpose of communication is to transfer information, feelings, and beliefs from one person to another. This communication can be nonverbal or verbal. Nonverbal communication includes personal gestures like smiles or body language, religious and political symbols like flags, stars, and crosses, and so on. Verbal communication is either oral (spoken) or written.

Verbal communication is done through the sentence, the basic grammatical unit. Sentences make statements that communicate in terms of absolute and conditional language, vocabulary, and logic. Absolute statements assert that something is always true, and conditional statements say that something is generally true, or true only under certain circumstances. Vocabulary concerns the meaning of individual words, influenced by the context of the sentence. The logic of a sentence has to do with whether or not its idea is reasonable. All these characteristics are important in shaping sentences that make sense, that communicate clearly and precisely.

## Absolute and Conditional Language

*Absolute* statements are formed by saying something *is* something, or by using words such as "always," "must," "all," "never." The purpose of absolute language is to say something is true at all times and in all circumstances. *Conditional* statements, on the other hand, say that something is generally or usually true, and they are formed by using such words as "frequently," "generally," "often," "could."

When you want to make a statement that is true at all times and in all circumstances, you ordinarily use absolute language. Such statements usually present a fact you know is true:

>  Coal is combustible.
>  Clouds always contain water vapor.
>  John F. Kennedy was the youngest man ever elected president.
>  A foot has 12 inches.

A little thought, however, will reveal that very few things are true at all times and in all circumstances. For example, although coal is combustible—that is, it will burn—it will not burn if it is under water. The statement "Coal is combustible" means that under normal circumstances coal will burn.

Most statements that are true at all times and under all circumstances are definitions or historical facts. "A foot has 12 inches" is always true because it is a definition of a unit of measure. "Two plus two equals four" is another kind of definition which is true because our number system makes it so. Historical dates are true because an event either did or did not happen at a particular time.

Almost every other kind of statement can be seen as possibly untrue. "Clouds always contain water vapor" is a statement of scientific fact nobody would seriously doubt. But science is constantly revising "facts" that were once thought to be true. Therefore, although there is little reason to believe that science will come up with a new description of clouds, all scientific statements should be qualified by saying, "This is true according to our current understanding."

That so few things can be seen to be absolutely true does not lessen the value of absolute statements. If we can communicate clearly one fact that is true at all times and in all circumstances, we have accomplished a great deal. But two things need to be considered to be sure you are using absolute language correctly: (1) facts and (2) opinions. Absolute language is used to express facts, and therefore it is your responsibility as a writer to be sure your facts are correct—that is, that they are true at all times and under all circumstances. Most often, however, you will be expressing an opinion rather than a fact, and you must therefore be careful to give the reader the correct clues by your choice of words and expression.

*Stating Fact.* Suppose you want to state a fact about intelligence. Consider the following to see if they are absolutely true:

> Intelligent students get higher grades.
> Intelligent parents have intelligent children.
> Intelligent people think fast.
> Intelligent students are bored by school.
> Good verbal ability is one measure of intelligence.

All these statements are expressed in absolute language, but only the last can be seen as true at all times and in all circumstances. Verbal ability is used as *one* measure of intelligence. The others should be qualified—that is, they should be shown to be generally true, and expressed in conditional language:

> Intelligent students *often* get higher grades. (But sometimes they do not.)
> Intelligent parents *usually* have intelligent children. (But not always.)
> Intelligent people *generally* think fast. (But some intelligent people think rather slowly.)
> Intelligent students are *sometimes* bored by school. (But often they are not.)

*Giving Opinions.* When you are expressing your opinion, you are not stating that something is a fact. Opinions should be indicated as such or expressed in conditional language. For example, you could express the statements about intelligence as opinions:

> *I believe* that intelligent students get higher grades.
> *I think* that intelligent parents have intelligent children.
> *I have concluded* that intelligent people think fast.
> *I have seen* intelligent students bored by school.

All these sentences are now expressed as opinions. They do not have to be accepted by the reader—in fact, the reader is almost invited to contribute an opinion or some facts of his or her own.

Distinguishing between fact and opinion is an important thinking and writing skill. If you are sure of a fact, sure that something is true at all times and under all circumstances, use absolute language to make your statement. If you are aware of exceptions to the idea you want to express, or if you are stating an opinion, use conditional language.

## Vocabulary

Words communicate meaning. In composing sentences, you should find precisely the right word to express what you want to say. As you write, try to recall words so that you will be able to complete sentences. Occasionally, you will face two problems: (a) you are not exactly sure that the word you have remembered says what you want it to, or (b) you cannot quite think of a word that fits the context of your sentence. Two reference books can help you with these difficulties: a dictionary and a thesaurus.

A dictionary helps you check the meanings of words. Suppose you wanted to say that intelligence is difficult to measure because it is not a physical object like a foot or a hand. You might write a sentence such as the following:

Intelligence is difficult to measure because it is not physical.

This is not a bad sentence, but perhaps, as you think about it, you remember that there is a word for nonphysical things. Maybe you recall that the word is "intangible." If you are not sure "intangible" is correct, you could consult a dictionary, and find the following:

in tan gi ble

not tangible: IMPALPABLE

You still might not be sure you have the right word. But if you check "tangible," you will get more help:

tan gi ble

    1a. capable of being perceived esp. by the sense of touch: palpable b: substantially real: MATERIAL 2: capable of being precisely realized by the mind 3: capable of being appraised at an actual or approximate value. <~assets>*

Dictionary definitions are written in a kind of shorthand. The particular system used by a dictionary is explained in what is called the "frontmatter"

*Webster's Seventh New Collegiate Dictionary, (Springfield, Mass., Merriam, 1965).

or introductory section of the dictionary. The definition above is from a dictionary that arranges definitions chronologically—that is, the most recent usage of the word is given last. Therefore, you should pay most attention to definition 3:

> capable of being appraised at an actual or approximate value. <~assets>

The angled brackets provide a common example, "tangible assets," which means those things which can be "appraised at an actual or approximate value."

You will be home free if you know that "appraise" means to set the value of something. Then you can determine that something *in*tangible is something that cannot be appraised, something for which you cannot set a value. Finally, you can look over the early definitions and figure out that "tangible" is something that can be touched; therefore, "intangible" is "untouchable." This is where you began, but now you have confirmed your recollection of a better word:

> Intelligence is difficult to measure because it is *intangible*.

The process of checking a word in a dictionary might seem to take a lot of time and effort, but it is worth it. The dictionary is the most valuable reference tool a writer has. Finding the right word is one of the most important writing tasks, and a dictionary will help you do it well and easily.

Sometimes, however, you cannot think of a word to express your idea. You know what you want to say, but the right word just will not come to mind. In such cases, a thesaurus can help.

For example, if you looked up "physical" in a thesaurus, you might find the following list of related words:

> substantial
> intrinsic
> real
> objective
> natural
> material
> concrete
> solid
> *tangible*
> palpable

A number of these words can be made into negatives that express something like what you have in mind:*

> *Note:* *In* and *im* are common prefixes that make the meaning of a word negative; that is, they are the same as saying "not" before the word.

*in*substantial
*im*material
*in*tangible
*im*palpable

If, when you reviewed this list, "intangible" jumped out at you as the word you wanted because seeing it reminded you of its meaning, you would have the word you need. You should still check the word in a dictionary to be sure, since a thesaurus does not provide definitions.

If, on the other hand, you are still not sure which word you want, you can check each of the thesaurus listings in a dictionary until you find one that fits your sentence. If you do this, you will probably conclude that "intangible" is the best because it includes the notion of setting a value on something, and you are talking about measuring, or setting a value on, intelligence. The other choices—"insubstantial," "immaterial," and "impalpable"—all suggest something that cannot be touched, but they do not include the same emphasis on measuring value.

## Logic

Absolute and conditional language determine the quality of the statement made by a sentence. Absolute language declares that the statement is true at all times and under all circumstances, and conditional language qualifies the statement by saying that it is usually, or generally, true. As we have seen, facts can be expressed in absolute language, and opinions in conditional language.

Expressing opinions is a natural activity, but they should result from clear thinking. Certain common problems in stating opinions can be identified: faulty generalizations, either-or reasoning, "persuasive language," incorrect cause-effect relationships, and non-sequiturs. Some of these problems are caused by using absolute language instead of conditional language, and others show fuzzy or unclear reasoning.

### Faulty Generalizations

This problem usually occurs when the writer states an opinion as a fact:

Higher education is good for everyone.
Developing nuclear energy is necessary for our economic growth.

Both of these statements are generalizations: they state that something is true in broad, unqualified terms. Generalizations such as these are useful because they allow us to summarize different ideas and information on a given subject.

However, generalizations should be phrased carefully and should result from careful thinking. The statement that declares that higher education will benefit everyone is a faulty generalization because the thinking behind it is questionable. Higher education is a good idea for many people, but not everyone. Some people should consider an alternative to college because their talents or their goals would be more suited to beginning their careers immediately. This generalization can be restated by changing it into conditional language, or by limiting its focus:

> Higher education is good for most people.
> Higher education is good for those people whose career goals require advanced study.

Similarly, the second statement should be qualified:

> Developing nuclear energy might add to our economic growth.

This restatement permits the reader to recognize that nuclear energy development is one way to improve our economy, but not the only way as the original generalization suggested.

## Either-Or Reasoning

Another common problem in sentence logic is falling into the trap of seeing an issue as black and white. A few things in life are truly and fairly expressed in these terms: *either* it will rain today, *or* it will be sunny; either a candidate will be elected, *or* he or she will not. Many other situations are stated in these terms when they should not be because a third or fourth possibility might also be true:

> Either we vote for this candidate or face disaster.
> If we do not cut taxes, the ordinary citizen will not be able to live.

Both these statements ignore other possibilities. Even if we vote for candidate A, we might still face disaster, and if we vote for candidate B, we might well avoid trouble. Cutting taxes may help the ordinary citizen pay his or her bills, but economic questions are always complicated. It is also possible that cutting taxes can cause an increase in the inflation rate, and therefore make it more difficult for people to manage their budgets.

These statements should be rephrased to take them out of the either-or box:

> This candidate is better suited to handling the challenges of the next few years because of his or her greater experience.
> Cutting taxes might help the ordinary citizen to live better by leaving him or her more money to pay for necessary expenses.

The first revision provides a reason for voting for the candidate without using the false either-or reasoning of the original. The second qualifies the statement by being more specific and by using conditional language.

### Persuasive Language

Although persuasive language is a useful writing tool, it should not substitute for logical thought. Persuasive language works on an emotional level, and when it is misused it prevents the reader from seeing the truth of your statement:

> Only a revolutionary would support the elimination of the peacetime army.
> That was not a debate but a circus.

The words "revolutionary" and "circus" are examples of persuasive language: they cause the reader to react emotionally instead of rationally. There are many reasons why a peacetime army is necessary, and the debate might not have been an orderly exchange of ideas. These statements would be better expressed in less emotional language so that the reader can respond to the ideas reasonably:

> The international situation is so unstable that a peacetime army is necessary.
> Because the debate was so poorly managed, nobody learned anything.

### Incorrect Cause-Effect Relationships

Understanding cause and effect relationships permits us to see how one situation happened as a result of another. But often, we are tempted to say that something caused something else only because it happened first:

> Ever since the fare was raised service has gotten worse.
> Herman began to get in trouble after he started hanging around with Little Arnie.

These sentences say that one thing caused another thing because it happened first: increase in fare, followed by worse service; Herman hangs around with Little Arnie, then gets in trouble. Although both of these cause and effect relationships might be correct, the situations they describe probably cannot be explained so simply. Both should be restated:

> Even though the fare was raised, service has gotten worse.
> Herman began to get into trouble, and at about the same time he started to hang around with Little Arnie.

Both revisions no longer insist on a cause and effect relationship, and allow the reader to consider that service might have gotten worse anyway, and that Herman might have been heading for trouble before he started his friendship with Little Arnie.

**Non Sequiturs**

*Non sequitur* means "it does not follow," and it describes statements that present conclusions that are not necessarily true:

> Because the store has added a new line of specialty items, it should attract more customers.
>
> I've put a lot of money into repairing my car, and so I shouldn't have to buy a new one for a long time.

The problem with these statements is that the conclusions they express might very well be untrue. If the store is in a neighborhood where potential customers do not have the money for, or interest in, specialty items, the new line might not produce more business. And repairing an old car is not a guarantee that it will not suffer further breakdowns. These statements have to be made in such a way as to make the conclusion probable or to recognize that it might not be sound:

> Because the potential customers for imported cheeses and other gourmet items have no place nearby to buy them, the store's new line should attract these customers.
>
> The money I have put into repairs for my old car might keep it on the road for a while longer.

The first revision provides more specific evidence for the conclusion, and the second makes the statement conditional. Both now avoid being *non sequiturs*.

WRITING EXERCISE

I. Write an absolute (unqualified), and a conditional (qualified) statement using each of the following words:

1. Summer

    Absolute _____

    _____

    Conditional _____

    _____

Sentence Sense 93

2. Work
   Absolute _____
   _____
   Conditional _____
   _____

3. Oil
   Absolute _____
   _____
   Conditional _____
   _____

4. World War II
   Absolute _____
   _____
   Conditional _____
   _____

5. Hamburger
   Absolute _____
   _____
   Conditional _____
   _____

II. State a fact and then an opinion about each of the following. Indicate whether you are using absolute or conditional language.

1. Marriage
   Fact _____
   _____
   Opinion _____
   _____
                                    A/C _____

2. Retirement

Fact _____

_____

Opinion _____

_____

A/C _____

3. Jogging

Fact _____

_____

Opinion _____

_____

A/C _____

4. Presidential elections

Fact _____

_____

Opinion _____

_____

A/C _____

5. Medicine

Fact _____

_____

Opinion _____

_____

A/C _____

III. Use a dictionary and/or a thesaurus to find the best words to complete the following sentences. Write the dictionary definition(s) beneath the sentences.

1. Professional athletes are paid _____ salaries.

Definition _____

_____

_____

Sentence Sense                                                                 95

2. The _____ speaker aroused the emotions of the audience.

   Definition _____
   _____
   _____

3. The delicate white wine had an _____ taste.

   Definition _____
   _____
   _____

4. The high cost of fuel makes _____ engines necessary.

   Definition _____
   _____
   _____

5. After Herman hurt his hand, his handwriting became _____.

   Definition _____
   _____
   _____

6. Newspaper editorials attempt to _____ the reader that a certain position is right.

   Definition _____
   _____
   _____

7. The police decided that the case was _____ because they lacked sufficient evidence.

   Definition _____
   _____
   _____

8. Since the beginning of the twentieth century, technology has been changing at an _____ rate.

   Definition _____

9. Student loans generally have a _____ rate of interest compared to other loans.

    Definition _____

    _____

    _____

10. Eating soda and potato chips for breakfast is _____ to good nutritional habits.

    Definition _____

    _____

    _____

IV. Use encyclopedias or other reference books to find five facts about one of the following:

   1. Unemployment
   2. Water pollution
   3. Computers
   4. Schizophrenia
   5. Stereo components

Topic: _____
Facts:

1. _____

   _____

2. _____

   _____

3. _____

   _____

4. _____

   _____

5. _____

   _____

Sentence Sense 97

List your source(s):

_____

_____

_____

_____

V. Each of the sentences below contain an error in logic. Identify the error (faulty generalization, either-or reasoning, persuasive language, incorrect cause-effect relationship, *non sequitur*). Then rewrite the sentence in the space provided.

1. I didn't have any problem with my teeth until I went to the dentist.

   Error _____

   _____

   _____

2. After his dog died, John began to lose interest in Mabel.

   Error _____

   _____

   _____

3. I'm not going to bother to vote in this year's election because all politicians are crooks.

   Error _____

   _____

   _____

4. If you do not take this job, you will never have as good an opportunity again.

   Error _____

   _____

   _____

5. We should build bigger prisons, if we have to, so that we can get all these hardened criminals off the streets.

   Error _____

   _____

   _____

6. The committee has been talking things over for hours, and that means it must agree with our position.

Error _____

_____

7. In today's times, I can't see how pet owners spend so much money on feeding their cats and dogs.

Error _____

_____

8. Bleeding heart liberals should spend a day in my neighborhood before they decide to give these people any more money.

Error _____

_____

9. Conservatives should understand that you first have to have something to conserve, and then maybe they will not be so eager to take advantage of the downtrodden masses.

Error _____

_____

10. The way she can add and subtract in her head, she must be a math major.

Error _____

_____

11. The party died the minute I walked into the room.

Error _____

_____

12. If I can't get into Professor Perkins' class, I won't be able to major in biology.

Error _____

_____

# 6
# The Simple Sentence

PREVIEW

A sentence expresses a complete thought by showing a relationship between a *subject* and a *verb*. This subject-verb relationship can take different forms: (1) in an *equation sentence,* a verb serves as an equals sign between the subject and some quality of the subject; (2) in an *action sentence,* the verb shows that the subject does or did something; (3) in an *action with object sentence,* the verb shows that the subject does or did something to something or someone.

These three sentence types provide ways of stating different kinds of ideas. Each of these types is suited to one kind of idea, and each is therefore limited in what it can say. Therefore, effective communication depends on a blend of all three types.

An understanding of basic sentence structure is important in both reading and writing. For the reader, familiarity with sentence types eases and improves understanding. For the writer, these sentence types provide the structures for expressing ideas.

**Key Terms**

    **Sentence.**  A group of words containing at least one subject-verb relationship.
    **Subject.**  What the sentence is about.
    **Verb.**  The word or words that establish a relationship between the subject and a quality or action of the subject.

**Equation sentence.** A type of sentence in which the subject is shown to have a certain quality.
**Action sentence.** A type of sentence in which the focus is on what the subject does or did.
**Action with object sentence.** A type of sentence in which the focus is on what the subject does or did to something or someone.

## READING SENTENCES

Reading is thinking. When you read, you recognize each word. You also try to understand how the words work together in a sentence by thinking about what the words in that sentence mean in relation to one another. Both oral and silent reading involve thinking about the meaning of the words in front of you. The attempt, always, is to get the message of the words. When that message becomes clear—that is, when you understand what you have read—your thoughts as a reader have matched those of the writer.

The *sentence*, a group of words that expresses a complete thought, is a basic tool of communication. To obtain meaning from a sentence, the reader has to see a relationship between its parts. For a sentence to express a complete thought, it must have at least two parts: (1) a someone or something that the sentence is about; and (2) a part that tells something *about* that someone or something. In other words, each sentence has a *subject,* the someone or something it is about, and a *verb,* the word that tells about the someone or something. Without both parts, there is no sentence or complete thought.

### The Basic Form

Every sentence has a subject and a verb, but every sentence does not, of course, express the same idea. Different ideas require different sentence forms. Even the desire to express the same idea in a different, perhaps more exciting, way may cause a writer to choose a different sentence form. But *all* sentences have a subject and a verb:

Jesus wept.
Snow melts.
Children sing.
Grass grows.
Birds chirp.
Bells ring.
Dogs bark.

Each of these sentences is in the simplest form: two words, one for the subject, and one for the verb. And while each of these communicate a complete thought, each raises *questions:*

> Why did Jesus weep?
> When do children sing?
> How does the grass grow?
> What makes dogs bark?

Sentences with only subjects and verbs are limited in what they can express. The following more complicated sentences answer some of the questions raised by the two-word sentences:

> Jesus wept out of sadness.
> Children sing when they are happy.
> Grass grows fast in the spring.
> Dogs bark when they are hungry.

These added words provide the reader with additional information.

Most sentences have more words than just one for the subject and one for the verb. These additional words form phrases, clauses, and transitions that increase the length of the sentence and separate the subject from the verb:

> *Jesus*, walking slowly among the poor and the sick, *wept* out of sadness.
> *Children* of all ages, and from all countries, *sing* sweet-sounding songs when they are happy.
> *Grass*, which is dormant during the winter and therefore brown in color, *grows* fast when the rains come in the spring.
> The chained *dogs*, hungry for their food, *bark* until they are fed.

In each instance, the sentence carries the same basic information as it did in the two-word version. The additional words provide more information for the reader, even though the sentence gets longer and the subject is separated from the verb. As a reader you must always be alert to the basic message of a sentence in spite of its length or the distance between the subject and the verb sometimes created by the addition of words.

As you may have noticed, the punctuation of a sentence can help you to identify interruptors so that you do not become confused about what the sentence means and therefore misinterpret the idea communicated by the sentence. (Sentence punctuation is discussed in Appendix B.)

## Types of Sentences

Effective communication involves not only *what* is said, but *how* it is said. Therefore, the reader gets information not only from the content of a sentence, but also from how it is formed. Let us look now at some common patterns.

*Equation Sentences.* Read these sentences and see if you can recognize how the words on either side of the verb are related. The verb in each sentence is in *italics:*

Gold *is* a metal.
Plums *taste* delicious.
I *am* very hungry.
The boys *are* athletes.
My mother *seemed* tired.
Sandra *became* eighteen today.

In each sentence, the verb connects the subject on one side of the sentence to *something it is, seems to be like,* or *is changed into.* The reader could substitute an = sign for the verb:

Gold = metal.
Plums = delicious.
I = very hungry.
The boys = athletes.
My mother = tired.
Sandra = eighteen.

Sentences like these use *linking* verbs that connect the subject to the word or words on the other side of the verb. Identifying this sentence form helps the reader understand that the writer wants to show a relationship between the subject and some characteristic or quality of the subject.

Here are more equation sentences, but this time the sentences are longer and contain "extra" words. See if you can recognize the basic message of each:

Fruits and vegetables, available at supermarkets and farm stands, are perishable.
The tall, beautiful brunette standing outside the movie theater that night was a famous actress.
Usually pleasant and pretty, Mary appeared ugly when angry.
The sweating, gasping drivers were, by the end of the race, tired.
According to our calendar, no month is shorter than 28 days.
A good watch, whatever the cost, is worth the money.

Here are the basic communications of each:

Fruits and vegetables are perishable.
The brunette was a famous actress.

Mary appeared ugly.
The racers were tired.
No month is shorter than 28 days.
A good watch is worth the money.

Being able to understand the basic message of a sentence by recognizing equation patterns helps you to read more efficiently. You have a category with which to classify sentences, and you can link *what* you are reading with *how* the idea is expressed.

*Action Sentences.* The action sentence emphasizes the action the subject of the sentence performs. In an action sentence, it is important to focus on the verb:

John *shouts*.
The audience *applauded*.
The couples *danced*.
Children *played*.

These sentences describe subjects performing or doing something. Unlike equation sentences, there is a direct relation between the subject and the verb, and not between the subject and the words that show a quality or characteristic of the subject. Such sentences usually contain additional words that give the reader more information:

Silly, ill-tempered *John* often *shouts*.
The opera house *audience applauded* loudly for several minutes.
The gaily dressed *couples* in the contest *danced* to the rock music.
Nancy's six *children* always *play* quietly.

But the basic message of each sentence remains the same: John shouts; the audience applauded; the couples danced; children played. The other words in the sentences provide additional information or detail to fill out the thought each sentence expresses.

Try to see the author's basic message in these action sentences:

The newly married couple searched eagerly for their dream house.
Yesterday, a new movie theater opened in the mall.
That young, unhappy child runs away from home every day.
These new brown shoes fit too tightly on my feet.
My uncle, bless his soul, visits too often for my comfort.

You should have seen the following as the basic messages of the sentences:

The couple searched.
A theater opened.
Child runs.

Shoes fit.
Uncle visits.

The action sentence category provides the reader with a classification of the author's message in terms of the action performed by the subject. That action is always expressed by the verb of the sentence. As with the other sentence forms, however, action sentences are limited in what they can express. Writers use such sentences in combination with equation sentences to increase the variety of the kinds of ideas they want to express. Compare the way different kinds of idea relationships are expressed in the sentences in the following paragraph:

> The day was a day to forget. Nothing went right. I fell out of my bed onto my back. Then, I was late for school. I was not ready for my chemistry test. I flunked. Later, I left to go home. My house keys were missing. And of all things, the money in my secret hiding place in the drawer of my desk had disappeared. The burglar's day was better than mine.

| | |
|---|---|
| Equation sentence: | The day was a day to forget. |
| Action Sentence: | Nothing went right. |
| Action sentence: | I fell out of my bed onto my back. |
| Equation sentence: | Then, I was late for school. |
| Equation sentence: | I was not ready for my chemistry test. |
| Action sentence: | I flunked. |
| Action sentence: | Later, I left to go home. |
| Equation sentence: | My house keys were missing. |
| Action sentence: | And of all things, the money in my secret hiding place in the drawer of my desk had disappeared. |
| Equation sentence: | The burglar's day was better than mine. |

*Action with Object Sentences.* A third sentence form or category, the action sentence with object, increases the writer's ability to communicate. With this form, the author can say not only that the subject did something but that the subject did that something to someone or something. The someone or something to which something is done is called the *object*. When reading action with object sentences, the reader focuses on the verb that shows the action, the subject that performs the action, and the object that receives the action:

Patricia hit the ball.
My father scolded me.
The baby hit her finger.
Computers save time.

These sentences give the reader images of a subject doing something to someone or something. This sentence form also gives the writer a chance to show an action relationship between the subject and someone or something different from that subject:

| Subject | Object |
|---|---|
| Patricia | ball |
| father | me |
| baby | finger |
| computers | time |

Read the following sentences, and see if you can identify the subject, the action performed by the subject (the verb), and the someone or something involved in the action (the object):

Hairdressers cut hair.
Mary slapped Bill.
Janet watched television.
David plays tennis.

In the first sentence, "hairdressers" is the subject, "cut," the verb, and "hair," the object. In the second, "Mary" is the subject, "slapped" the verb, and "Bill" the object. "Janet" serves as the subject of the third with "watched" as the verb and "television" as the object. In the fourth sentence, "David" is the subject, "plays" the verb, and "tennis" the object. To make sure you locate the object, first say the subject, then say the verb, and then ask the question *who?* or *what?*

Hairdressers cut *what?*
Mary slapped *who?*
Janet watched *what?*
David plays *what?*

Now read these longer sentences and determine the subject, the verb, and the object:

Benny, tired and hungry after the ten-inning game, drove his car down the expressway at seventy miles an hour.
On the way to the airport, somehow Karla lost her airplane tickets.
The new luxury liner cruised the ocean smoothly and swiftly.
Parents frequently scold their young children for their poor behavior.

The subjects, verbs, and objects are as follows:

| Subject | Verb | Object |
|---|---|---|
| Benny | drove | his car. |
| Karla | lost | her tickets. |
| The liner | cruised | the ocean. |
| Parents | scold | their young children. |

In each sentence, the basic message becomes clear when the subject, verb, and object are identified. Though additional words give more information, the basic message gives you the writer's idea.

If a writer were to use only action with object sentences, he or she would be limited in expressing ideas. Seeing the same form over and over would also bore the reader. So writers usually combine equation, action, and action with object forms to express themselves with clarity and variety, as in the following paragraph:

> The bones of the human body are important. They create the body's shape. They hold and protect the organs of the body. The muscles of the body attach to the bones. Bones make the movements of the body possible. Without bones, we would all fall in a heap onto the ground.

| | |
|---|---|
| Equation sentence: | The bones of the human body are important. |
| Action with object: | They create the body's shape. |
| Action with object: | They hold and protect the organs of the body. |
| Action sentence: | The muscles of the body attach to the bones. |
| Action with object: | Bones make the movements of the body possible. |
| Action sentence: | Without bones, we would all fall in a heap onto the ground. |

## READING EXERCISE

I. Read each of the following sentences. Indicate the sentence type each represents by placing E (equation), A (action), or AO (action with object) after each sentence.

1. The children, dressed in Halloween costumes, knocked at the doors of the houses on the street. _____
2. Despite their various shapes and sizes, all clocks tell time. _____
3. Luisa, the game's newest winner, was ecstatic. _____
4. The partial or complete covering of one celestial body by another is called an eclipse. _____
5. Arms stretched high in the air, Mel caught the whirling Frisbee. _____

II. Read the following paragraphs. In the spaces provided, indicate (1) the sentence form of each italicized sentence and (2) the basic message of each italicized sentence.

The Simple Sentence

1. The experimenters who created hybrid corn carried out a great many tests in the years between 1900 and 1926. *They controlled the fertilization of corn plants by tying paper bags over the tassels and over the growing ears.* At just the right time, they transferred the pollen from the tassel to the silk on the ear. Then, they replaced the bag that covered the ear. No airborne pollen was allowed to touch the corn silk on a growing ear. In this way, each plant was fertilized with its own pollen, and inbred corn plants were the result. Several generations of inbreeding could fix good qualities in the corn plants, but the stalks tended to be weak and the ears small.

   Sentence form _____

   Basic message _____

2. Some graphs have keys. The key for a graph is very much like the key for a map. The key shows you the symbols that will be used in the graph, and it tells you what the symbols mean. Usually a picture graph has a key. *The graph which showed you actual pictures of boxes is a picture graph.* This type of graph is sometimes called a pictograph.

   Sentence form _____

   Basic message _____

3. But men do not always improve the land they use. *Sometimes, because of ignorance or carelessness, they ruin it.* This is what the fishermen did to Riche Island. As the years passed, they cut down more and more trees. As the trees became fewer, the wind and the sea began to eat away at the land. The sand piled up in great drifts, or dunes. In time, the trees and grass completely vanished beneath the sand. Today Riche Island is nothing more than a narrow, sandy island about twenty miles long and one mile wide—a tiny speck in the North Atlantic.

   Sentence form _____

   Basic message _____

4. During the latter half of the nineteenth century, a different art movement began in France. *Called impressionism, it introduced different subjects, techniques and uses of light.* Impressionists, including Renoir, used nature and contemporary society as their subjects. Applying pure dots of color onto the canvas was a new technique. The viewer's eyes blend the colors when the painting is seen from a distance. Impressionists investigated the use of light at different times of day. Impressionist paintings were appealing because of their warmth and intensity.

Sentence form _____

Basic message _____

5. *The United States Supreme Court decision on the Bakke case promises to be one of the landmark decisions relating to education and human (or civil) rights in American history.* It is, perhaps, the most important case relating to the rights of black Americans since the days of the Reconstruction Era.

Sentence form _____

Basic message _____

6. Nick Carroway comes to New York to work for a brokerage firm. *He rents a house in West Egg, L.I. next to a magnificent estate owned by a Jay Gatsby.* He calls on his cousin, Daisy, whom he discovers had once been in love with Jay. He also discovers that Daisy's husband, Tom, is having an affair with a Myrtle Wilson, the wife of a garage owner.

Sentence form _____

Basic message _____

7. *The ash thrown out of Paricutin is a fine black dust.* During the early life of the volcano it filled the air almost constantly. *On one occasion it traveled to Mexico City, 200 miles to the east.* Street lights often burned in daytime at Uruapan, a town 15 miles away. Near the volcano, ash was everywhere. *People and animals inhaled it with every breath.* It sifted into clothing, into food, even into watches and other machinery. *It covered the countryside like an unrelenting snow of coal dust.* As it grew into layers inches deep, natives brushed it off their roof-tops to keep their wooden houses from collapsing.

Sentence forms _____  _____  _____  _____

Basic messages _____

_____

_____

_____

8. *Sweden, the other side of the mountain range that remained after the great Arctic plateau had disappeared beneath the waves of the Atlantic, is a very different country from Norway.* People often wonder why these two nations do not decide to form a single nation. *It would mean a great saving in the cost of administration.* On paper such an arrangement looks eminently practicable. *But their geographical background makes it impossible.* For

whereas Norway on account of the Gulf Stream enjoys a mild climate with lots of rain and little snow, Sweden has a continental climate, with long, cold winters and a heavy snowfall. Whereas Norway has deep fjords that penetrate for miles into the interior, Sweden has a low coast with few natural harbors. And whereas Norway has no raw materials of its own, Sweden is possessed of some of the most valuable ore deposits of the whole world. *The unfortunate absence of coal still forces Sweden to export a great deal of these ores to Germany and France.* But during the last twenty years the taming of many important waterfalls has made Sweden increasingly independent of coal while the forests that cover such a great part of the kingdom account for the enormously rich Swedish match trust and the far-famed Swedish paper factories.

Sentence forms _____  _____  _____  _____

Basic messages _____

_____

_____

_____

## WRITING YOUR OWN SENTENCES

As you have already seen, a sentence is a unit of thought. In order to communicate an idea, you as a writer must identify what it is you want the reader to learn something about. This identification takes the form of the *subject* of the sentence. The *verb* expresses what you want to say about the subject.

For a sentence to be complete—that is, for it to express a thought—it must have a subject and a verb. Without the verb, the sentence does not "say" anything. Without the subject, the sentence is not about anything. The key to writing good sentences is to establish a clear relationship between subject and verb to form a complete thought.

### Types of Sentences

*Equation Sentences.* Different kinds of thoughts require different kinds of sentences. Suppose you want to say something about yourself during a job interview so you will impress the interviewer. Your subject would probably be "I" in a sentence like "I am a hard worker." This type of sentence is like an equation with the verb *am* serving as an equals sign. The words on both sides of the verb are directly related to each other. In this case, "I" (the subject) is defined as a "hard worker."

The same experience of looking for a job could be described with these sentences:

> I am industrious.
> He is the boss.
> Jobs are hard to find.

All these sentences use a form of the verb "to be" ("am," "is," "are"). Here are some other verbs that can be found in this type of sentence:

> I *grew* angry.
> He *became* sad.
> She *seemed* lucky.
> They *appeared* lonely.
> The day *looked* good.
> The weather *turned* bad.
> The cake *tasted* sweet.
> The singer *sounded* off key.

In all these sentences, the verb establishes a close relationship between the subject and some quality of the subject. Because these verbs work in this way, we call them *linking verbs*. The following paragraph contains only linking verbs.

> He <u>is</u> an outrageous egotist. The world <u>seems</u> to be his stage. All his friends <u>appear</u> to be only a supporting cast. His self-centered behavior <u>has grown</u> tiresome to everybody. One day, perhaps, he <u>will become</u> aware of the dangers of his character flaw. Then, he <u>will be</u> a lot better off.

Although this paragraph does communicate clearly, it is difficult to write using only linking verbs. You may want to state not only what a subject is, seems to be, or is becoming, but also what a subject does. To express these kinds of ideas, you use two other types of sentences.

*Action Sentences.* Often, you will want to say that the subject *did* something, took some action. For example:

> I *searched* for a job.
> I *walked* to the employment agency.
> My car *has died*.
> My mother *rejoiced*.
> My father just *smiled*.

In these sentences, the focus is on the action communicated by the verb: "searched," "walked," "died," "rejoiced," "smiled." Compare these to the equation, or linking, sentences:

I *am* a hard worker.            Linking
I *looked* for a job.            Action

Action verbs complete the thought unit of the sentence by themselves, but they are often followed by additional information:

I *walked*.

I *walked* to the store.

I *searched*.

I *searched* for a job.

The following paragraph contains only action verbs:

> I woke up at seven A.M. Monday morning. I hurried out of the house to my car. It had died. I walked to the employment agency, two miles from my house. Sweat poured down my face and into my eyes. The man behind the desk frowned at me. I left with an empty feeling and no job.

Again, this paragraph communicates, but its range of expression is limited by using a single sentence form.

*Action Sentences with Objects.*   In addition to stating a relationship between the subject and some quality of the subject, or telling what the subject does, you will often want to say that the subject did something to somebody or something:

I *bought* a car.

My father *loaned* the money to me.

The car *made* my life simpler.

The cost of gasoline *broke* my budget.

This type of sentence establishes a different kind of relationship. By adding an object of the verb, the subject is related to something completely different from itself. The following paragraph contains only action verbs with objects:

> I needed a job for over six months. I wrote letters to dozens of companies. I called all my friends and relatives two and three times. I read books on how to improve my appearance and my vocabulary. I even consulted an astrologer to determine the best job-hunting days. Finally, I saw a "Help Wanted" sign in the window of a deli. After a short interview, the owner hired me.

As with the other types of sentences, the action verb plus object form is limited in what it can express. In the paragraph above, this structure almost demands that each sentence begin with the same subject, and it can only express that subject doing something to somebody or something.

Each of the patterns in this chapter is a basic tool for the writer. In the next chapter we will see how these basic tools can be combined in various ways to expand the writer's range of choice.

## WRITING EXERCISE

I. Fill in the blanks of the paragraph below with one of the following verbs: appear, sound, seem, become, grow, look, feel, continue. Use each only once. You may need to change the form of the verb.

The weather _____ nasty yesterday. It _____ too cold to go to the beach as we had planned. Instead, my friends and I decided to go to Jim's house. However, Jim _____ unhappy with that decision. He _____ uneasy because he knew that his sister would _____ annoyed with his friends. We had no other place to go, and we _____ afraid that the day would _____ bad. Just as we _____ sure we would have nothing to do, the sun came out.

II. Fill in the blanks in the following paragraphs with the appropriate verbs.

1. The stranger _____ into the room. He _____ at the other people as though they couldn't possibly _____. He _____ to no one in particular, "How much time do we have?" Some people _____, but nobody _____. Finally, the door to the inner office _____, and everybody _____ in relief.

2. She _____ distance she would have to swim. The challenge of the distance _____ her. Gritting her teeth, she _____ the water. A voice in the back of her head _____ her to take it easy. After a few minutes in the water, she _____ her stroke. She _____ the water and _____ her way over and through the waves. Hours later, with her last store of energy, she _____ the distant shore at the end of the race.

The Simple Sentence

III. Choose one of the following subjects and write five equation sentences: "my friend," "my parents," "I," "an apple," "music." Try not to use forms of "to be" ("is," "are," "am," and so on) for this exercise. Refer to the chapter text for other verbs that can be used in equation sentences.

1. _____
2. _____
3. _____
4. _____
5. _____

IV. Provide subjects and action verbs for the following:

1. _____in the morning.
2. _____every chance I get.
3. _____through the traffic.
4. _____for six hours.
5. In the meantime, _____.
6. At certain times. _____.
7. Just by chance, _____.
8. _____like a lion.
9. _____through life.
10. _____just in time.

V. Provide subjects and objects for the following action verbs:

1. _____ read _____.
2. _____ frightened _____.
3. _____ seek _____.
4. _____ helped _____.
5. _____ found _____.
6. _____ lost _____.
7. _____ handled _____.

8. _____ captured _____.

9. _____ tried _____.

10. _____ considered _____.

VI. Fill in the blanks in the following paragraphs. Each sentence is numbered. In the corresponding blanks below, indicate by E, A, or AO whether the sentence is an equation, action, or action plus object type.

(1) We _____ along the beach. (2) The surf _____ against the shore. (3) Overhead, clouds _____ patterns of white fluff. (4) The sun _____ our skin, turning it a bright red. (5) The water _____ our attention. (6) It _____ so tempting, cool and refreshing. (7) Without waiting any longer, we _____ into the waves to cool off. (8) After a long swim, we _____ back through the hot sand to our blanket. (9) All day we _____ in the sun, and _____ in the water.

1. _____
2. _____
3. _____
4. _____
5. _____
6. _____
7. _____
8. _____
9. _____

(1) My first car _____ a thing of character, if not beauty. (2) It _____ easily only on seventy degree days. (3) Hotter or colder, it _____ its displeasure with the weather by refusing to start. (4) The engine would _____ for a couple of seconds. (5) Then it would _____. I _____ a lot on those days. (6) Occasionally, I would _____ my fist against the steering wheel in anger. (7) But the car only _____ more unresponsive. (8) On a beautiful spring day, however, the car would _____ on the first try. (9) Then I would _____ its previous failures. (10) And at this time, I could _____ the rusted chrome, dented fenders, squeaky doors, and pervasive body rot.

The Simple Sentence

1. _____
2. _____
3. _____
4. _____
5. _____
6. _____
7. _____
8. _____
9. _____
10. _____

VII. Write a sentence about each of the following, and then note what kind of sentence you have composed (E, A, AO):

1. pride

_____ _____

2. smoking

_____ _____

3. success

_____ _____

4. power

_____ _____

5. youth

_____ _____

# 7

# The More Complicated Sentence

## PREVIEW

The simple sentence forms are only the starting points in analyzing and constructing more complicated and interesting sentences. Simple sentences can be expanded into compound and complex sentences by using coordinating and subordinating conjunctions. And information contained in simple sentences can be compressed into smaller grammatical units called phrases.

In reading and writing these more complicated sentences, the key is to focus on the relationships between ideas expressed in the sentences. The complexity and variety of sentence forms provide the structures within which effective communication of ideas from the simplest to the most complicated can be accomplished.

**Key Terms**

**Clause.** A group of words containing a subject and a verb and making up part of a sentence, or, in some cases, a simple sentence by itself.
**Sentence.** A group of words containing at least one subject-verb relationship.
**Simple sentence.** A sentence consisting of one subject-verb relationship.
**Compound sentence.** A sentence consisting of at least two equal subject-verb relationships.
**Complex sentence.** A sentence containing two subject-verb relationships of unequal value.
**Coordinating conjunction.** A word that combines two subject-verb relationships or other parts of speech of equal value.

**Subordinating conjunction.** A word that combines two subject-verb relationships of unequal value.
**Correlatives.** Matched coordinating conjunctions.
**Phrase.** A group of words that expresses a thought in a conpressed or shorthand form within a sentence.
**Sentence combining.** Compression of several ideas into the phrases and clauses of larger sentences; word economy.

## READING MORE COMPLICATED SENTENCES

A *simple sentence* consists of one subject-verb relationship and generally conveys one idea. If a writer chooses to discuss more than one thought or idea in a sentence, he or she can show the relationships between and among these ideas by combining sentences and parts of sentences in several different ways. One is the compound sentence, and another is the complex sentence.

### The Compound Sentence

The compound sentence consists of two simple sentences joined into one larger one. The smaller sentences are combined by using *coordinating conjunctions*, words that link ideas of equal value. Sometimes, coordinating conjunctions link two subjects together in a simple sentence:

John and Jim walked into the room.

In fact, any part of a simple sentence can be compounded by linking two or more sentence parts together with coordinating conjunctions. If the sentence still only has one basic subject-verb relationship, however, it remains a simple sentence.

When two or more subject-verb relationships are included in one sentence, the sentence becomes *compound*. The coordinating conjunction tells the reader to see one idea as equal to the other. The two smaller parts of the sentence should be understood as carrying the same weight.

Four coordinating conjunctions are most often used to join ideas in a compound sentence: "and," "or," "but," and "for." Each expresses a different relationship between the ideas of the sentence. Notice how the same two ideas in the following compound sentences change when the relationship between them is presented with different coordinating conjunctions:

Mary is a good athlete, *and* she is a good student.
Mary is a good athlete, *or* she is a good student.
Mary is a good athlete, *but* she is a good student.
Mary is a good athlete, *for* she is a good student.

Although the same ideas are expressed in each sentence, the coordinating conjunction in each determines the kind of relationship between the ideas. "And" indicates that Mary is both a good athlete and a good student; "or" says that Mary is either a good athlete or a good student (but not both); "but" suggests that Mary is a good student in spite of the fact that she is a good athlete; and "for" makes the point that Mary is a good athlete because she is a good student.

Joining words like "and," "or," "but," "for," "yet," and "so" provide the reader with a *signal* of the writer's purpose: they call attention to the relationship between two ideas in a sentence. Here are some more examples:

Alan was happy about the team's victory, *but* David was not.
Karen's parents will drive, *or* Monica's father will make the trip.
Roses and violets are flowers, *but* pears and raisins are fruits.
The boys were good swimmers, *and* the girls were good runners.
I liked Dolores, *yet* I felt she did not like me.
Steve worked all day, *and* he danced all night.
She won the contest, *for* she was the prettiest contestant.

Whenever coordinating conjunctions are used, they join ideas of *equal* importance. The differences among the conjunctions concern the kind of relationship between ideas they establish:

| | |
|---|---|
| and | Adds one idea to another. |
| but | Shows a change in direction in the sentence. |
| or | Compares one possibility to another. |
| for | Establishes a cause and effect relationship. |

In addition to these coordinating conjunctions, there are two which are used in pairs and are called *correlatives:*

*Either* John will come soon, *or* we will have to start without him.
*Neither* did John come on time, *nor* could we wait for him.

The first half of the pair in each case, "either" and "neither," comes before the subject of the first part of the sentence. The second half, "or" and "nor," comes before the subject of the second half of the sentence.

## The Complex Sentence

The *complex sentence* contains two ideas that are *not* equal in value. A writer uses a complex sentence to show that one idea in the sentence is more important than the other idea. To indicate this unequal relationship, the writer joins the ideas with *subordinating conjunctions* such as these:

The More Complicated Sentence

| before | if | so that |
| although | though | after |
| unless | since | as |
| whether | because | while |
| until | where | when |

Here are some examples of complex sentences:

I lost the game *because* I didn't practice.
*Although* I started out on time, I was late for the movie.
*If* she studied harder, she would pass the driver's test.
You may not watch television *until* you do your homework.
*Whether* it rains or not, graduation ceremonies will be held Sunday.
*After* Mary's preparations were complete, the party started.

In each sentence, the less important idea is introduced by a subordinating conjunction, and its content adds information to the basic message:

I lost the game.
I was late for the movie.
You may not watch television.
Graduation ceremonies will be held Sunday.
The party started.

The basic message, the most important idea of the sentence, is expressed in an *independent clause*. An independent clause has a subject and a verb, expresses a complete idea, and can stand alone as a simple sentence. The less important idea is called a *subordinate clause*. It has a subject and a verb, but it cannot stand alone because it does not express a complete thought. The thought it expresses must be understood in relationship to the more important idea of the independent clause. Every complex sentence has a subordinate clause and an independent clause. Your goal, as a reader, is to be able to use the signals given by the conjunctions in complex sentences to determine which idea is the most important.

## Additional Relationships within Sentences

In both compound and complex sentences, the relationship between ideas always focuses on whether the ideas are equally important or not. But besides the question of greater or less importance, sentences often present additional information about a particular relationship.

*Time.* If a writer wants to show that the information in a sentence is related in terms of time, he or she might use certain joining words like "before," "while," "when," "after," and "as":

Joan is going shopping *before* she returns home.
*While* I sat waiting for my appointment, I studied for my chemistry test.
Kevin was washing the car *when* the rain started.
Sheila cooked supper *as* she talked with us.
I felt rested and relaxed *after* we had taken a vacation.

In each sentence, the joining words signal that one event in the sentence took place before, after, or at the same time as another.

*Cause and Effect.* If a writer wants to show that one thing or event did or could cause another to happen, he or she may do so by using joining words like "because," "since," "if," "so that," and "although":

| | |
|---|---|
| Cause: | *Because* he was improperly dressed |
| Effect: | he couldn't enter the club. |
| Cause: | *Since* she won the lottery, |
| Effect: | she is a millionaire. |
| Cause: | *If* Eric is on time, |
| Effect: | the test will start at ten o'clock. |
| Cause: | Foundations have given money |
| Effect: | *so that* scholarships can be awarded. |
| Cause: | *Although* she had trouble making the call, |
| Effect: | she finally reached her mother. |

In each sentence, the joining words signal the reader that one thing or event did or could have caused the other. Notice that "if" tells you that the effect *might* occur, and that in this sentence "although" tells you that the effect was achieved with some difficulty. "Although" can also suggest that the effect was delayed or did not happen at all:

| | |
|---|---|
| Delayed: | *Although* the plane's departure was postponed for several hours, we had a good trip. |
| Did not happen: | *Although* we expected him to come, he told us later that he hadn't been able to make it. |

*Identification.* Should an author wish to point out or clarify something that relates to the central idea of the sentence, he or she may use joining words like "who," "where," "that," "which," and "when":

Wendy is the girl *who* lives in the room next to mine.
This is the place *where* we first met.
I read the book *that* you recommended.
I live on Elm Street, *which* is three blocks north of here.
That was a time *when* I had no worries.

In each of these sentences the joining word indicates that the subordinate clause will identify the time, place, person, or circumstance of the idea expressed in the independent clause.

*Dilemma.* An author may choose to establish a relationship between ideas in a sentence which shows that the subject faces a problem, predicament, or difficulty. Joining words like "although," "unless," "if," or "as if" can be used in such sentences:

*Although* I needed the money, I couldn't work.
Valerie would miss the bus *unless* it was late.
He ran *as if* he were being chased by the devil.

In each of these sentences, the subject faces a problem which is stated in the independent clause of the sentence, and which is further explained in the subordinate clause.

These relationships are only a few of the possible kinds a writer can establish. You should be able to grasp them by being aware of and recognizing how joining words signal the reader.

**Sentence Combining and Word Economy**

A simple sentence presents one subject-verb relationship. Compound sentences present two subject-verb relationships of equal value. Complex sentences present subject-verb relationships in two clauses of unequal importance. All these possibilities communicate ideas in terms of combinations of clauses. A *clause* contains one subject and verb relationship. If it can stand by itself, it is also a simple sentence. Compound and complex sentences involve two or more clauses in differing relationships. Such sentences increase variety and efficiency of expression. They provide *word economy*.

Word economy can also be achieved by reducing clauses to phrases. A *phrase* communicates an idea; a clause presents an idea relationship between subject and verb. Phrases therefore enable writers to compress information and also increase sentence variety and efficiency. The following examples show how the information presented in several simple sentences, or clauses, can be incorporated into one, longer sentence by using compound, complex structures and phrases.

| Longer sentence: | Denise is pretty and Daniel is handsome. |
|---|---|
| Contains these clauses: | Denise is pretty. Daniel is handsome. |

Here the two simple sentences are combined into a compound sentence with two clauses of equal value.

|  |  |
|---|---|
| Longer sentence: | Although the weather is hot and humid, and although the rain falls infrequently, summer is my favorite season. |
| Contains these clauses: | The weather is hot and humid. Rain falls infrequently. Summer is my favorite season. |

Here the first two simple sentences have become subordinate clauses introduced by the signal word "although," and the last simple sentence is the independent clause of the complex sentence.

|  |  |
|---|---|
| Longer sentence: | Laura, shy and a good listener, and Ruby, friendly and a great talker, are sisters. |
| Contains these clauses: | Laura is shy. Ruby is friendly. Laura and Ruby are sisters. Laura is a good listener. Ruby is a great talker. |

Here, by compressing information into phrases, six simple sentences have been compressed into one sentence that expresses the basic message, "Laura and Ruby are sisters." All the other information has been compressed into phrases that provide further detail within the structure of the one equation sentence.

|  |  |
|---|---|
| Longer sentence: | Although I sent my payment on time, the mail was slow, and since the bank did not receive payment on the due date, I now have to pay a late charge. |
| Contains these clauses: | I sent my payment to the bank. The payment was on time. The mail was slow. The bank did not receive payment on the due date. I now have to pay a late charge. |
| Subordinate clause: | Although I sent my payment on time |
| Independent clause: | the mail was slow. |
| Subordinate clause: | Since the bank did not receive payment on the due date |
| Independent clause: | I now have to pay a late charge. |
| Longer sentence: | The hot and thirsty construction worker put his tools down when his helper brought him a cold drink. |
| Contains these clauses: | The construction worker was hot. The construction worker was thirsty. He put down his tools. His helper brought him a drink. The drink was cold. |

Independent clause: The hot and thirsty construction worker put down his tools

Subordinate clause: *when* his helper brought him a cold drink.

When authors use these longer, sometimes complicated, sentences to express ideas and details, the reader must be able to identify each of the ideas and details in the sentence, and see the relationships among them.

READING EXERCISE

I. Read each of the following sentences. Indicate in the spaces provided (1) the coordinating conjunction used in the sentence and (2) the relationship between the two ideas in the sentence.

1. Laura likes to jog, and Luke likes to play tennis.

    Coordinating conjunction _____

    Relationship between ideas _____

    _____

2. Sarah will cook dinner for them, or they will go out to eat.

    Coordinating conjunction _____

    Relationship between ideas _____

    _____

3. Elizabeth bought Sam a tie, for she knew he would like it.

    Coordinating conjunction _____

    Relationship between ideas _____

    _____

4. David danced with the girls at the party, but Mark sat in a corner all night.

    Coordinating conjunction _____

    Relationship between ideas _____

    _____

5. I like eggs for breakfast, and I like meat and potatoes for dinner.

    Coordinating conjunction _____

    Relationship between ideas _____

    _____

II. Read each of the following sentences. Indicate in the spaces provided (1) the subordinating conjunction used in the sentence and (2) the most important idea of the sentence.

1. Before I could get in the door, the phone rang.

Subordinating conjunction _____

Most important idea _____

2. My car insurance will be canceled unless I pay the premium.

Subordinating conjunction _____

Most important idea _____

3. Whether John goes or not, Kenny is going fishing.

Subordinating conjunction _____

Most important idea _____

4. Bystanders were helpful when I had the accident.

Subordinating conjunction _____

Most important idea _____

5. I dreamed of ice cream and chocolate candy while I was on a diet.

Subordinating conjunction _____

Most important idea _____

6. Because he was kind to her, the woman left him part of her fortune.

Subordinating conjunction _____

Most important idea _____

7. Alfred took the blame so that Alan wouldn't get into trouble.

Subordinating conjunction _____

The More Complicated Sentence                                    125

Most important idea _____

_____

8. He is the man who stole my car.

Subordinating conjunction _____

Most important idea _____

_____

9. If the thief is caught he will go to jail.

Subordinating conjunction _____

Most important idea _____

_____

10. When the thief is caught he will go to jail.

Subordinating conjunction _____

Most important idea _____

_____

III. Read the following sentences. In the spaces provided, list the separate ideas that have been condensed to create the sentence.

1. Donald, withdrawn and sensitive, and Frank, outgoing and popular, live together and are brothers.

_____

_____

_____

2. The unexpected rain drowned my car, leaving me stranded on an unfamiliar road.

_____

_____

_____

3. Jason, a four-year-old adventurer, wandered far away from home though his mother warned him to play in front of the house.

_____

_____

_____

4. Unless you lived more than one mile from your school, you could not get a bus pass to ride to school during the school year.

5. Since I was fired by my boss for being late too many times, I faced starvation and the loss of a roof over my head.

## COMPOSING MORE COMPLICATED SENTENCES

As you have seen, a sentence can be as short as a few words, or it can be long and complicated. Every sentence, however, establishes a relationship or relationships. The length, complexity, and form of a particular sentence are determined by the ideas it expresses.

### Compound Sentences

On the simplest level, a sentence presents a relationship between a subject and a verb so that a statement about the subject can be made: "I called my boss." Sometimes, for purposes of sentence variety and efficiency, two simple sentences are combined into one longer sentence: "I overslept, and I called my boss." In this sentence, two ideas of equal importance are joined by the coordinating conjunction "and." Other coordinating conjunctions establish different kinds of relationships between the ideas expressed in the sentence:

I could call my boss, *or* I could just hope for the best.
I called my boss, *for* I knew she would be looking for me.
I called my boss, *but* her line was busy.

Each of these conjunctions expresses a different kind of relationship. "And" adds one piece of information to another; "or" compares one possibility to another; "for" suggests a cause and effect relationship; "but" changes the direction of the sentence to say that something other than what was expected happened.

Coordinating conjunctions enable a writer to increase the length of sentences by joining two or more ideas together. But since conjunctions also signal relationships between ideas, they permit the writer to express ideas more clearly and efficiently. The following paragraph contains only simple sentences:

> It was a hot, muggy day. The streets seemed to be turning into liquid asphalt. The sun shone down intensely. It sent waves of heat into the houses. All day, there was not a sign of a breeze. At six o'clock, the curtain in the window fluttered. The air began to feel a little cooler. Clouds darkened the sky. Rain brought welcome relief.

Coordinating conjunctions can join these sentences together:

> It was a hot, muggy day, <u>and</u> the streets seemed to be turning into liquid asphalt. The sun shone down intensely, <u>and</u> it sent waves of heat into the houses. All day, there was not a sign of a breeze, <u>but</u> at six o'clock, the curtain in the window fluttered. The air began to feel a little cooler, <u>for</u> clouds darkened the sky. Rain brought welcome relief.

The coordinating conjunctions "and," "but," "for" in the second version of the paragraph lengthen the sentences. The longer sentences read fluidly, while those in the first paragraph are unpleasantly choppy. More important, the conjunctions aid in establishing relationships between the ideas:

It was a hot, muggy day,
  *and*      Two related ideas
the streets seemed to be turning added together
into liquid asphalt.
The sun shone down
intensely,
  *and*      Two related ideas
it sent waves of heat    added together
into the houses.
All day, there was
not a sign of a breeze,
  *but*      Conjunction "but"
at six o'clock the curtain   changes direction of
in the window fluttered.   the ideas
The air began to feel a
little cooler,
  *for*      Two ideas in a cause
clouds darkened the sky.   and effect relationship

The last sentence, "Rain brought welcome relief," could also be added to the preceding sentence with another "and." However, the short, simple sentence may be more effective standing alone to provide an emphatic ending. As you construct sentences, you can decide which to compound with coordinating conjunctions and which to leave alone as simple sentences.

Those which are compounded will show a relationship between the ideas. Those which are left as simple sentences can provide useful emphasis at key places in the paragraph.

**Complex Sentences**

Although coordinating conjunctions show how two ideas of equal importance can be related to each other in one sentence, it is often desirable to show how one idea in a sentence is more important than another. For this purpose, different signal words can be used:

*Before* I left for work, I called my boss.
*After* I overslept, I called my boss.
*Because* I overslept, I was late for work.
*Although* I overslept, I still managed to be on time.

Each of the signal words serves two purposes. Like the coordinating conjunctions, each suggests a relationship between the idea it introduces and the information in the rest of the sentence. In addition, these signal words show that the information they introduce is less important than the idea communicated by the rest of the sentence.

The first half of each sentence above is a *subordinate clause,* and it is introduced by a *subordinate conjunction.* The important idea in the second half of each sentence is called the *independent clause.* A sentence containing a subordinate clause and an independent clause is a *complex sentence.* As indicated earlier in the chapter, subordinate clauses can indicate time relationships and cause and effect relationships, provide identification information, or explain a dilemma. Coordinating conjunctions can serve some of these same purposes in combining two independent clauses, but the subordinating clause structure also establishes degrees of importance between the two clauses:

| | |
|---|---|
| Two independent clauses | I called my boss, *for* I had overslept. |
| Independent clause and subordinate clause | I called my boss *because* I had overslept. |

Both sentences indicate a cause and effect relationship between the ideas stated in each clause. The difference is that the first makes no distinction between the importance of the ideas, but the second focuses on one idea as more important ("I called my boss"). The rest of the information becomes background or secondary to the statement made by the independent clause.

Generally, subordinate clauses enable you to write more precisely. First, they separate one idea from another in terms of which is more important. Second, they permit you to express a wider range of relationships than do coordinating conjunctions. Notice how more precision can be added to the description of the hot summer day with the use of some subordinating conjunctions:

> <u>Because</u> it was a hot, muggy day, the streets seemed to be turning into liquid asphalt. The sun shone down intensely <u>so</u> <u>that</u> it sent waves of heat into the houses. <u>Although</u> there was not a sign of a breeze all day, at six o'clock the curtain in the window fluttered. The air began to feel a little cooler <u>when</u> clouds darkened the sky. Rain brought welcome relief.

When written with a combination of subordinate and independent clauses, the independent clauses stand out more clearly:

The streets seemed to be turning into liquid asphalt.
The sun shone down intensely.
At six o'clock the curtain in the window fluttered.
The air began to feel a little cooler.
Rain brought welcome relief.

As you learn to write sentences more carefully, you will find that a mixture of simple, compound, and complex sentences will make your writing varied, emphatic, and clear.

## Sentence Combining and Word Economy

A compound sentence joins two ideas of equal importance. A complex sentence joins an idea of lesser importance to an idea of greater significance. Sometimes, however, you will want to *compress* an idea so that it becomes a detail in a larger context:

| Compound: | I overslept, *and* I called my boss. |
| Complex: | *Because* I overslept, I called my boss. |
| Compressed: | *Having overslept,* I called my boss. |

In the last sentence, the information about oversleeping has been reduced to a *phrase,* which is a grammatical unit smaller than either an independent or subordinate clause. Phrases communicate an idea, but not a relationship.

Compression of information into phrases permits you to pack more details into a sentence without losing sight of the most important idea:

The snow was heavy.
It clogged the roads.
It was unexpected.
It buried my car.
I could not get to my car.

becomes:

> The unexpected and heavy snow buried my car so that I could not reach it on the clogged road.

In this example, three ideas—(1) the snow was heavy; (2) it clogged the roads; and (3) it was unexpected—are reduced to phrases.

> I missed work on Monday.
> I had missed work several times.
> My boss had warned me about my absences.
> He had said I would lose a day's pay.
> I needed the money for my rent.

becomes:

> Because of my boss's warning not to miss work again, I faced the prospect of losing a day's pay, and the rent money, when I was out on Monday.

Here again information is compressed into phrases so that the main idea can be presented clearly and emphatically. "I faced the prospect of losing a day's pay, and the rent money" is the independent clause of this sentence and communicates the most important information. The other information becomes detail expressed in phrases and one subordinate clause at the end of the sentence:

| | |
|---|---|
| Phrase | Because of my boss' warning not to miss work again |
| Independent clause | I faced the prospect |
| Phrase | of losing a day's pay and the rent money |
| Subordinate clause | when I was out on Monday. |

Reducing clauses to phrases makes your writing even tighter, more economical, and more sharply focused. Notice what happens to the hot, muggy day paragraph when some of the information is compressed into phrases:

> On a hot muggy day, the intense sun turned the streets into liquid asphalt. Without a sign of a breeze all day, the houses received only waves of heat until six o'clock when the curtain in the window fluttered. Against a background of dark clouds, the air began to feel a little cooler. Rain brought welcome relief.

Now, we are left with only the following independent clauses:

> (On a hot muggy day) the intense sun turned the streets (into liquid asphalt).
> (Against a background of dark clouds) the air began to feel a little cooler.
> Rain brought welcome relief.

The material in parentheses has been compressed into phrases that are attached to the independent clause to provide context for the more important information it expresses. The independent clauses also contain detail that has been reduced to a word:

The sun shone down intensely

becomes:

The *intense* sun

In the revised paragraph, only one subordinate clause remains, and it stands out in a key place: the houses received only waves of heat *until six o'clock when the curtain in the window fluttered*.

This revision of the hot, muggy day paragraph is only one of dozens of possibilities. The same basic information can be expressed in many different combinations of phrases and independent and subordinate clauses. Each combination will provide a different emphasis and a different focus. And each will effectively communicate the individual perceptions of the writer who composed it.

WRITING EXERCISE

I.  A. Write compound sentences for the following:

   *Independent clause*         *Independent clause*

   1. _____, and _____.

   2. _____, but _____.

   3. _____, for _____.

   4. _____, or _____.

   5. Either _____, or _____.

   6. Neither _____, nor _____.

   B. Revise the following paragraph, which contains only simple sentences. Combine these simple sentences into compound sentences, using "and," "but," "for," and "or." Try to use each conjunction only once.

   My dog has fleas. He scratches himself from morning to night. Sometimes he uses his hind paw to work on his ear. Sometimes he works on his belly with his teeth. He tries everything. Nothing works. I would like to be able to help him. After all, he is my best friend.

_____
_____
_____
_____

II. A. Write complex sentences for the following:

*Subordinate clause*          *Independent clause*

1. After _____, _____
2. Because _____, _____
3. Although _____, _____
4. If _____, _____
5. Since _____, _____

*Independent clause*          *Subordinate clause*

6. _____ who _____
7. _____ when _____
8. _____ which _____
9. _____ unless _____
10. _____ so that _____

B. Revise the following paragraph, which contains only simple sentences, by using subordinating conjunctions:

    I went to see the film. My friend had recommended it. She was going to see it with me. She decided not to go. I was disappointed. I had wanted her to explain it to me. I never understand these foreign films. I can't read the subtitles fast enough. These foreign directors also like fuzziness a lot. They never seem to focus their cameras right. It's like looking at people in a fog. My friend enjoys these films. I can't understand why.

_____
_____
_____
_____

The More Complicated Sentence

C. Rewrite Exercise IB or IIB using a combination of simple, compound, and complex sentences:

_____
_____
_____
_____

III. Rewrite the following into several sentences by using compound and complex sentences and by compressing some information into phrases.

A.
1. Mr. and Mrs. Smith were divorced yesterday.
2. Mrs. Smith is an actress.
3. They had been married for three weeks.
4. Mr. Smith is a writer.
5. Mrs. Smith has been married four times.
6. Mr. Smith has been married five times.
7. They met on the set of Mrs. Smith's latest film.
8. Their courtship lasted two days.
9. In the divorce papers, they accused each other of infidelity.
10. They had returned from their Caribbean honeymoon last week.

_____
_____
_____
_____
_____

B.
1. The first television shows were live.
2. The performers could not correct mistakes.
3. These shows were like live theater.
4. Sometimes the unexpected happened.
5. These unexpected happenings were often very funny.
6. Sometimes they were embarrassing.
7. But they were real.
8. Today, nearly all shows are taped.
9. Performers have the chance to redo lines and scenes.
10. These shows are flawless.
11. They are predictable.
12. They are often boring.

C. 
1. More and more discount stores are opening.
2. They sell merchandise at much lower prices.
3. Some of the merchandise is slightly damaged.
4. Some of the merchandise is irregular.
5. Some of the merchandise is last year's model.
6. Some of these stores accept only cash.
7. The service in these stores is sometimes not very good.
8. The shoppers are looking for good prices.
9. They will tolerate some inconvenience.
10. For some people, these stores are an answer to inflation.

# 8

# Main Idea and Topic Sentences

PREVIEW

Paragraphs present one major thought that is clarified and explained in a series of sentences. The major thought is called the *main idea*. The main idea is usually stated in a *topic sentence* that expresses the general thought of the paragraph.

For a reader, it is important to be able to identify main ideas in paragraphs. When a reader makes this identification, he or she is stating in his or her own words the general thought communicated by the paragraph. Main ideas can be located by asking three questions:

1. Who or what is the topic of the paragraph?
2. What part of the topic is being discussed?
3. What does the writer want the reader to understand and/or remember about the part of the topic being discussed?

For a writer, it is just as important to determine what main idea he or she wishes to communicate in a paragraph. By modifying the three questions above, a writer can focus his or her approach to the topic of the paragraph and construct a topic sentence.

It is useful to note that topic sentences can occur in different places throughout the paragraph. They usually appear at the beginning of a paragraph, but they can also be located at the middle or at the end. In some cases, the main idea will be implied but not stated in a topic sentence.

**Key Terms**

**Paragraph.** A group of related sentences that focus on one idea.
**Main idea.** The general statement contained in a paragraph.
**Topic sentence.** The expression of the general statement.
**General statement.** The expression of a conclusion or broad idea.
**Specific statement.** The expression of particular or detailed information.

When you read a page in a book, you see that the writing is divided into paragraphs. Writers organize ideas into paragraphs so that the reader can easily understand how the ideas relate to each other, and how they develop into the broader statement that the writer makes. The first step for the reader is to understand that the paragraph focuses on one main idea.

By this time you have had a lot of experience with main ideas. You can probably even explain that they take the form of broad, general statements, or that when they appear in written form they are called topic sentences. You might also say that topic sentences are usually the first sentence of a paragraph, and that topic sentences tell what the paragraph is about.

However, even though you are familiar with these descriptions, you might not know *how* to identify main ideas. And even when you do identify them in topic sentences, you probably do so intuitively. That is, you somehow *know* that a certain sentence within the paragraph expresses the main idea, but you can't explain why.

The purpose of this chapter is to provide you with a more systematic approach to determining main ideas in paragraphs and composing your own topic sentences.

## DETERMINING MAIN IDEAS

In order to determine main ideas, you must first recognize that the main idea expressed in a topic sentence can appear almost *anywhere* in a paragraph: beginning, middle, or end. Each of the diagrams in Figure 8.1 shows the placement of main ideas expressed in topic sentences within paragraphs.

It is better not to expect that the first sentence of a paragraph will automatically be the topic sentence. Placement of the topic sentence depends upon the writer's intent and the style he or she chooses to express ideas. A better method for determining the main idea and then locating the topic sentence is to ask yourself three questions:

1. Who or what is the topic of the paragraph?
2. What part of the topic is being discussed?
3. What does the author want the reader to understand and/or remember about the part of the topic being discussed?

# Main Idea and Topic Sentences

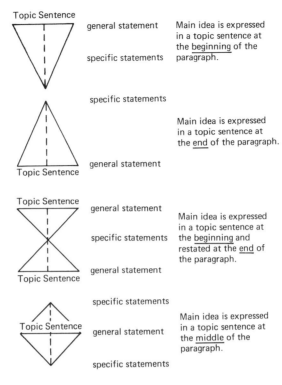

**Figure 8.1**

Read the following paragraph:

> It is not unusual these days to see men shopping for the family's groceries in the local supermarket, or requesting paternity leave to care for newborn infants. Once thought to be "woman's work," these activities are becoming the responsibilities of men and are therefore altering the functions of men in marriage. What caused this to happen? The Women's Liberation Movement has changed the man's role in marriage.

*Who or what is the topic of the paragraph?* This question is the most general of the three, and it enables you to identify what, in a broad sense, the writer is discussing in the paragraph: marriage.

*What part of the topic is being discussed?* This question asks you to be a little more specific. Since it is impossible to discuss a topic like marriage in one paragraph, in answering this question you should focus on the part or element of the topic that is discussed in the paragraph: the man's role in marriage.

*What does the author want the reader to understand and/or remember about the part of the topic being discussed?* Now that you know the part of the topic on which the paragraph concentrates, you can ask, "What am I supposed to know, in a general sense, about this part of the subject?" Because authors usually have a point to make in each paragraph—something the reader should understand and remember—you must locate the general statement or topic sentence. The answer to this question (based on the answers to the first two questions) leads to determining the main idea and locating the topic sentence that expresses it.

The example of marriage as the answer to the first question, refined to "man's role in marriage" as an answer to the second question, becomes "Man's role in marriage has changed with the advent of the women's movement." This is the answer to the third question and the main idea. The sentence which states that main idea is therefore the topic sentence of the paragraph.

## Direct Statements

Read the following paragraph. Using the three questions to find the main idea, see if you can determine which sentence in the paragraph best states the main idea.

> For centuries, no one questioned France's preeminence* in the world of fine perfume. But within the next few months, the French will be challenged—and on their own native grounds—as American designers introduce their fragrances in Paris.

1. Who or what is the topic? *France.*
2. What segment of the topic is being discussed? *France's leadership in the world of fine perfume.*
3. What does the author want the reader to understand and/or remember about the segment of the topic being discussed? *American designers will challenge France's position when they introduce their perfumes in Paris.*

The last sentence of this paragraph best states the author's main idea in the form of a topic sentence: "But within the next few months, the French will be challenged—and on their own native grounds—as American designers introduce their fragrances in Paris."

As you can see, the main idea is the idea the author has in mind as he or she writes the paragraph. When using the three questions to find the main idea, you as a reader are doing some detective work: you are attempt-

---

*Prominence, leadership.

Main Idea and Topic Sentences   139

ing to think as the author did when writing the paragraph so you can identify the central thought or main idea. Try the following examples:

> After graduation, I faced the job market with expectation. Unlike many of my fellow graduates who were waiting to be accepted into professional schools, I anxiously looked for my first job as a professional. However, these people understood what I would have to learn: my liberal arts education had not prepared me for a particular job. Today's economy seems to require college graduates to have skills directly related to the careers they desire.

1. Who or what is the topic? _____

2. What part of the topic is being discussed? _____

3. What does the author want the reader to understand and/or remember about the part of the topic being discussed?

Try this paragraph from the same article:

> I was a classics major. As an undergraduate I studied Plato, Aristotle and Socrates to help me better understand life. I was often asked what I would do with a classics degree. I thought that such a course of study would make me a knowledgeable person, someone an employer would hire at a respectable wage.

1. Who or what is the topic? _____

2. What part of the topic is being discussed? _____

3. What does the author want the reader to understand and/or remember about the part of the topic being discussed?

**Indirect Statements**

Not all paragraphs state the main idea *directly,* as in the previous examples. So far, in each paragraph you could choose a topic sentence that stated the main idea. Some authors, however, may state the main idea *indirectly;* that is, they may give a main idea without actually stating it. In paragraphs like this, all the sentences provide information to help you compose the main idea. In such instances, you can still apply the three questions. However, the topic sentence for such paragraphs must be written in your own words on the basis of what is stated about the topic and the segment of the topic discussed. Consider the following example:

"The No. 280 reflects character and station in life. It is superb in styling and provides a formal reflection of successful living." This is quoted from the catalogue of Practical Burial Footwear of Columbus, Ohio, and refers to the Fit-A-Foot Oxford, which comes in patent, calf, tan or oxblood with lace or goring* back. The same firm carries the Ko-Zee, with its "soft, cushioned soles and warm, luxurious slipper comfort, but true shoe smartness." Just what practical use is made of the footwear is spelled out. Burial footwear demonstrates "consideration and thoughtfulness for the departed." The closed portion of the casket is opened for the family, who on looking see that "the ensemble is complete although not showing. You will gain their complete confidence and good will." The women's lingerie department of Practical Burial Footwear supplies a deluxe package, in black patent box with gold-embossed inscription, of "pantee, vestee" and nylon hose, "strikingly smart—ultimate in distinction." Also for the ladies is the "new bra form, Post Mortem Form Restoration," offered by Courtesy Products at the demonstrably low price of $11 for a package of 50—they "accomplish so much for so little."

Here the author provides sufficient information so that the topic, burial attire, and the segment of the topic, those who supply it, is easily identified. The main idea, "Burial wear suppliers appeal to the family's desire to give the dead an image of style and luxury," must be concluded from the information presented in the paragraph.

Read the following paragraph and see if you can identify the implied (indirectly stated) main idea:

When I think of hills, I think of the upward strength I tread upon. When water is the object of my thought, I feel the cool shock of the plunge and the quick yielding of the waves that crisp and curl and ripple about my body. The pleasing changes of rough and smooth,

*Cloth.

pliant* and rigid, curved and straight in the bark and branches of a tree give truth to my hand. The immovable rock, with its juts and warped surfaces, bends beneath my fingers into all manner of grooves and hollows. The bulge of a watermelon and the puffed-up rotundities** of squashes that sprout, bud, and ripen in that strange garden planted somewhere behind my finger tips are the ludicrous* in my tactual** memory and imagination.

READING EXERCISE

Read each of the following paragraphs. Using the three questions to find the main idea, identify the main idea for each. Where the main idea is directly stated, underline the topic sentence that expresses it. Where the main idea is indirectly stated, write the main idea in your own words. Use a dictionary to look up unfamiliar words. Use the spaces that follow each paragraph for writing implied main ideas and/or definitions.

1. Crib death, more formally known as sudden infant death syndrome, and shortened to SIDS, has been described as the silent killer that stalks the nursery. Apparently healthy, apparently normal babies are put to bed and simply don't wake up. There is no noise, no struggle, no suffering. The sleeping, or just awakening, baby stops breathing and dies. The cause is unknown. There is no cure.

_____

_____

_____

_____

2. If a woman wants a field cleared, the first thing she does is cook up some food and send the word around that a party is being prepared. In the morning her working guests arrive and each does his allotted share. About two in the afternoon they gather around the food pots for an extended dinner hour. In this way, whatever they do is accomplished through work parties, an ingenious combination of work and play.

*Flexible.
**Round objects.
*Humorous, silly.
**The sense of touch.

3. Hawks are generally regarded as ruthless enemies of the farmer and are generally condemned to be shot on sight. But as a rule, the hawk is the farmer's friend, for he feeds on rats, mice, gophers, locusts, and other pests. There are many tall tales from nature which are widely believed but without scientific foundation. There is the belief that birds always return to the same nest each spring, but, according to scientists, this is not true. Again, owls have been called the wisest of birds, perhaps because of their solemn expressions, but there is no scientific evidence to vouch for their wisdom.

4. One of the most romantic legends in the world of wine involves the glass traditionally used for Champagne, the glass known as the *coupe*, or cup, that resembles a wide-mouthed bowl with a short stem attached. Because it is shallow, spills its contents easily and causes Champagne bubbles to dissipate readily, it is perhaps the most impractical wine glass known to man. Yet its creation is steeped in Greek mythology, for it is said that the first coupe was molded from the breast of Helen of Troy to enable the gods on Mount Olympus to drink toasts from a chalice of the most sensual shape from the most beautiful woman of her time.

5. Webster College graduates have discovered many types of employment. An anthropology major serves burgers at Cowboy Ranch. A psychology major sells cosmetics at the counter of a local department store. Another classics major sells encyclopedias door to door. I work in a bookstore. Although I am near the books I love, I am in the same predicament as those graduates who serve burgers and sell

cosmetics. In truth, I am not in any better position than many other recent college graduates in the United States.

6. Unlike the heroin addict, the speed freak is a hyperactive, suspicious person. He may sharpen and re-sharpen the same pencil a dozen times or start a fight for no apparent reason. His behavior can't be predicted. And, he is an intolerable burden to those around him. The only people that can stomach him are other speed freaks. He is completely undependable. He is a clear example of the person who does his "own thing" no matter what. People who try to help him receive no thanks. Although no one loves him, the speed freak is the result of the drug scene started in the 1960's.

7. Egypt was an especially attractive land. Its warm climate was eminently suited for human beings who had not yet learned how to live with ease in colder areas. The great Nile, with its annual overflow, gave fertility to the valley through which it ran; and the abundant vegetation springing up from the rich soil and growing to maturity under the vital sun in a long season minimized the struggle for existence. There was just enough geographic protection to make invasion difficult, but not enough to foster isolation and stagnation. Protection, food, and warmth—these were the factors that made Egypt so attractive to the hordes who sought the security of its bosom and founded the civilization that was to be the basis for so many of the institutions of the Western world.

8. Scientific observation is systematic. A scientific investigation defines

a problem, then draws up an organized plan for collecting facts about it. Suppose the question is, "How does the drop-out rate of college students who marry while in college compare with the drop-out rate of unmarried students?" One might try to answer the question by simply recalling the students he has known; but this sample would be small; it might not be typical; and one's memory is imperfect. Conclusions based on casual recollections are not very reliable. If our research plan calls for a systematic check on the college records of several thousand students, then our drop-out rates for the single and married students are based on dependable factual data. Unless these data have been collected as part of an organized systematic program of scientific observation, they are likely to be spotty and incomplete. Anecdotes, personal recollections, off-hand opinions, and travelogue impressions may suggest an hypothesis which is worth testing; but no scientist would base a conclusion upon such data.

9. It is a miracle that New York works at all. The whole thing is implausible. Every time the residents brush their teeth, millions of gallons of water must be drawn from the Catskill Mountains and the hills of Westchester. When a young man in Manhattan writes a letter to his girl in Brooklyn, the love message gets blown to her through a pneumatic tube—pfft—just like that. The subterranean system of telephone cables, power lines, steam pipes, gas mains and sewer pipes is reason enough to abandon the island to the gods and the weevils. Every time an incision is made in the pavement, the noisy surgeons expose ganglia that are tangled beyond belief. By rights New York should have destroyed itself long ago, from panic of fire or rioting or failure of some vital supply line in its circulatory system or from some deep labyrinthine short circuit. Long ago the city should have experienced an insoluble traffic snarl at some impossible bottleneck. It should have perished of hunger when food lines failed for a few days. It should have been wiped out by a plague starting in its slums or carried in by ships' rats. It should have been overwhelmed by the sea that licks at it on every side. The workers in its myriad cells should have succumbed to nerves, from the fearful pall of smoke-fog that drifts over every few days from Jersey, blotting out all light at noon and leaving the high offices suspended, men groping and depressed, and the sense of world's end. It should have been touched in the head by the August heat and gone off its rocker.

## COMPOSING TOPIC SENTENCES

All effective expression demands clarity and organization. As you have seen, paragraphs generally explain and develop one main idea. This main idea is usually found in a topic sentence somewhere in the paragraph. As you begin to write a paragraph, you first have to decide what you want to express; that is, you have to determine the main idea for the paragraph. Then, in most cases, you will state that main idea in a topic sentence.

Determining a main idea is similar to taking a picture with a camera. Both activities involve making choices. Just as you would not pick up a camera and trip the shutter without looking through the viewfinder, so you should not begin writing a paragraph without careful thought. Suppose you are hiking in the White Mountains of New Hampshire, and you pause before a waterfall that plunges straight down over its rocky bed. You decide this scene is worth capturing, and that the fall, with its brilliant splashes of water, should be the center of attention. You aim your camera through the viewfinder in such a way as to show off the waterfall against a background of green trees and rocky ledges, and then you trip the shutter.

Composing paragraphs, like photographing the scene in the mountains, requires that you decide what you want to emphasize, just as you have to figure out what angle of vision to use when aiming your camera. In the first half of this chapter, you saw how to read paragraphs to discover the main idea of the writer. As a writer, you must determine your own approach to your subject, and then you can compose a topic sentence which will express that idea.

### Three Questions for Composing Main Idea Sentences

These three questions are the same as those you used to identify the main ideas in the paragraphs you read, except as the writer you must make the choices:

1. Who or what do you want the topic of the paragraph to be?
2. What part of the subject do you want to discuss?
3. What do you want the reader to understand and/or remember about the part of the topic you are discussing?

Assume you are writing a paragraph that describes the scene in the mountains. Instead of taking a picture of it, you will use words. The task of determining emphasis remains, and you can use the three questions to help you determine a main idea and to express it in a topic sentence.

1. *Who or what do you want to be the topic of the paragraph?* The subject of your paragraph could be the mountain scene itself.

2. *What part of the topic do you want to discuss?* The scene involves a variety of elements—the waterfall, the surrounding vegetation, the bright blue sky. Perhaps you want to concentrate on the waterfall.

3. *What do you want the reader to understand and/or remember about the part of the topic you are discussing?* You still have to decide what you want to say about the waterfall. To help you make this decision, you could ask yourself what about the waterfall interests you. Is it extremely high? Is it exciting in its constant motion against the solid and unmoving rocks? Is it dangerous? In answering this question, you will determine your main idea for the paragraph—what you want the reader to understand and/or remember about this scene.

Suppose you pick the second possibility, the one about the movement of the water. Your main idea, then, might be something like the following: "The constant motion of the waterfall stands out against the rocks." This main idea would determine the direction and emphasis of the paragraph about the waterfall. Each detail you provide would support this statement. You might begin the paragraph by writing your main idea into a topic sentence:

> The constant motion of the waterfall stands out against the rocks. From a height of four hundred feet, the water rushes almost straight down and crashes against the still rocks at the bottom. The rocks, though, seem undisturbed and unmoving. They present the same quiet surface to the fury of the water that they have presented for thousands of years.

The first sentence, "The constant motion of the waterfall stands out against the rocks," is a topic sentence that expresses the main idea of the paragraph. Sometimes the topic sentence will be almost the same as the statement of the main idea. The important thing to remember is that first you determine the main idea, and then you write the paragraph with a topic sentence which states that main idea. The exact wording of the topic sentence will take shape as you write the paragraph.

The paragraph about the mountain waterfall is a physical description. Some paragraphs concentrate on ideas rather than on physical objects. But the procedure is the same: you determine the main idea, and then shape that main idea into a topic sentence as you write the paragraph. For example, suppose you want to write a paragraph about the shift away from liberal arts degrees to majors in business. Your topic is college degrees. You decide you want to write about the fact that many college students are choosing majors in business areas. And to answer the third question, you think you will tell the reader that the increase in business majors is a reaction to difficult economic times. Your paragraph would state this main idea in a topic sentence, and then provide other statements to explain and clarify the idea:

> More and more college students are choosing to major in business related degree programs because of the uncertain state of the economy. Students today start college with their eyes focused on job opportunities after they graduate. College is no longer only a place to learn about literature, philosophy, or history. These areas are still important, but more important is the need to increase the college graduate's chance for a job. This need seems to be met best, according to the new business majors, by choosing a degree program which prepares them for a specific career.

The details in this paragraph concern ideas rather than physical facts, as in the waterfall example, but they follow the emphasis and direction provided by the main idea as expressed in the topic sentence.

## Placement of the Topic Sentence

Once you have your main idea, you still have to decide where you want to express it in a topic sentence in the paragraph. The most likely place is at the beginning, since this position clearly tells your reader what to expect in the rest of the paragraph. But the effect would be boring if you began each paragraph this way. Therefore, for variety, sometimes you will want to put the topic sentence in different places.

The different positions of the topic sentence can also help you create other effects. Placing it at the end of the paragraph builds interest as the reader wonders where the details will lead. Placing it in the middle enables you to balance the details in the first half of the paragraph against those in the second half. For added emphasis, you can state the topic sentence at the beginning and repeat it at the end. As your skill in composition increases, you might want to write paragraphs with an implied rather than stated topic sentence.

The paragraph about business majors began with the topic sentence, but placing it at the end could create more interest:

> Students today start college with their eyes focused on job opportunities after they graduate. College is no longer only a place to learn about literature, philosophy, or history. These areas are still important, but more important is the need to increase the college graduate's chance for a job. This need seems to be met best, according to the new business majors, by choosing a degree program which prepares them for a specific career. More and more college students are choosing to major in business related degree programs because of the uncertain state of the economy.

Here the details in the paragraph lead to the statement of the more general idea at the conclusion.

Putting the topic sentence in the middle of the paragraph can permit you to balance details in the first and second halves:

> Students today start college with their eyes focused on job opportunities after they graduate. College is no longer only a place to learn about literature, philosophy, or history. More and more college students are choosing to major in business related degree programs because of the uncertain state of the economy. Literature, philosophy, or history are still important, but more important is the need to increase the college graduate's chance for a job. This need seems to be met best, according to the new business majors, by choosing a degree program which prepares them for a specific career.

Added emphasis can be achieved by stating and restating the topic sentence (in slightly different words) at both the beginning and the end of the paragraph:

> More and more college students are choosing to major in business related degree programs because of the uncertain state of the economy. Students today start college with their eyes focused on job opportunities after they graduate. College is no longer only a place to learn about literature, philosophy, or history. These areas are still important, but more important is the need to increase the college graduate's chance for a job. This need seems to be met best, according to the new business majors, by degree programs which prepare them for a specific career. Hard economic times, they have decided, demand practical educational choices.

Whether the topic sentence is stated at the beginning, middle, or end of the paragraph, the main idea it expresses must be chosen before the paragraph is written. Once the main idea is determined, you can decide how you want to formulate it in a topic sentence and where to place that sentence in the paragraph. If you have difficulty keeping your paragraph focused on your main idea, you should write the topic sentence at the beginning as a guide. As you become more experienced, you can experiment with different placement, and finally with implied topic sentence paragraphs.

Main Idea and Topic Sentences 149

WRITING EXERCISE

I. Using the three questions, determine the main ideas for the following topics. Remember, it is important to determine main ideas that provide emphasis and direction for a paragraph.

Marriage
A beautiful scene
Career choices
A good film
Your neighborhood

II. In the following exercise, the first two questions have been answered for each topic. Provide the third answer for each.

A.  1. Topic: *airplane hijacking.*
    2. Part of the topic you want to discuss: *precautions to prevent airplane hijackings.*
    3. Part of the topic you want the reader to understand and/or remember.
    _____

B.  1. Topic: *cars.*
    2. Part of the topic you want to discuss: *buying a used car.*
    3. Part of the topic you want the reader to understand and/or remember.
    _____

C.  1. Topic: *my girlfriend/boyfriend.*
    2. Part of the topic you want to discuss: *his/her most annoying habit.*
    3. Part of the topic you want the reader to understand and/or remember.
    _____

D.  1. Topic: *maturity*
    2. Part of the topic you want to discuss: *the first time I felt mature.*
    3. Part of the topic you want the reader to understand and/or remember.
    _____

E.  1. Topic: *studying.*
    2. Part of the topic you want to discuss: *studying at home.*

3. Part of the topic you want the reader to understand and/or remember

   _____

III. Write a paragraph based on one of the main ideas in Exercise I. State the main idea in a topic sentence at the beginning of the paragraph. Then rewrite the paragraph with the topic sentence placed in a different position. Underline the topic sentence.

_____
_____
_____
_____
_____
_____
_____
_____
_____

IV. Discrimination is usually thought of as a broad social problem, and all of us have felt discriminated against at one time or another. Jot down some times when you have felt discriminated against.

_____
_____

Now use the three questions to determine a main idea for a paragraph.

1. Who or what do you want to be the topic of the paragraph?

   _____

2. What part of the topic do you want to discuss?

   _____

3. What do you want the reader to understand and/or remember about the part of the topic you are discussing?

   _____
   _____

# Main Idea and Topic Sentences

The answer to the third question is a main idea sentence. Now write a paragraph, and underline the topic sentence.

_____
_____
_____
_____
_____
_____
_____
_____
_____

V. Pick your own topic, and use the three questions, outlined below, to determine a main idea:

1. Who or what do you want to be the topic of the paragraph?
   _____

2. What part of the topic do you want to discuss?
   _____

3. What do you want the reader to understand and/or remember about the part of the topic you are discussing?
   _____
   _____

   Write the paragraph; underline the topic sentence.

   _____
   _____
   _____
   _____
   _____
   _____
   _____

# 9
# Paragraph Patterns

PREVIEW

A topic sentence can occur at the beginning, middle, or end of a paragraph; sometimes it is repeated at both the beginning and the end. Placement of the topic sentence shapes the way the main idea of the paragraph is communicated in terms of clarity, emphasis, tension, and balance.

Placing the topic sentence at the beginning of the paragraph provides the greatest clarity because the topic sentence immediately announces the main idea. If the topic sentence occurs at the end of the paragraph, a tension or interest is created because the specific information in the paragraph leads to a conclusion that is not expressed until the end. Added emphasis can be achieved by stating the topic sentence at the beginning and at the end of the paragraph. Finally, a topic sentence positioned in the middle of a paragraph provides a way to balance the details that precede the topic sentence with those that follow it.

Recognizing and using these positions for the topic sentence will increase your reading comprehension and add to the style and precision of your writing.

**Key Terms**

    **Clarity.**   Clear presentation of ideas in a paragraph.
    **Emphasis.**   Placement of stress on key ideas in a paragraph.
    **Tension.**   Quality of creating suspense or interest in paragraphs.
    **Balance.**   Grouping details to emphasize relationships among them.

Paragraph Patterns

In the previous chapter, you learned how to determine the main idea of a paragraph, how that main idea is expressed in a topic sentence, how to formulate your own approach to composing a paragraph, and how to compose your own topic sentences. These topic sentences could be placed at the beginning, the middle, or the end of the paragraphs you studied and wrote. Remember that a topic sentence is the written expression of the main idea.

## IDENTIFYING PARAGRAPH PATTERNS

It is important to be able to locate and to compose the main idea of a paragraph. It is also important to understand *why* the topic sentence appears where it does. This placement is determined by the writer's purpose and style.

For example, if the author wishes to supply information so that the reader knows from the start what the paragraph is about, the topic sentence might appear at the beginning of the paragraph. Textbook authors and reporters use this pattern because the most important value in texts and news stories is clarity. Clarity can be achieved by telling the reader right away what the paragraph is about:

<u>On the stage of the Broadway Theater, home of the Tony Award-winning musical, Evita, Terri Klausner leads a double life.</u> Six nights a week, she is just one of the "descamisados" (shirtless ones) in the crowd. She plays most of the show in the shadows, and in the big balcony scene she is one of the multitudes gathered outside Argentina's presidential palace chanting "Evita, Evita, Evita."

<u>But at the Wednesday and Saturday matinees, Klausner is that Latina Lady MacBeth, the glamorous Eva Peron herself.</u> She is up there on the balcony, tiara glittering in the spotlight, singing "Don't Cry for Me, Argentina," to the supplicating masses below.

<u>This week, however, Klausner will give up the matinee performances to take on the evening shows for vacationing Patti LuPone, who won the best-actress-in-a-musical Tony for her portrayal of Eva Peron.</u> Nancy Opel, who has been understudying the part for more than a year without ever performing it, will take the matinees.

In this news item, the writer achieves maximum clarity by stating a topic sentence at the beginning of each of the three paragraphs of the story.

Sometimes, though, it is important to increase the reader's curiosity, to build suspense, or to show how certain details lead to a conclusion. In such cases, the topic sentence can come at the end of the paragraph. The idea of delaying the most important information until the end builds tension, and it is this tension that makes you turn the pages of a mystery or detective story to see how it will come out.

A different kind of emphasis can be achieved by beginning a paragraph with a topic sentence and then restating its idea at the end of the paragraph. This pattern or arrangement is often found in longer paragraphs to make sure the reader does not lose track of the focus of the paragraph.

A final pattern places the topic sentence in the middle of a paragraph. In such a paragraph, one set of details leads up to the statement of the main idea in the topic sentence, and then another set of details, which can be compared or contrasted to the first, follows. This arrangement produces a rising and falling tension and is useful in providing variety in paragraph structure. The diagrams in Figure 9.1 represent these four paragraph patterns.

All paragraphs in which the main idea is stated in a topic sentence contain both general and specific sentences. The general, or topic, sentence states the main idea. The specific sentences are always clearly related to one another. They develop, extend, clarify, explain, describe, and prove or

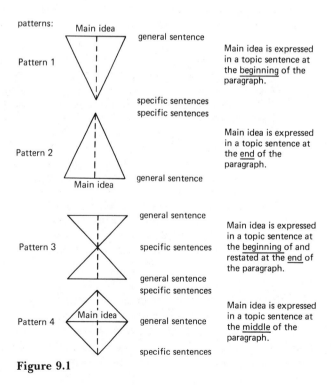

Figure 9.1

Paragraph Patterns

disprove the main idea stated in the topic sentence. Let us look more closely at each of the four types of paragraph patterns.

**Pattern 1**

According to one entomologist,* the queen bee develops to adulthood more rapidly than the worker. She emerges as a full-fledged queen after eight days of pupal change and sixteen days from the time when she was a tiny blue comma-shaped egg. The workers, on the other hand, require twenty-one days to complete the cycle from egg to adult, and the drones** procrastinate until the twenty-fourth day to get on their brand-new legs and start ambling† around for food.

*Organization.* Pattern 1 presents the main idea first. In the example above, the topic sentence is first:

According to one entomologist, the queen bee develops to adulthood more rapidly than the worker.

It is followed by two specific sentences that add detail:

She emerges as a full-fledged queen after eight days of pupal change and sixteen days from the time when she was a tiny blue comma-shaped egg. The workers, on the other hand, require twenty-one days to complete the cycle from egg to adult, and the drones procrastinate until the twenty-fourth day to get on their brand-new legs and start ambling around for food.

*Author's Purpose.* In this paragraph, the main idea appears in a topic sentence at the beginning. Clarity is emphasized by this pattern because the following sentences provide details that reinforce and explain the general statement.

**Pattern 2**

You have natural curiosity. This curiosity needs to be fed. You can feed your curiosity by obtaining new information on a topic which interests you. But you must take the first step. Your natural curiosity will continue to draw you into exciting new areas of investigation as long as you respond to its call.

*Scientist who studies insects.
**Male honeybee.
†Walking.

*Organization.* Pattern 2 gives you details that build up to the conclusion/topic sentence. It begins with specific sentences:

> You have natural curiosity. This curiosity needs to be fed. You can feed your curiosity by obtaining new information on a topic which interests you. But you must take the first step.

Then comes the general sentence:

> Your natural curiosity will continue to draw you into exciting new areas of investigation as long as you respond to its call.

*Author's Purpose.* Here, the first sentence draws you into the paragraph by stating a specific detail you will want to know more about. This detail leads to others and finally to the topic sentence, which explains the main idea. This pattern increases the reader's interest by creating a tension that is resolved at the end of the paragraph.

**Pattern 3**

> Sports offer many opportunities for excitement. When you are preparing to serve at match point and deliver an ace which whistles by your opponent, you feel the joy in your bones. When the game is tied in the closing seconds, and you go up for your jump shot with a defender right in your face, and see the ball swish through the net, you think you will never touch the floor again. When you are in goal and the attacking wing swoops down on you and kicks the ball in a hard line toward the far corner, and you must manage to deflect it with your straining hand, you feel that life will never again be so good to you. These are the moments of bliss offered by sports, and they cannot be matched easily in other life situations.

*Organization.* Pattern 3 has the topic sentence at the beginning and at the end of the paragraph. Here is the first:

> Sports offer many opportunities for excitement.

It is followed by specific sentences:

> When you are preparing to serve at match point and deliver an ace which whistles by your opponent, you feel the joy in your bones. When the game is tied in the closing seconds, and you go up for your jump shot with a defender right in your face, and see the ball swish through the net, you think you will never touch the floor again. When you are in goal and the attacking wing swoops down on you and kicks the ball in a hard line toward the far corner, and you just manage to

Paragraph Patterns

deflect it with your straining hand, you feel that life will never again be so good to you.

Now the paragraph concludes with the general statement:

These are the moments of bliss offered by sports, and they cannot be matched easily in other life situations.

*Author's Purpose.* In this paragraph, the main idea is expressed in topic sentences at the beginning and at the end of the paragraph. The details are expressed in three sentences that describe the joys of sports in tennis, basketball, and soccer. This pattern emphasizes clarity by stating and restating the main idea.

**Pattern 4**

The early Americans led hard lives that left little time for the pleasures of the table; at least that is the modern view. Certainly, Europeans who journeyed to America reinforced the idea that the American diet was both limited and tasteless. Journals, letters, and notes from Americans, however, belie this depressing picture of American cooking (or "cookery," as it was then called); on the contrary, Americans seem to have enjoyed a variety of delicious foods. Game, for example, was one of the staples of the American diet since wild turkeys, passenger pigeons, and canvasbacked ducks were all plentiful. Food from the sea was also available, and oysters, terrapin, and turtles are mentioned in letters describing American fare. Most families raised vegetables, and broccoli, asparagus, and cauliflower were enjoyed in season.

*Organization.* In pattern 4, the topic sentence appears in the middle, after some introductory specific sentences:

The early Americans led hard lives that left little time for the pleasures of the table; at least that is the modern view. Certainly, Europeans who journeyed to America reinforced the idea that the American diet was both limited and tasteless.

Here is the general sentence:

Journals, letters, and notes from Americans, however, belie this depressing picture of American cooking (or "cookery," as it was then called); on the contrary, Americans seem to have enjoyed a variety of delicious foods.

It is reinforced by additional specific sentences:

> Game, for example, was one of the staples of the American diet since wild turkeys, passenger pigeons, and canvasbacked ducks were all plentiful. Food from the sea was also available, and oysters, terrapin, and turtles are mentioned in letters describing American fare. Most families raised vegetables, and broccoli, asparagus, and cauliflower were enjoyed in season.

*Author's Purpose.* In this example, the main idea is set in the middle of the paragraph so that the details in the second half can disprove the case made by the details in the first. This topic sentence in the middle of the paragraph underscores the change in direction by using the phrase "on the contrary," which leads to the information that early Americans enjoyed the pleasures of good cooking. This pattern communicates the meaning of the paragraph by balancing contrasting details on either side of the topic sentence.

## Analyzing Paragraphs

Read the following paragraphs. See if you can locate the topic sentence and then identify the paragraph pattern. Draw the correct diagram in the space provided.

> Nature is awesome. It has created the vast fjords of Norway, the spectacular glaciers of the Antarctic, the startling volcanic "fairy chimneys" of central Anatolia south of Ankara, Turkey, the dank, beautiful rain forests of the Philippines. I've stood hypnotized by the beauty of them all.

Topic sentence _____

_____

Diagram:

Explanation: In this paragraph, the main idea is stated in the first sentence. The second sentence provides specific examples of extraordinary geographical features. In the last sentence, the author introduces a personal note to support the main idea.

Interior decorators adore them, landscape designers recommend them, nursery people feature them and gardeners and home owners love and grow them. They're the ancient family of ferns, beautiful and easy to grow. Perhaps you should get involved in a fern-growing project.

Topic sentence _____

Diagram:




Explanation: In this example, the main idea is expressed in the topic sentence in the middle of the paragraph, "They're the ancient family of ferns...." Details in the first sentence heighten the reader's interest in learning what various people "adore," "recommend," and "love." The topic sentence answers the interest created by these details. The last sentence offers the reader a suggestion and changes the direction of the paragraph.

Read the following paragraph. Once you locate the topic sentence and draw the correct diagram to represent the pattern, see if you can explain how the pattern works to fulfill the author's purpose in emphasizing clarity, tension, and/or balance.

Since women bear children, it seems to be taken for granted that they should care for them too. For example, it is said that a man is too awkward to hold a baby. He hasn't the touch. This is pure nonsense. A baby is so soft that anybody with a firm grip can hold one. All you have to remember is to keep the right side up. But women will tell you it's an art. Another fiction is that no man can properly dress a child. Once again, nonsense. I knew a man who was an expert at it, better than any woman. He was a skilled automobile mechanic, much in demand at races, where he had to whisk tires on and off. He used the same technique in the home. Carrying a mouthful of safety pins, he would toss the youngster to the floor. Even before her head had bumped, he was hard at work. Arms flying, he would have his task completed before the child could begin to cry. Often the youngster was too astonished to make a sound, and my friend would turn her over to her mother with a triumphant smile.

Topic sentence _____

Diagram:

Author's purpose _____

Explanation: In this paragraph, the topic sentence is at the beginning. It suggests that what is taken for granted may not be true. The information that follows the topic sentence clearly makes this point. These detail sentences also fall into two groups which balance against each other. The first group states the "fictions" about taking care of babies. The second group disproves these "fictions" by showing how a particular man changes a baby as easily as he changes a tire on a car.

Try another:

> He went up to her silently and kissed her. It was the first kiss he had ever given her without being asked. And the poor lady, so small in her black satin, shrivelled up and sallow,* with her funny corkscrew** curls, took the little boy in her lap and put her arms around him and wept as though her heart would break. But her tears were partly tears of happiness, for she felt that the strangeness between them was gone. She loved him now with a new love because he had made her suffer.

Topic sentence _____

Diagram:

Author's purpose _____

*Pale.
**Tight, spiral-like.

Paragraph Patterns 161

Explanation: The creation of tension is most important in this paragraph. The reader is drawn into the situation and wants to know the significance of "the first kiss." This necessary information is delayed until the end of the paragraph as the action itself is described. Finally, in the last sentence, which is the topic sentence, the reader understands that the relationship between the child and the "poor lady" has been clarified.

READING EXERCISE

Read each of the following paragraphs. Indicate in the spaces provided the topic sentence, the correct diagram that represents the pattern of the paragraph, and the author's emphasis on clarity, tension, or balance.

1. There was not a sound in the huge stadium while Cosgrove carefully measured his paces behind the place where the ball would be held. The snap came back in a perfect and efficient spiral into the waiting hands of Jablonski, the backup quarterback who was the holder on placekicks. Jablonski set the ball down in one, smooth motion as Cosgrove began his approach. Cosgrove swung his foot into the ball and drove it towards the goalposts. The silence thickened between the sound of the kicker's foot thudding against the ball and the explosion of cheers as the ball split the uprights for the touchdown which gave the Titans their first championship.

Topic sentence _____

Diagram:


Author's purpose _____


2. Si Ling-Shi, a lovely Chinese empress, sat drinking tea in her garden one day. As she gazed up into the mulberry tree above her, she saw a fat white worm moving its head back and forth. From the worm's mouth came a shiny golden strand. Si Ling-Shi watched as the worm wrapped the strand round and round itself to make a cocoon. The cocoon was so beautiful she began to wonder how she would look in a gown made of the threads of many such cocoons. When she

returned to the palace, she persuaded her husband to give her a whole grove of mulberry trees, where she could grow thousands of the worms that spun the golden strands. In the years that followed, Si Ling-Shi spent many hours working in her garden, until she had enough thread to weave a gown. The Chinese named the delicate cloth *si* for their empress. *Si* has been the Chinese word for silk down to the present day.

Topic sentence _____

_____

Diagram:

Author's purpose _____

_____

3. Motion pictures and television have created subtle make-up problems that seem more closely related to the physics and chemistry of light, lenses, and film emulsions than to the cosmetic art. As the art has developed, experts have appeared, but none quite so odd as the Hollywood "fly man." Because grease paint is vitamin-rich and contains sugar, movie studio flies are attracted. So, while actors and actresses await their camera call, the "fly man" brushes the insects from their faces, which the performers themselves dare not touch.

Topic sentence _____

_____

Diagram:

Author's purpose _____

_____

4. We think of the United States as a rich and plentiful nation. It is; but it isn't self-sufficient. Our reliance on foreign sources is apparent

every day in the year. Take sugar. Cane sugar ranks first in value among imported foodstuffs. Or take coffee. Coffee drinking couldn't be an American habit if we cut off our imports from Brazil. You wouldn't have your newspaper without printing ink, and we get much of that from Canada. The chief source of raw silk is Japan. A wrist watch may or may not be a Swiss watch, but the inner movements are probably imported. Ninety per cent of them are.

Topic sentence _____

Diagram:


Author's purpose _____


5. His average annual income is one-half the amount which has been determined to be the general poverty level for the poor in the United States. He can expect to live to age 42. His segregation from the rest of society makes the Negro's degree of acceptance look good. The level of unemployment among his people is seven or eight times that of his nation's average unemployment. He suffers more from poor health, malnutrition and ignorance than does any other ethnic group in his country. Who is he? Any American school child should know that the American Indian and only the American Indian answers to that description. Conquered, dispossessed, exploited, abandoned, the American Indian confronts the nation as its primary challenge.

Topic sentence _____

Diagram:


Author's purpose _____

6. Two summers ago in England, after being conceived in a dish, Louise Brown was born. For many, her birth was a reason for joy. Women like Mrs. Brown, who had not been able to have babies, lined up for the procedure and doctors all over the world moved to duplicate the achievement. For others, those who believe conception, like birth control, belongs in God's hands, the birth represented a dark beginning. But for most, joyous or angry, the main feeling was one of amazement that it could be done, that a child could be conceived outside the body. What the birth of Baby Louise meant was that a man and woman need not be together, they need only donate sperm and egg. With the amazement came the sense that something fundamental was going on, had been going on quietly for some years. With the birth of Baby Louise, it became clear what had happened: As the man who delivered her, Dr. Patrick C. Steptoe, put it, "The whole field of human reproduction has been transformed."

Topic sentence _____

Diagram:

Author's purpose _____

7. One of the commonest beliefs about reptiles concerns the existence of a "hoop snake." This reptile is supposed to grasp its tail in its mouth and roll along at terrific speed. Yet science declares no such creature exists. There is also a belief among cowboys and hunters that they can protect their camps by stretching horsehair ropes around them, that the prickly hairs will repel any snakes—particularly rattlers. Actually, rattlers crawl over ropes as if they didn't exist. Like most nature "fables" there is a shred of truth here, but it has been stretched out of all proportion. It is probable that snakes detect the human odor and, since they fear humans, turn and crawl away. There are many other "whoppers" just as fantastic, but these examples show why the widespread belief in them is unjustified.

Topic sentence _____

Diagram:




Author's purpose _____


8. Franklin D. Roosevelt collected stamps, welcomed Boy Scouts, rode in an open car down Pennsylvania Avenue on State occasions and traveled to far-distant lands for weighty confabulations* with heads of state. In these ways he was not unique. In one way only he differed from his contemporaries and from his predecessors. He had high regard for the popular consensus. When Congress fought him on the so-called "packing of the Supreme Court," he didn't call in the Democratic whips for a tongue-lashing, he went on the radio. And when critics inside and outside Congress accused his New Deal of being a concoction of "alphabet soup" he didn't upbraid Congress or send them messages; he scheduled another fireside chat.

Topic sentence _____


Diagram:




Author's purpose _____


## ARRANGING DETAILS IN YOUR PARAGRAPHS

Written communication builds from words to sentences and then to paragraphs. As you have seen, paragraphs are information packages that can take a variety of different shapes, depending upon the writer's pur-

*Meetings, conferences.

pose. Each paragraph makes or implies a general statement, and then provides details to make the general point clearer, more interesting, and more emphatic.

When you prepare your own paragraphs, your first job is to figure out what you want to say. In a classroom situation you will often be assigned a topic, or you might be asked to write a certain number of words in a broadly defined area, such as a response to something you have read. In life situations you will often have to write reports or letters, and these circumstances will provide you with your subject matter. No matter what the situation is, however, the procedure is the same. You first determine what you want to say, and then how you want to say it. In terms of paragraph arrangement, this second step involves deciding on the placement of specific details in relationship to your general idea.

**Determining What You Want to Say**

You cannot begin to write until you know what you want to say. You might begin by asking yourself, "What do I know about the topic?" Suppose you have been asked to write about the energy problem. To see what you know about the topic, you can jot down the items that come to mind:

OPEC
high gas prices
nuclear power plants
solar energy
gas-guzzling cars
coal heat
nuclear waste
air pollution

This list can help you find a direction for your writing assignment, but it is only a start. Your next step is to decide which of these items you know the most about and can therefore write about most comfortably. You have probably heard about all these subjects, but some of them may be no more than words you have seen in headlines or heard on the news. Look at the list and cross out any item you really do not know that much about:

~~OPEC~~
high gas prices
nuclear power plants
~~solar energy~~
gas-guzzling cars
coal

nuclear waste
~~air pollution~~

Having eliminated the approaches to the subject you know least about, you are still left with a number of possibilities.

You can next ask yourself, "Which of these do I know *most* about?" If you happen to own a 1973 Buick Electra with an oversized V8 engine and enough extra power to propel two or three small trucks, and which gets about eight miles to the gallon, you could choose "gas-guzzling car." If, on the other hand, you live in a building heated by a coal furnace, you might know something about soot, if not air pollution, and therefore you could choose "coal." Or if you are old enough to remember when gas cost about 30 cents a gallon, or if you have heard older members of your family telling stories about how they used to "fill up" for two or three dollars, you might choose to focus on "high gas prices."

Suppose you decide on "high gas prices." You have two more questions to ask yourself:

1. What can I figure out about the topic?
2. What do I feel about the topic?

An answer to the first question could be that since gas now costs so much, the development of mass transportation has become much more important. In answer to the second question, you might decide you feel very strongly that you cannot afford to support your car, and that you would like to find some relief from the drain on your finances. Putting these two together, you could finally decide that the way you want to write about the energy problem is to write about the need for gas-efficient engines.

## Arrangement of Details

The process of determining what you know about a topic and how you would like to write about it prepares you to formulate a topic sentence.

1. Who or what do you want the subject of the paragraph to be? *High gas prices.*
2. What aspect of the subject do you want to discuss? *The need for gas-efficient engines.*
3. What do you want the reader to understand and/or remember about the aspect of the subject you are discussing? *High gas prices make the development of gas-efficient engines more necessary.*

The answer to the third question becomes the topic sentence for your paragraph.

The topic sentence is your general statement, which you will support with more specific information. Before you can decide which of the four paragraph patterns discussed earlier you might want to use, you have to do a little more preparation. Your concern now is what details you are going to use, and then how you will arrange them.

The details of a paragraph relate to the general statement the paragraph makes. They make that general statement clearer, more interesting, and more emphatic. Think of details that relate to your topic sentence, and divide them into facts and reasons.

| Facts | Reasons |
|---|---|
| Gas used to cost 30 cents a gallon. | We cannot afford gas guzzlers anymore. |
| It now costs well over a dollar. | |
| Gas prices have increased very fast over the past couple of years. | The price of gas will continue to increase. |
| Many cars get poor gas mileage. | High gas prices make everything else cost more (inflation). |
| The cost of running a car has increased dramatically. | Inflation is a major problem. |

From these lists, you can select details that support your topic sentence. You might choose to work only with the facts, only with the reasons, or with a combination of both. As you consider these details, you can also think about how they can best be arranged.

For example, if your purpose is to be absolutely clear, you might begin your paragraph with a topic sentence and then provide the specific details that emphasize your point:

*High gas prices make the development of gas-efficient engines more necessary.* Not so long ago, you could fill up your tank for less than five dollars. Now when you pull up to the pump, you have to be prepared to spend fifteen or twenty dollars, and there seems to be no end in sight to these rising costs. It is no longer easy to enjoy the power of that big engine as it zooms you out of the gas station when you realize that before long you will have to empty your wallet again.

Another approach to the arrangement of details can be to ensure your reader's interest by delaying the topic sentence to the end of the paragraph:

The days of the gas guzzlers must end. As the price of gas continues to rise, as it most certainly will, the average citizen finds it increasingly difficult to afford basic transportation. Moreover, the trucks which transport our goods run on diesel fuel. So do the locomotives which pull our trains, and the jet engines of our airplanes, not to mention the mighty engines of the oil tankers themselves as well as other ships. Since transportation is a base cost in all areas of the economy, rising fuel costs feed inflation. *These high gas prices make the development of a gas-efficient (and diesel-efficient) engine most necessary.*

Paragraph Patterns

The following pattern 3 paragraph combines tension and clarity by stating and restating the topic sentence at the beginning and the end. The specific details in the middle further expand the general idea of the topic sentence:

*High gas prices make the development of a gas-efficient engine more necessary.* Because the price of gasoline and related fuels has risen sharply over the past few years, there is every reason to believe that it will continue to increase. American car manufacturers have begun to downsize their engines in response to the demand for fuel economy. But these efforts have been proceeding too slowly to stop the accelerating inflation caused by the skyrocketing rise in the cost of gasoline. *It is time now for the automobile manufacturers to redouble and triple their efforts to produce engines that consume not at the rate of thirty or forty miles to the gallon, but rather at eighty or a hundred.*

In the example of this pattern earlier in the chapter, the restated topic sentence was only slightly different from the sentence that introduced the paragraph. In this example, the restated topic sentence is reworded more significantly. Although it still makes the same point, it makes it more dramatically.

Pattern 4, which has the topic sentence in the middle of the paragraph, can easily be used in an arrangement of contrasting details:

My great-grandfather tells the story of filling up his Model-T for literally pennies. My grandfather and father remember the good old days of gas for nickels and dimes. *It occurs to me that today's high prices will leave a very different legacy for me to pass on to my children and grandchildren; unless a gas-efficient engine is developed, the family car may become obsolete.* I may then tell my carless children what it was like to be able to afford to take a ride on a Sunday afternoon just for the feeling of freedom and adventure that experience could provide. Maybe I will tell my grandchildren that I didn't have to live within walking distance of the supermarket. And perhaps I will show my great-grandchildren pictures of a family sedan as they prepare to hike across town to a neighborhood movie.

Here the realistic details of the first half of the paragraph are contrasted with the exaggerated possibilities of the second half to emphasize the point made by the topic sentence in the middle.

WRITING EXERCISE

I. Choose one of the following topics, and then determine what you know about that topic.

Zoos for animals, not people.
Bad breath need not be fatal.
Trees, not paper.
Legs for locomotion.
Astrology for everyone.

A. What you know about the topic you have chosen:

_____
_____
_____
_____

B. Now apply the three questions to develop a topic sentence:

_____
_____
_____
_____

II. Imagine you are preparing a paragraph on fast food restaurants. Use the three questions to determine your main idea. Since you want to emphasize clarity in this paragraph, write it in pattern 1:

Topic
Sentence

Paragraph Patterns    171

III. Suppose you want to invite a friend to a party and want to build a feeling of excitement. Write a pattern 2 paragraph:

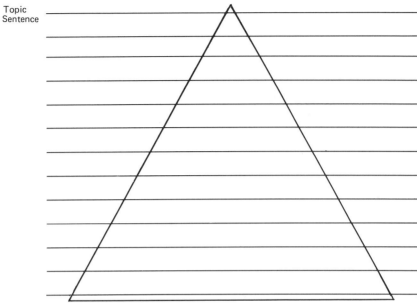

IV. Suppose you want to impress somebody with an important point, perhaps asking your boss for a raise. Write a pattern 3 paragraph:

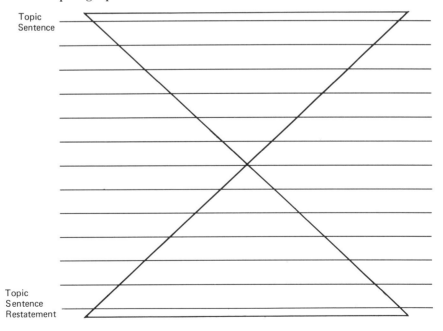

V. Imagine you have been wrongly accused of doing something. In a pattern 4 paragraph present the contrasting details that make your case:

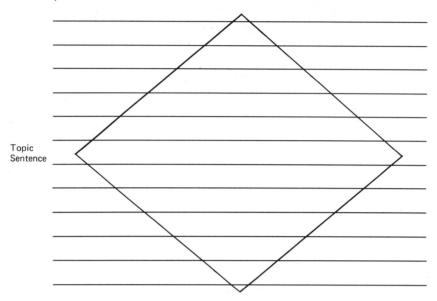

# 10

# Paragraph Development

PREVIEW

Paragraphs shape information into units that can be understood. Each paragraph generally presents one main idea, often stated in a topic sentence. The rest of the paragraph expands and refines that idea so the whole paragraph communicates successfully and efficiently. Expanding and refining the main idea requires development of that idea—that is, the addition of specific information to support the point made by the topic sentence. This additional information can be presented in a variety of different ways: by examples; by comparison and contrast; by process; by analogy; by definitions; by classification; and by showing cause and effect.

The particular arrangement depends upon the writer's style and also upon the kind of information being presented. Certain types of subject matter lend themselves to a particular kind of development and arrangement. Instructions on how to fix something, for example, fall naturally into a process arrangement; historical material often seems best developed in a cause and effect arrangement, and so on. Many paragraphs, of course, combine one or more of these arrangements; one does not have to be used alone. But nearly all paragraphs can be shown to have a predominant kind of development, and these categories are useful for both reader and writer because they focus on one more tool to help express ideas clearly.

**Key Terms**

    **Development.**   Specific information that explains the general statement expressed in the topic sentence.

**Examples.** The most common method of development; providing illustrations of the idea expressed in the topic sentence.
**Comparison and contrast.** Method of development that clarifies the idea expressed in the topic sentence by showing similarities and differences.
**Process.** Method of development that shows how a series of events or steps leads to a result.
**Analogy.** Method of development in which an unfamiliar idea is explained in terms of a familiar one.
**Definition.** Method of development in which the characteristic features of something are identified.
**Classification.** Method of development in which an idea is broken into smaller categories according to a particular feature.
**Cause and effect.** Method of development in which one event is shown to determine another.

The topic sentence and the related specific statements that serve to extend, clarify, explain, describe, exemplify, and prove or disprove, work together in an arrangement of detail to communicate the main idea of the paragraph. Different main ideas lend themselves to different kinds of paragraph development. A writer chooses the arrangement that will best express his or her message. To do this, he or she decides *how* the message will be communicated best. Depending upon the content of the paragraph and the audience to which it is directed, the writer may choose examples, comparison and contrast, process, analogy, definition, classification, and cause and effect.

## METHODS OF DEVELOPMENT

### Examples

Suppose, for example, a writer wants to discuss the idea that people spend more on the things they use up—that is, on things they consume—than in the past, and therefore have less money to save and invest. He or she might use details, examples, and/or illustrations to support that idea. These supporting sentences present the reader with "evidence." Here is such a paragraph.

Another consequence of the excessive stresses on consumption has been a noticeable decline in savings and investment. During the 30 years, 1948 through 1977, savings averaged 6.2 percent of disposable personal income. However, over the last two years, the fraction averaged 4.7 percent, and it decreased further to about 3 percent in the first half of this year.

This paragraph begins with a topic sentence which expresses the main idea that people are spending more money on consumption than on investment and savings. The sentences that follow show how this idea is true by providing statistics to prove the accuracy of the point.

In a different paragraph that uses the same method of development, the author explains the law of supply and demand:

> What is a candy bar worth? Usually you pay a certain price for it, but that price could change. Suppose twenty people wanted to buy the same candy bar? This might change the price. Demand could make the price higher. However, if only a few people wanted to buy thousands of surplus candy bars, the price could be very low. The effect on price is called the law of supply and demand.

Here the topic sentence, which is at the end of the paragraph, is supported by details in the sentence that precede it. These sentences explain the law of supply and demand by illustrating how the price of a candy bar changes, depending on how many candy bars are available and how many people want to purchase them.

Details, examples, and/or illustrations are also employed in other kinds of paragraphs. However, when they are the primary source of evidence to support the main idea, as expressed in the topic sentence, we can say that the writer has used the *example* method of development.

## Comparison and Contrast

A second method of development is *comparison and contrast*. A paragraph based on this method shows the reader the similarities (comparisons) and the differences (contrasts) among the subjects discussed in the paragraph. Comparison and contrast enable the reader to understand the subjects both individually and in relation to one another.

Comparison and contrast can be arranged in different ways. An author may choose to present all the similarities and then all the differences, or to demonstrate how the subjects are alike and how they are different throughout the paragraph.

In the following paragraph, the author shows how jealousy and envy are alike, and how they are different:

> Jealousy and envy are both unpleasant, but envy is like getting stung by a mosquito or, at worst, a bee. It hurts, but it's not overwhelming. Jealousy can be like having a rusty jagged knife stuck in your gut and—depending on the circumstances—slowly twisted. You rarely hear of people killing because of envy.

In another paragraph the author chooses to discuss only the differences between dry ice and ordinary ice.

Dry ice was first manufactured in 1925. It has since fulfilled the fondest hopes of its inventor. It can be used for making artificial fog in the movies (when steam is passed over dry ice, a very dense vapor rises). It is more practical than ordinary ice because it takes up less space and is 142 degrees colder. Since it evaporates instead of melting, it is cleaner to use. For these reasons it is extremely popular, and many people prefer it to ordinary ice.

In a third paragraph, the author discusses only the similarities between monkeys and human beings.

Are monkeys like people? Well, as a matter of fact, they are! When certain kinds of monkeys are domesticated, they act just like human beings. They smoke cigars, drink beer, and look almost human when dressed in children's clothing. If you invite them to dinner, they can sit quite comfortably in real chairs and use a knife and fork exactly as you do.

Comparison and contrast, as a method of development, is an effective way for an author to communicate the specifics of a paragraph to the reader because it focuses clearly on important characteristics of the subjects being compared and/or contrasted.

**Process**

A third method of development, called *process*, is used when a writer wishes to tell the reader how something is done. The description of that process can be as simple as the steps in a recipe or as complicated as constructing a car engine. In other words, the writer wants the reader to understand that following the step-by-step approach expressed in the specific sentences of the paragraph will enable the reader to grasp the message. The writer has decided that this method of development best expresses the details suggested by the topic sentence. Process may be used in a variety of ways with a variety of subjects:

Principles of physical law are responsible for helping scientists create the abundant energy needed to launch a vehicle into space. Fuels are converted into gases and these chemical reactions create extremely high temperatures in the rocket's engine. Then the heat places pressure on the engine walls. As the gases are released, and if the total pressure within the space vehicle is enough to overcome its inactivity, they force the rocket skyward. Finally, rocket lift-off is achieved, and Newton's third law of action and reaction is demonstrated.

Here the writer uses specific sentences to indicate how a series of actions results in lifting a rocket into space.

> If an insect were to irritate a hair of the Venus' flytrap just once, no change would take place. But if within sixty seconds another shock were applied, a rapid snapping would occur. For here we have a remarkable example of a plant requiring more than one shock to cause the tightening of the leaves. If a fair-sized insect has been closed in upon, the outline of the body can be traced from without.

The author of this paragraph describes the working of the Venus' flytrap as a series of actions.

> Addition done with the ten-key machine requires that you enter each number that has to be added. Press the figure keys to enter each number's digit. Digits should be taken from left to right, just as you would write them. After you press the key for the final digit of a number, press the motor bar. This will insure that the whole number will be printed. Continue in this way until you complete the numbers. After entering the last number, press the total key, and then the motor bar. The sum will appear on the printed tape.

In this paragraph the author very effectively uses the step-by-step method to explain addition with a ten-key listing machine.

## Analogy

*Analogy,* a fourth method of development, helps a writer clarify an idea for the reader. Usually, the author has chosen a complicated, unfamiliar subject and wishes to simplify the explanation of it. To do so, he or she will show how the complicated subject is similar to a simpler subject with which the reader is probably familiar. In other words, as a method of development, analogy employs an idea, person, or event that the writer thinks you know about in order to explain an unfamiliar idea, event, or person. Consider the following paragraphs:

> Imagine you are visiting your first English pub and your host challenges you to a game of darts. Never having played, you graciously decline and then—in the finest American spirit—run out, buy a set and begin practicing in your hotel. After the first hundred tosses you begin getting a feel for the game; by the next day, you're ready to go out and challenge the Queen's finest.

You have learned your dart game well. But let us pretend you were forced to practice your throws blindfolded, with plugs in your ears. Could you ever perfect your toss under these conditions? No. Improvement would be impossible because you lacked the vital component of learning: feedback concerning your performance. Deprived of visual feedback—unable to gain knowledge of results concerning your throwing accuracy—your predicament would be hopeless.

Here two paragraphs familiarize the reader with the concept of feedback. Playing darts blindfolded is compared to an absence of "feedback," the idea the author wants to explain to the reader. Learning to throw darts when you can see where your darts land is similar to gaining "knowledge of results" in the learning process.

Going to college is like getting married. It requires lots of preparation. When the long-awaited day arrives you discover that the real work has just begun. You must sacrifice. No longer can you do what you like when you like. Instead you must conform to another's wishes, if you hope to succeed. And you must work at it. College, like marriage, is a responsibility that forces you to schedule duties, activities, meetings, trips, meals, and even sleep, if you hope to get them all in! And you must have money. Without it, neither is possible.

Writing for a group of adults about to go to college, the author of this paragraph explains college life in terms of married life. Her goal is to make her reader understand what to expect of college by reminding the reader of what marriage requires, a subject many members of her audience are familiar with.

In the following paragraph, the author compares the state of the economy to a sinking ship.

As our economic ship of state slowly sinks into the briny deep, the bridge is manned by a captain, President Carter, who has led it into disaster. Down in the engine room a would-be captain, Ronald Reagan, is planning to restart the ship's hot engine by throwing economic gasoline on it. Back on the deck another would-be captain, John B. Anderson, is trying to still the economic gales with old sea tales of 50-cent gasoline taxes.

**Definition**

When a writer develops a paragraph by using *definition,* he or she has decided that the reader needs to review carefully the meaning of a word, term, or concept. The writer may provide, in addition to the simple meaning, a restated definition, characteristics, or qualities of the thing being defined, and perhaps examples to help show how the definition may be applied. Consider the following paragraphs:

> A promise a seller makes to a buyer is called a warranty. Such a promise may be a written guarantee that a television will work without repair for a year. If it does not work, the seller repairs the set or provides a new one. On the other hand, a warranty may be unwritten. It may suggest that a bottle of soda is suitable to drink. If the soda contains pieces of glass, it is not suitable to drink. Even if the warranty is unwritten, the seller must replace the soda or give back the buyer's money.

In this paragraph the author defines the word "warranty" in the topic sentence. The specific sentences describe characteristics of a warranty and provide examples that reinforce those characteristics.

> A set of points all a given distance from a given point on a plane is a circle. Parts of a circle include its diameter, radius and center. The diameter is the longest chord of the circle containing the center. The radius is a segment which joins the center with any point of the circle. It is half the length of the diameter. The center is a given point within the circle that is equidistant from the set of points on the plane that creates the circle.

Like the previous author, the author of this paragraph states the definition in the topic sentence. The specific sentences following the topic sentence describe the various parts (characteristics) of the circle.

Definition is perhaps the easiest method of development to recognize. Usually the definition is given in the topic sentence and usually a form of the verb "to be" is used to make this sentence an *equation* sentence (see Chapter 6). Frequently, you will find these paragraphs in informative materials like textbooks and newspapers.

## Classification

*Classification* is a method of development that allows a writer to use categories (groups, types, kinds) as a means of arranging and expressing the specific information of the paragraph. Suppose, for example, that a writer wanted to discuss play activities. He or she might decide to categorize those activities as "indoor" and "outdoor":

> There are two types of play activities: (1) indoor and (2) outdoor. Indoor activities involving play are very often restricted to games and

hobbies. These indoor activities are usually limited by space and by how careful you must be when playing indoors. Outdoor activities are far more varied. Swimming, skiing, running, jumping rope, wrestling, playing ball and skating are just a few of the many outdoor activities involving play.

In the following paragraph the author categorizes memory as short term and long term. Each type is illustrated with a basic feature and example:

>Studies indicate that human beings use two kinds of memory: short term and long term. When we use short-term memory, we retain information for a very brief period of time. For example, we use short-term memory when we look up a phone number and remember it only long enough to dial. When we use long-term memory, we retain information for a considerable length of time. A young child, for example, may memorize a poem and remember it for the next twenty years.

Classification enables the careful reader to associate the specifics of what he or she reads with a type, group, class, or category that separates or distinguishes various ideas, events, or things.

**Cause and Effect**

When something happens, there is usually a reason for it and a result, an outcome or a consequence. Whenever an author wishes to make the reader aware of the *cause* (reason) and the *effect* (result) or describe the relationship of an event as cause and effect, he or she uses the cause and effect method of development. History, for example, is almost always written in this style because history attempts to show relationships between one occurrence and another in terms of their cause(s) and effect(s). Read the following paragraph:

>Between 1890 and 1900, millions of people from the southern and eastern parts of Europe left their own countries in search of a new one, one that would give them peace and security. With this dream in mind, they immigrated to America, but unfortunately, the land they entered was for many a far cry from what they had imagined. The new immigrants had hoped to find a comfortable place to live where they could settle and live out the rest of their lives. But the cities to which they came were not prepared to house so many new arrivals, and many immigrant families ended up living in ugly tenements that were poorly supplied with light, heat, and water. They had dreamed of finding work, work that would make them independent and, if possible, rich. They found instead that jobs were scarce. Fre-

quently they were forced to take jobs for which they were not suited, jobs that left them exhausted and depressed. Many immigrants found that instead of the warm welcome they had expected, they were treated as outsiders with funny customs and an even funnier way of speaking.

In this paragraph the author tells us why millions of people left Southern and Eastern Europe for America (reason or *cause*), and that many were disappointed (result or *effect*) with what they found. But history is not the only subject that can be discussed in terms of cause and effect:

In the early 1920's, one by one, the King Model Houses began to be sold to blacks who were for the most part, professional people and therefore comparatively wealthy—doctors, lawyers, and educators. And the new black residents of these houses decided, at the outset, that their two streets would not be sucked into the rapidly growing slum beyond. The trees were cared for, the hedges clipped, the stone vases and window boxes were kept filled with flowering plants. Entrance railings and balustrades were painted; brass doorknobs and knockers were polished. Gardens and courtyards were maintained. Each neighbor tried so hard to compete with the others for the best-clipped shrubbery, the best polished brasswork, the best-washed steps, and the prettiest garden that the two consecutive blocks were humorously given the name "Strivers' Row."

In this paragraph the author writes that the wealthy black professionals decided to try to prevent their streets from becoming part of the growing slum (cause). By keeping their streets attractive and well cared for, these blocks became known as "Strivers' Row" (effect).


**Combined Methods**

Each of the methods of development has been presented separately. But often an author will *combine* methods. Details, examples, and illustrations frequently appear in paragraphs developed in all the other ways described. Process paragraphs can combine cause and effect, just as paragraphs that classify can also define. Careful attention to the major method of development, however, will tell the reader how the paragraph is organized.

As you grow in ability to recognize the major method of development, you may be able to recognize several methods in the same paragraph:

Automobile makers give free cars to TV series if their brand is made to look good. The "good guys" on the show will use the free cars provided. The "bad guys" will use a different brand. Mannix always used to drive a Chevrolet Camaro. Mod Squad members drove a Chrysler. Starsky and Hutch drive a Ford Torino. A Firebird is used on "The Rockford Files." Notice how "good" shots or scenes using the free car show up in programs of this type. A Chrysler official says that the cars they "donate" to the program must be used right. If they aren't, they point it out to the TV show's producer. The number of cars given is reduced if their product isn't given enough show time.

READING EXERCISE

For each of the following paragraphs, indicate in the spaces provided (1) the method(s) of development and (2) an explanation for each answer you chose. Only two of the paragraphs have more than one major method of development.

1. Mead is an alcoholic beverage that is often mentioned in history books. Surprisingly, it is not hard to make. Mix two quarts of water, two cups of honey, two lemons cut in slices, and one-half tablespoon of nutmeg. Boil the mixture until no scum comes to the top, removing any scum as it rises. Add a pinch of salt and the juice of one lemon. Strain and cool. Let ferment and drink.

Method(s) of development _____

Explanation _____

2. Possessed by the desire to modernize his country and his subjects, Peter the Great, King of Russia, actually tried to whip his subjects into living in the style of the modern world. The nobles of his court were told to clip their beards and shorten their robes while their wives were summoned to court. The ladies, who had previously been told to stay at home, were terrified and tended to huddle in a corner; still, they were forbidden to go home. To import new ideas from the West, Peter demanded that young Russians go abroad to study, and he invited Europeans to come and visit Russia. The Europeans he invited could have refused if they chose, but his subjects had no such freedom of choice. If they refused to become modernized, they were beaten and in some cases executed.

Method(s) of development _____

Explanation _____

_____

3. An ideal teacher, then, is one who reflects a real interest in his students and their education by keeping himself knowledgeable and up-to-date on the subject, by making his lectures as interesting and lively as possible. He must also provide a fair means of evaluating the progress that the student has made in the subject. If a teacher is truly motivated to help the student, the results should be obvious.

Method(s) of development _____

_____

Explanation _____

_____

4. The emotion of fear sets off many changes in your body. When you become frightened, you breathe more deeply, giving your muscles more oxygen and greater energy. Your heart beats more powerfully so that your blood circulates faster, carrying oxygen to all parts of your body. Your stomach and intestines no longer contract and all digestive action stops. No saliva flows in your mouth and your throat becomes dry. Your face becomes pale because the tiny blood vessels shrink under the skin so that less blood would flow if you were cut. The blood can clot faster so that there would be less bleeding from a wound. The pupils of your eyes enlarge, admitting more light during the emergency. You might be able to perform great feats of strength in this condition.

Method(s) of development _____

_____

Explanation _____

_____

5. Common among most whites are the false understandings and images which they retain about Indians. For many, the moving pictures, television, and comic strips have firmly established a stereotype as the true portrait of all Indians: the dour, stoic, warbonneted Plains Indian. He is a warrior, he has no humor unless it is that of an incongruous and farcical type, and his language is full of "hows," "ughs," and words that end in "um." Only rarely in the popular media of communications is it hinted that Indians, too, were, and are, all kinds of real, living persons like any others and that they included peace-

loving wise men, mothers who cried for the safety of their children, young men who sang songs of love and courted maidens, slow-witted people, statesmen, cowards, and patriots. Today there are professional men and women, jurists, ranchers, teachers and political office holders. Yet so enduring is the stereotype that many a non-Indian, especially if he lives in an area where Indians are not commonly seen, expects any American Indian he meets to wear a feathered headdress. When he sees the Indian in an ordinary business suit instead he is disappointed!

Method(s) of development _____

_____

Explanation _____

_____

6. Anxiety frequently expresses itself in two types of behavior known as obsessions and compulsions. Obsessions are recurring thoughts that a person cannot seem to get out of mind. For example, a young man who thinks continuously about the possible death of his parents is suffering from an obsession. Compulsions, on the other hand, are recurring activities that a person must perform to avoid anxiety. A woman who insists on washing her hands every few minutes even though her hands are not dirty is showing compulsive behavior.

Method(s) of development _____

_____

Explanation _____

_____

7. For some strange reason, the unmarried American woman is an "old maid," while the unmarried man is a swinging bachelor. The forty-year-old man with a family and a career is an admirable success. A woman in the same position is often accused of not tending to the needs of her family. The hostess planning a dinner party is happy to accommodate the unattached male; the unattached woman, however, is considered a worry and a bother.

Method(s) of development _____

_____

Explanation _____

_____

8. Robert Falcon Scott (1868–1912) hoped to be the first to explore the South Pole, but he failed in his attempt, and the Norwegian explorer, Roald Amundsen, reached the Pole before him. Scott and his party set out from Cape Evans, a site about nine hundred miles away from the Pole, and although the ponies on which they were relying did not take well to the Antarctic conditions, the group thought they were ahead of Amundsen. They did not realize that the Norwegian was four hundred miles beyond them. As the ponies grew weaker and blizzards slowed down their progress, Scott and his companions grew steadily more discouraged. Their depression increased when they found traces of Amundsen's party. When they finally reached the Pole, they discovered that their fears had been well founded; Amundsen had camped at the Pole and was already returning home. Scott's party had no other choice but to turn around and try to make their way back home; the return journey was a nightmare filled with cold weather and hunger. None of the men survived.

## DEVELOPING YOUR PARAGRAPHS

Composing paragraphs involves a number of steps: formulation of an approach to the topic and statement of that approach in a topic sentence; selection of details to provide the necessary supporting information for the topic sentence; arrangement of those details into an effective pattern, including the placement of the topic sentence somewhere in the paragraph.

It is possible to vary the order of these steps and still write good paragraphs, but each step is important. It makes sense to discuss the arrangement of supporting information in a paragraph as a step to be taken *after* formulating the topic sentence and selecting appropriate information, because the arrangement of this information often is determined by the approach to the topic, and by the nature of the information itself.

An appropriate arrangement of specific information in a paragraph frequently flows quite naturally from the topic sentence itself:

> After the terrible devastation of the Civil War, Lincoln saw the need to begin pulling the divided nation back together.

This topic sentence could easily lead into a paragraph in which the supporting information is arranged in a cause and effect pattern, since the topic sentence itself establishes a cause and effect relationship:

| Topic sentence | After the terrible devastation of the Civil War, Lincoln saw the need to begin pulling the divided nation back together. |
|---|---|

| | |
|---|---|
| Causes | The economies of both the victorious North and the defeated South were in a shambles. And, of course, the cost in human life and deep-rooted hostility on both sides was immeasurable. The President only had to walk across the scarred earth of the Gettysburg battlefield, for example, or read hurt and anger in the eyes of the woman or man who had lost a son to know that the country needed time to heal. |
| Effect | In order to prepare the American people for the long period of reconciliation which would follow the War, Lincoln shaped his Second Inaugural Address around the theme of binding the nation's wounds. He proposed forgiveness, rather than punishment, for the South, and hope for the future, rather than bitterness about the past. |

In this paragraph, the topic sentence states a cause and effect situation: the devastation of the Civil War *caused* Lincoln to attempt to prepare the people for a period of reconciliation. The first half of the paragraph provides further explanation of the cause, and the end of the paragraph further defines the effect.

As in this example, often the approach to the topic, and the supporting information itself, will determine how the paragraph is developed and how the details can best be arranged.

## Examples

One of the most common methods of paragraph development is through examples. In fact, specific examples of a general statement can be the basis for developing almost any paragraph, since the point made by the topic sentence must always be explained.

If there is no other organization necessary or desirable, a paragraph can be developed simply through a series of examples. One of the clearest instances of such development is a paragraph that *describes* an object, person, or scene. The topic sentence introduces and presents the general features, and the specific sentences isolate individual physical details.

Suppose you want to describe your father to somebody who has never met him. You would first decide which feature you wanted to emphasize.

Let us suppose you decide on his face. Your topic sentence is "My father's face shows his strong will." The details are these: strong jaw, firm lips, ready smile, blue eyes, angular bone structure.

>My father's face shows his strong will. His face is angular with the shape of the bone structure clearly visible from forehead to chin. His jaw juts forward at all times, but even more when he is angry or upset. His lips are firm, but slide back easily into a bright smile. His blue eyes often twinkle, but turn as cold and deep as the ocean when he wants an answer to an important question. All of his moods can be found in his eyes and his smile, and his strength in the sharp, bony features of his face.

This descriptive arrangement of examples can be applied to any object, person, or scene.

In addition to physical description, examples can be used to develop ideas. For example, a general statement, such as "Music appeals to a wide variety of people," can easily and naturally be developed with examples from the following details:

1. Teenagers always look for new forms of popular music.
2. Adult music lovers develop tastes for particular types of music.
3. Some like folk.
4. Some like classical.
5. Some like opera.
6. Some like jazz.

These details are sufficient to form the skeleton of a paragraph, but they are not enough. You could ask yourself "why?" after each of these details:

1. Teenagers view music as part of their social behavior.
2. Adults see music as a permanent source of enjoyment.
3. Folk offers naturalness.
4. Classical offers intellectual challenge.
5. Opera combines a theatrical element.
6. Jazz is exciting and emotional.

A paragraph can now be written on the basis of these expanded details:

>Music appeals to a wide variety of people. Teenagers have always seen popular music as something especially their own, and for them rock or disco or whatever is as much a social as a musical experience. Adults develop more permanent tastes. Some become attracted to folk music because of its naturalness, and occasional flashes of moral idealism. Others turn to classical music to appreciate its structure and nuances of composition. Another group finds the combination of theater and stirring melodies in opera irresistible. And still

others become addicted to the driving rhythms and spontaneous invention of jazz.

Here, the specific sentences all illustrate the idea stated in the topic sentence by presenting examples. The order of these examples is not particularly important, since each is equally important as an illustration of the general idea. In other paragraph arrangements, the order in which the details are presented is determined by the approach to the topic and the nature of the details themselves.

**Comparison and Contrast**

If your approach to a topic involves two or three related subjects, and if the list of details can be grouped according to these subjects, then a natural arrangement would be *comparison and contrast.*

Suppose, for example, that you want to write about different types of music. After figuring out what you know about this topic, you discover you are most interested in folk music and jazz. You could then group details for each subject:

| **Folk** | **Jazz** |
|---|---|
| Often tells a story. Has a regular structure in lyrics and musical line. Often is performed by one singer with little accompaniment. | Usually involves improvisation. Recently has featured electronically amplified instruments. Can feature one player, but group is important. Lyrics involve blues themes of lost love and other personal problems. Sometimes almost popular, even disco flavored, but "pure" form is always more inventive. |

Most of these details can be easily paired for purposes of comparison and contrast. It is always easier to understand something in relationship to something else, and the relationship itself is often interesting. The details about folk and jazz then can be paired as follows:

| **Folk** | **Jazz** |
|---|---|
| Tells a story | Blues theme in the lyrics |
| Structured | Improvisation |
| Solo | Group and solo |
| Acoustic guitar or banjo | Electronic amplification |

The detail about "popular and pure" jazz, though, does not easily match anything in the folk category. You might find a similar statement to make about folk music, which you could then add to your list. Or perhaps you will decide that in this area, the two forms of music cannot really be compared or contrasted.

A paragraph written in a comparison-contrast pattern based on these details would probably emphasize the points of contrast between the two music forms. The details could be arranged by grouping all the information about folk first, and then all the material concerning jazz, as in the paragraph below. Or the folk and jazz details could be alternated.

> The folk singer often strides onto the stage accompanied only by a guitar or banjo slung over the shoulder. The idea is to emphasize the story that the songs will tell by keeping the performance simple and uncluttered. Then, the strong structure, choruses, and simple melodies, communicate the story-telling art of the music. <u>Although folk music presents an idea of simplicity and attention to story line, jazz concentrates on emotional energy and spontaneous variations in the music.</u> The expression on a jazz player's face will often appear intense, eyes closed in concentration on the music. The group begins to set down the rhythm, and the lead player joins in for a while until the moment arrives when the lead begins to improvise, to stretch for the possibilities of the music. Frequently, the other players will also improvise before they all come back to the starting melody. If a vocal is part of the performance, the lyrics will usually concern a blues theme of lost love. Music and words will then combine to create jazz' unique emotional experience.

Notice that the topic sentence is located in the middle of the paragraph to emphasize the balance of the folk and jazz details. The following paragraph begins with the topic sentence and then presents alternating details.

> <u>Folk music can be contrasted with jazz in several ways.</u> Lyrics in a folk song will often tell a simple story of the people and the land or the sea, while jazz lyrics usually develop blues themes of lost love. The melodic line in folk music is highly structured and repetitive. Jazz, on the other hand, builds from the base melody into free form improvisations. And though the folk singer generally accompanies himself or herself on a guitar or banjo, jazz usually involves ensemble playing. Finally, folk musicians are much less inclined to experiment with electronic amplification, since such modern gimmickry would not be in keeping with the original sound of the music. Jazz musicians, though, feel much freer to try different ways of producing sound with which to weave their magic.

Of these two methods, the second—alternating details—is more highly structured and demands an exact match of details for comparison or contrast. The first arrangement, with its blocks of details, is a little looser and more natural. Both, however, are effective ways to explain how different subjects can be understood in relationship to one another, as well as individually. Comparison and contrast is one of the most useful methods of paragraph development because it so clearly improves understanding.

## Process

*Process* paragraphs explain how something works. The process arrangement can be applied to something as simple as a recipe for baking a cake, or as complicated as calculating the gross national product. In either case, the key to this development and arrangement of details is a step-by-step presentation of the information.

Technique in sports, for example, readily falls into a process arrangement. Here is the topic sentence for a paragraph on basketball: "Successful foulshooting in basketball depends on concentration and repetition." The details are these:

Eye on the front rim
Comfortable body position
Feel of the ball in your hand
Deep breaths for relaxation
Easy motion
Follow-through

In such paragraphs, the topic sentence is usually placed at the beginning:

<u>Successful foul-shooting in basketball depends upon concentration and repetition.</u> The first thing to do when you approach the foul line is to concentrate on remembering how it should feel to shoot fouls. Walk to the line the same way each time. Bounce the ball the same number of times. Take a breath to relax, and settle your body in a comfortable position, just as you have done hundreds or thousands of times before. Stare at the front rim of the basket. It is the only thing that counts at this moment. Balance the ball in your shooting hand so that it feels like part of your body. Take another breath, and focus on that front rim. With an easy motion stretch your legs and extend your body while you direct your arm towards the basket. Let the ball release from your hand as though it were on a string. Continue your arm motion to a full follow-through, and wait for the swish of the ball through the basket. Next time, and every time, shoot exactly the same way.

Sometimes, for dramatic effect, the topic sentence in a process paragraph can be placed at the end. The steps will then create a tension in the reader, who will want to know the conclusion to which the steps lead.

Keep your mind on other things, pleasant things, such as fresh air, the sun, the waves. Avoid stress at all costs. Literally run away from trouble. Say "yes" to anything so as to remove the possibility of anxiety and conflict. Find new ways to go to work or school, preferably through unpopulated areas. The woods, if possible, would be fine. Do not venture near drug stores or supermarkets. Watch only public television so as not to chance seeing a dangerous commercial for a related vice. Better yet, if you must watch anything, stay with Sesame Street. Anything else might be too stimulating. Go to sleep early, and sleep as much as possible. Eat all you want, and more. <u>By doing all this, and with a little luck, you might just get through your first week without cigarettes.</u>

**Analogy**

One of the most important ways to learn about new things is by *analogy*, a comparison between two things. Usually, one of the subjects is very ordinary, and the other is unfamiliar. Analogy demonstrates how the unfamiliar can be understood by comparing it to what is known and understood.

In constructing an analogy paragraph, details should be matched in the same way as for comparison and contrast. But for an analogy paragraph, the first step should be to jot down information you know about the subject you want to present through analogy. You may already know what you want to compare your subject to. If you do not, the list of details might give you an idea.

Suppose your topic is inflation, and you want to describe how rising wages and prices cause inflationary pressures.

>   Employees want higher wages because everything they buy costs more.
>   Manufacturers and merchants want to charge higher prices because labor and other costs have risen.
>   Each side tries to get an edge on the other by exerting pressure.
>   Government attempts to control inflation through regulations and voluntary guidelines.
>   More rigorous wage-price controls have never really worked.

To present this information in an analogy, you must discover a pattern in the details that can be applied to something simple and readily understood. Among these details, certain features can be isolated:

>   Pressure coming from two sources
>   Ineffective efforts to reduce these pressures

Having isolated a key feature of inflation—pressure—think of things that work by, or react to, pressure:

>   Balloons
>   Teapots
>   Steam engines
>   Dams
>   Jet engines

To make the analogy work, pick an item that can logically have two pressure sources.

A good choice might be an airplane with two jet engines. Add a pilot who cannot control the power going to the engines, and you have a detail to match "ineffective efforts." The idea of a plane also enables you to employ other details, such as the danger of a crash and the idea of heading in the wrong direction. A paragraph that compares wage-price sources of inflation can then be developed, using a topic sentence at the beginning and at the end:

> <u>The pressures for increased wages and prices are causing inflation to resemble a runaway, two-engine jet plane.</u> On one wing is the engine of wages. On the other is the engine of prices. Both are high-powered and capable of driving the aircraft. Government sits in the pilot's seat, and tries to control the plane. But as the pilot reduces power to one side, the other gains strength. Clamping down on the second engine enables the first to catch up. Cutting off the power to both engines too sharply might cause a crash. Letting both expand as they wish will permit the craft to zoom too far away from a safe landing. <u>It will take an extraordinary pilot to end this journey safely.</u>

Such paragraphs are informative and enjoyable as long as the analogy works—that is, as long as there is a real basis for comparison.

## Definition

*Definition,* like analogy, is a pattern often used to teach or present information. Both physical things and concepts can be presented. In either case, to define something is to identify the essential characteristics that separate the subject from all other subjects.

For example, a major oil company has been running a series of commercials that define the "gas guzzler" as the unthinking driver who wastes gasoline in a number of ways:

1. Doesn't keep tires properly inflated
2. Doesn't keep engine tuned
3. Warms up the car too long in winter
4. Runs air-conditioning too much in summer
5. Likes "jack-rabbit" starts

These details could be developed in a paragraph of definition:

> <u>The gas guzzler is no longer a car but the unthinking driver who wastes gas needlessly.</u> This kind of driver will ignore the reduced mileage caused by underinflated tires. He or she never has time to

tune the engine. In the winter, the gas guzzler lets the car warm up for half an hour before getting into it, and in the summer turns the air conditioner on full blast until the interior temperature is as cold as what the guzzler wanted to avoid in the winter. Finally the guzzler insists on zooming away from each stop, not realizing that he or she is really only speeding to the next fill-up at the service station.

The guzzler paragraph defines a type of person through physical details. But suppose you want to define something less physical, such as "success." Here are some possible details:

    A good job
    Happiness
    A big house
    A big car
    Achieving your goals

Some of these are physical details, such as the house and car. The others measure success differently. Although both physical and nonphysical measures can be applied, suppose you choose not to use the physical details. Then you are left with the following:

    A good job
    Happiness
    Achieving your goals

These three details would not work into a very interesting paragraph. "Happiness" is too vague. "A good job" is too limited. But "achieving your goals" can be developed by thinking of related ideas. It would be useful, then, to try to *define* what "achieving goals" means.

The key word is "goals." Defining it will lead to useful details. Ask yourself what goal is most important to you. Perhaps you decide that serving society is a goal you would strive to achieve. This idea could lead to further questions, such as which careers would fulfill the purpose of serving society:

    Health
    Education
    Arts
    Engineering
    Business

The paragraph might then be something like this:

> *Success involves finding a way to serve society.* Although success is often measured by how much money you make, money alone is not enough. To be truely successful, you have to feel that you are a useful

person. One way to do this is to try to find a way to make life better for other people. Service careers in the health area, for example, can provide opportunities to achieve the goal of serving society by taking care of the sick. Educators serve society by teaching skills and ideas which are necessary for each new generation to learn. Businessmen and women permit the economy of the society to function. Engineers make life more convenient through the application of technology. Researchers in all fields explore the future. Less obviously, artists serve society by making the world more beautiful. <u>By finding a career which helps you improve the lives of others, you will feel better about yourself. You will be successful in a most meaningful way.</u>

Here the topic sentence begins the paragraph and the main idea is restated at the end.

## Classification

*Classification* breaks a subject down into categories, or smaller groups. Much of our knowledge about the world comes from classification. The natural sciences describe the physical environment in terms of categories of animals, plants, minerals, chemicals, atoms, and so on. Diseases are classified—viral infection, bacterial infection, and so on. Language itself is a system of classification in which words represent classes of things, actions, attitudes, or qualities. For example, the word "red" represents a wide variety of colors, all of which are more like each other than they are similar to "blue" or "yellow," or "green" or "black" or "white." Without classification, we would not be able to think or communicate.

Classification paragraphs organize specific details into two or more categories. In this way, classification is similar to comparison and contrast. The major difference between the two is that in classification we divide a subject into smaller groups according to specific criteria. The comparison and contrast technique does not focus as strongly on the criteria that are used to form the categories.

In order to compose a classification paragraph, you should ask yourself this question: "What criteria can I use to divide my subject into categories?" For example, suppose your subject is "handwriting." You can divide different types of handwriting into categories according to the size and legibility of the letters.

Bold and clear
Cramped, compressed
Swirling
Neat and clear
Illegible

The topic sentence in classification paragraphs usually comes at the beginning and states the criteria for the categories.

> Handwriting can be divided into categories according to the size and shape of the letters, and these details seem to tell us something about the people who write in certain ways. A bold, clear handwriting in which the letters are large and strongly formed seems to indicate that the writer is certain of what he or she says. A cramped and compressed handwriting where the letters are bunched and twisted together might show somebody who is either insecure or very concerned about space and order. Swirling letters and free-flowing curves could come from the pen of somebody who desires freedom and a sense of movement. Perfectly formed, medium-sized letters would seem to result from the writer's concern for clarity and precision. An illegible scrawl shows haste, carelessness, or a desire to be somewhat mysterious.

**Cause and Effect**

One of the basic ways we think about events is the order in which they occur. We have watches and calendars to keep track of the passing of time. Chronology, or the sequence of events, is a fundamental way of ordering our understanding of our lives. However, it is often more interesting and important to think of events not only in order, but in terms of one event *causing* another. A more significant thought process is involved in determining this kind of relationship. We say that Monday comes before Tuesday every week because our calendar gives us this structure for separating one day from another. But to say "The storm Monday caused traffic delays Tuesday morning" is to build upon chronology into a cause and effect relationship. *Cause and effect* relationships tell us not only that event B happened after event A, but that A *caused* B. We may want to know *why* a particular event occurred for a variety of reasons. Cause and effect reasoning is an attempt to answer this question.

But the process of determining cause and effect is complicated. It is often impossible to find a single cause for an event, because often several factors seem to influence a particular result. Nonetheless, though determining cause and effect relationships may pose some problems, the problems are both necessary to face and exciting to solve.

Paragraphs based on cause and effect relationships answer the question:

Why did event B happen?

The answer to this question should be logically sound. One way of testing if an answer is sound is to ask:

Would event B have happened without cause A?

For example, suppose you are involved in an automobile accident with another car. Your insurance company will surely be interested in what caused the accident, because determining responsibility (or cause) establishes liability. The company would probably send you a form that asks you to describe the accident. Then, based on this report, as well as on the reports of the other driver, the police, and any witnesses, the company will decide whether one or both drivers caused the accident, or whether road and/or weather conditions were primarily responsible. Imagine that your report included the following details:

> You were driving at 20 mph on a city street.
> You slowed as you approached an intersection.
> It was raining heavily.
> The light turned green as you reached the intersection.
> The roads were slippery.
> Another car approached from the street on your left.
> You proceeded slowly into the intersection.
> The other car skidded as it tried to stop for the light.
> The other car veered toward the front of your car.
> You braked but the other car struck your front fender.

A paragraph based on these details would identify the causes of the accident by asking this question: "Would the accident have occurred without any of these circumstances?" The list of details includes several circumstances which might answer that question affirmatively:

> Raining heavily.
> Slippery roads.
> The light had just begun to change.
> The other car skidded.
> The other car veered into your path.

The first three details certainly contributed to the accident, but the last two seem most immediately responsible. The rain, slippery roads, and changing light created a dangerous situation. The other car's skid, and the direction of the skid, made the accident unavoidable.

This paragraph, which will emphasize clarity, should begin with the topic sentence. The paragraph would then focus on the causes and conclude with the result—the accident.

> <u>The accident was caused by bad weather, slippery roads, a changing traffic light, and most important, the other car's skid.</u> It was raining heavily. The roads were slippery and visibility was poor. As I slowly approached the intersection, the light was still green in my direction, but it began to change after I had entered the intersection. I

saw a car coming toward me from my left. It tried to stop, but skidded across my path. I applied my brakes when I saw the other car begin to skid, but I couldn't stop in time. The other car struck my left front fender with its right front fender, doing considerable damage to both cars.

Cause and effect relationships, as illustrated in the above paragraph, are important and interesting. Social scientists and natural scientists often focus on such relationships. They are central to legal and moral discussions. And they are used by novelists and filmmakers to establish tension in telling stories, because narratives are often a series of causes leading to one or more results.

**A Note on Combined Methods**

The underlying principle in all paragraph development is a central statement supported by specific details. The details can be arranged in any of a number of patterns. Sometimes, however, a combination of patterns is desirable. For example, description is often part of analogy, classification, and comparison and contrast. In fact, all these patterns can be, in one way or another, combined with the others.

As a writer, however, it is important that you have a predominant pattern in mind so that your paragraphs clearly express your approach to your subject. Therefore, it is wise to determine a specific arrangement and then blend other patterns if it seems natural and desirable to do so.

WRITING EXERCISE

I.  Write a paragraph of description on one of the following topics:

    A memorable face
    A scene of natural beauty
    A painting or piece of sculpture
    An outrageous outfit worn by a friend
    A delicious food

    List your details:

    _____
    _____
    _____
    _____

Write the paragraph below. Underline the topic sentence.

II. Chose one of the following topics for a paragraph developed through examples:

Energy saving
Popular magazines
Blue Monday
False promises
Free time

List your details:

Write the paragraph below. Underline the topic sentence.

# Paragraph Development

_____
_____
_____

III. Develop a comparison and contrast paragraph on one of the following topics:

Advantages and disadvantages of working for a small company
Advantages and disadvantages of living in the country
Sketch of two celebrities
Good friends, bad friends
Sun time, moon time

Note your details:
    Subject A                          Subject B

_____     _____
_____     _____
_____     _____
_____     _____

Write the paragraph below. Underline the topic sentence.

_____
_____
_____
_____
_____
_____
_____
_____
_____
_____

IV. Select one of the following topics for a process paragraph.

Buying a stero system
Learning a new dance step

Seeking a job
Living within a budget
Forming a car pool

List your details:

Step 1. _____

2. _____

3. _____

4. _____

5. _____

Write the paragraph below. Underline the topic sentence.

_____
_____
_____
_____
_____
_____
_____
_____
_____
_____
_____

V. Imagine you have to explain one of the following to a visitor from another country. Use the analogy pattern.

A presidential election
Shopping malls
Professional football (or basketball, soccer)
Western movies
Condominiums

List your details:

| Subject | Analogy |
|---------|---------|
| _____ | _____ |
| _____ | _____ |
| _____ | _____ |
| _____ | _____ |

Paragraph Development

Write the paragraph below. Underline the topic sentence.

VI. Write a paragraph of definition on one of the following:

Pride
Volcanos
Commercialism in art or literature
Depression
Inflation

List your details:

Write the paragraph below. Underline the topic sentence.

VII. Divide one of the following into categories, and write a classification paragraph:

    Newspapers
    Camera lenses
    Leisure athletics
    Telephone personality
    Retail stores

List your details:

_____
_____
_____
_____

State your criterion for classification:

_____
_____

Write the paragraph below. Underline the topic sentence.

_____
_____
_____
_____
_____
_____
_____
_____
_____

Paragraph Development

VIII. Analyze one of the following into a cause-effect relationship

Traffic congestion
A good harvest
Population increase or decrease
Inner city decay
Popularity of designer jeans

List your details:

_____
_____
_____
_____

Which details are necessary for the result to have occurred?

_____
_____

Write the paragraph below. Underline the topic sentence.

_____
_____
_____
_____
_____
_____
_____
_____
_____
_____

# 11

# Paragraph Coherence

PREVIEW

Since every paragraph develops one general idea by supporting it with specific details, the relationship between the specific information and the general statement should be clear. Each detail should clearly connect with the other details so that the pattern of the paragraph is easily visible. The paragraph should be *coherent*—its ideas should hang together and make sense.

A paragraph can be made coherent in several ways: (1) through repetition of a key word or phrase; (2) by the use of transitional words or phrases; (3) by the replacement of a noun with a pronoun; (4) by the use of parallel sentence structure. All these methods work to create a smooth flow in which one idea relates to another, and in which all the specific details can be understood as they develop the main idea stated in the topic sentence.

**Key Terms**

**Coherence.** Quality of unity and clear relationships in paragraphs.
**Repetition.** Repeating of words or phrases in paragraphs.
**Transitions.** Words or phrases that provide bridges between ideas in paragraphs.
**Parallel structure.** Repeating similar grammatical structures in sentences in paragraphs.

A paragraph is a group of sentences about one general idea. It has a topic sentence, either stated or implied, and a number of specific sentences that may explain, discuss, clarify, exemplify, prove, or disprove the topic sentence. In other words, the sentences in a paragraph are related. When a writer creates a paragraph, he or she decides how the information in each sentence relates to that in the other sentences.

In addition, a writer will take care to organize and place those sentences so that the reader can follow the flow of ideas throughout the paragraph. He or she aims for a smooth connection between one idea and another, one sentence and another so that the reader can more easily understand the reasoning behind the paragraph. If the reader is able to go from one idea to another and to see the relationship between and among ideas and sentences, the author has produced a *coherent* paragraph, one in which the parts stick together.

## READING FOR COHERENCE

There are four common ways by which a writer can make ideas and sentences cohere, or stick together, within a paragraph. He or she can

1. *Repeat a key word or phrase* to emphasize an important idea or concept.
2. *Use transitional words or phrases* like "since," "so," "and," "however," "but" "therefore," "further," "yet," "furthermore," "because," "nonetheless," "finally," "in spite of," "of course," "in addition," "on the other hand," "so that" to carry the reader from one idea or sentence to another, and to show the relationship between one idea and another.
3. *Replace a noun with a pronoun* to eliminate the need to repeat the name of a person, place, or thing throughout the paragraph.
4. *Use parallel sentence structure* by repeating the phrasing of one sentence in another, or by repeating similar phrasing within individual sentences.

### Repetition of Key Words or Phrases

The authors of the following paragraphs repeat an important word to emphasize the thing it refers to.

The central, or core, <u>cities</u> are themselves losing population. In every part of the nation people are moving out of the older <u>cities</u> into the suburbs. The countryside around the <u>cities</u> is being leveled by bulldozers—at a rate, according to one estimate, of some 3000 acres every day—and huge suburban housing developments are springing up almost overnight. Department stores and banks are opening branches in the new suburban shopping areas, more and more industries are following the population out of the <u>cities</u>.

We all came out of Warwick better criminals. Other guys were better for the things that I could teach them, and I was better for the things that they could teach me. Before I went to Warwick, I used to be real slow at rolling reefers and at dummying reefers, but when I came back from Warwick, I was a real pro at that, and I knew how to boost weak pot with embalming fluid. I even knew how to cut drugs, I had it told to me so many times. I learned a lot of things at Warwick. The good thing about Warwick was that when you went home on visits, you could do stuff, go back up to Warwick, and kind of hide out. If the cops were looking for you in the city, you'd be at Warwick.

The word "cities" in the first paragraph is repeated to stress the difference between cities and suburbs. The word "Warwick" in the second paragraph is repeated to emphasize the skills that were learned there.

## Transitional Words or Phrases

The following paragraphs use transitions to move the reader from one idea to another.

She was surprised to hear the fish talk, and a little frightened. But she had found no water that morning, so she handed him the pitcher, and he filled it with cold, clear water.

The words "but," "and," and "so" make the flow of very different ideas smooth, and the reader moves easily through the paragraph, from idea to idea, sentence to sentence. These words also show relationships among "she," "him," and the "water."

President and Congress are given many checks over the federal judiciary.* The President exercises a measure of control over the courts through his power to name all federal judges. A legislative check of both the executive and the judiciary is found in the power of the Senate to confirm these judicial appointments made by the President. The very existence of all federal courts, save one—the Supreme Court—depends upon congressional legislation. In the case of the Supreme Court the number of justices who serve on that tribunal is subject to congressional control. Further, the very power of the federal courts to hear cases is subject in many ways to the will of Congress. Finally, Congress may impeach and remove federal judges from office, and it has done so more than once.

The word "further" adds additional information to the sentence pre-

*Courts.

ceding it, and the word "finally" shows that the last sentence concludes the paragraph. Both words indicate the relationship of the last two sentences to those that come before.

> We have passed our bicentennial year. Our progress has been recorded in the annals of history. Most of it is good. Medical advances have eliminated and found cures for many dread diseases of the past. Transportation has gone from the horse and buggy to jumbo jets that fly across the continent in six hours. Communication is possible to anywhere in the world with the lifting of a telephone receiver. <u>Yet</u> despite our technical advancement made over the past two hundred years we are facing a time when, unless both government and industry take immediate action, we will have to pay dearly for our progress.

"Yet" establishes a cause and effect relationship between the advances that have been made in the past 200 years (cause) and the warning that unless certain action is taken, we will pay for our achievements (effect).

## Replacement of a Noun with a Pronoun

The authors of the following paragraphs use pronouns that refer to nouns already mentioned in the paragraph.

> Analogy is the most imaginative kind of reasoning. <u>It</u> attempts to predict the future, yet final proof occurs only when the predicted event does or does not happen. Biologists use the analogy method when they employ monkeys, mice, and other animals to discover serums for human diseases. The Wright brothers used analogy when they studied the anatomy of birds to discover the principles of airplane construction.

The word "it" refers to analogy and replaces that noun in the second sentence.

> The baby was really delightful; <u>he</u> took his food with a will, stuck out <u>his</u> toes merrily whenever <u>his</u> legs were uncovered, and did not have fits. <u>These</u> are supposed to be the strongest points of baby perfection, and in all these our baby excelled.

The words "he" and "his" refer to baby; the word "these" refers to the things that make the baby delightful and are the "strongest points of baby perfection."

> If children discover the beauty of nature while <u>they</u> are young, <u>they</u> will respect and try to preserve <u>it</u> when they are older. Parents

play an essential role in helping their children make this discovery. They are instrumental in providing an environment which is conducive to learning and in helping their children to gain important experiences. Although young children are not able to understand the complex relationship of man to his environment, they can gain a respect for nature and a simplified understanding of the importance of a healthy ecological environment. Helping children to gain such an appreciation and understanding can be an exciting adventure for parents and children. And this adventure is available to all who are willing to explore and use their senses of touch, taste, smell, sight, and hearing.

The first three "they's" refer to children; "it" refers to nature. The fourth "they" refers to parents, "their" to parents, "his" to man. The fifth "they" refers to young children, and "their" refers to "all who are willing."

**Parallel Sentence Structures**

The following paragraphs contain repeated sentence structures that put greater force or emphasis on the ideas of the paragraph.

While on vacation I am going to do all the things I cannot do at any other time of year. I will stay out all night carousing. I will stuff myself with creamed desserts and I will drink too much. I will spend money foolishly on trinkets I will never use once I get home and I will feel free, relaxed, and perfectly content for it all.

Here the author uses "I will" to begin each sentence to give greater emphasis.

Bones was my favorite dog. He was the dog who met me at the door each evening, who stayed close to my bed when I was ill, who brought help when I was drowning, and who died in my arms. Since he's been gone, I cannot bring myself to get another pet, and certainly not another dog. Somehow, it just would not be fair. He was a lovely dog, that Bones.

The repeated use of clauses beginning with "who" is an example of parallel sentence structure.

Each of these coherence devices appears frequently in materials you read. Your ability to recognize them and to see the relationships they reveal will help you to read more quickly and with greater understanding.

Paragraph Coherence    **209**

## READING EXERCISE

The paragraphs that follow all contain one or more of the devices described in the text. Read each paragraph carefully and decide which device each paragraph contains. In the spaces provided write the word(s), phrase(s), or clause(s) for each device you have identified:

1. The sea was here quite quiet; there was no sound of any surf; the moon shone clear; and I thought in my heart I had never seen a place so deserted and desolate. But it was dry land; and when at last it grew so shallow that I could leave the yard and wade ashore upon my feet, I cannot tell if I was more tired or more grateful. Both at least, I was; tired as I never was before that night; and grateful to God as I trust I have been often, though never with more cause.

Repetition _____
Transition _____
Replacement _____
Parallelism _____

2. In January, 1979, James Lewis of Lima, Ohio was reunited with his identical twin, James Springer, after 39 years. They were separated five weeks after their birth in simultaneous adoptions. Lewis, a security guard, asked the help of court authorities in locating his twin brother. Springer, a records clerk in Dayton, had been told by his adopted parents that his twin brother had died at birth. He was shocked to be contacted, but agreed immediately to meet.

Repetition _____
Transition _____
Replacement _____
Parallelism _____

3. Each year, more than 5,000 New York City teachers are beaten, robbed, raped or assaulted (70,000 nationwide, which is 4% of all U.S. teachers). They are attacked in their classrooms, in hallways, bathrooms. They lie awake at night, reliving their horrifying experience. Many are unable to cope with the reality that their private world has been violated. Many will not allow their names to be used. Fear of reprisal is constant.

Repetition _____

Transition _____

Replacement _____

Parallelism _____

    4. Motown. Within five years, the label and the sound synonymous with the ultimate soul revue: The Supremes, Mary Wells, Marvin Gaye and Tammi Terrell, The Four Tops, The Temptations and, of course, the Miracles. Lot of spiritual names. Smokey notes. Yes, it had some roots in pain, but it also had hope, a danceable counterpoint of aching and abandon. It was music born of black adolescents; the miseries hadn't time to settle deep in their bones. Besides, you can cross a hot tin roof barefoot if you dance fast enought. Let the voice skip through a phrase and punctuate it with a soulful OW! Felt so good it hurt. Smokey's song, "I Got To Dance To Keep From Cryin'," spoke volumes to the kids from the projects. And for the first time in any significant way, black music made inroads with the Brylcream and drive-in set.

Repetition _____

Transition _____

Replacement _____

Parallelism _____

    5. Tom said to himself that it was not such a hollow world, after all. He had discovered a great law of human action, without knowing it—namely, that in order to make a man or a boy covet a thing, it is only necessary to make the thing difficult to attain. If he had been a great and wise philosopher, like the writer of this book, he would now have comprehended that Work consists of whatever a body is obliged to do. And this would help him to understand why constructing artificial flowers or performing on a treadmill is work, while rolling tenpins or climbing Mont Blanc is only amusement. There are wealthy gentlemen in England who drive four-horse passenger-coaches twenty or thirty miles on a daily line, in the summer, because the privilege costs them considerable money; but if they were offered wages for the service, that would turn it into work and then they would resign.

Repetition _____

Transition _____

Replacement _____

Parallelism _____

Paragraph Coherence

6. To the child, the genius with imagination, or the wholly untravelled, the approach to a great city for the first time is a wonderful thing. Particularly if it be evening—that mystic period between the glare and gloom of the world when life is changing from one sphere or condition to another. Ah, the promise of the night. What does it not hold for the weary! What old illusion of hope is not here forever repeated! Says the soul of the toiler to itself, "I shall soon be free. I shall be in the ways and the hosts of the merry. The streets, the lamps, the lighted chamber set for dining are for me. The theatre, the halls, the parties, the ways of rest and the paths of song—these are mine in the night." Though all humanity be still enclosed in the shops, the thrill runs abroad. It is in the air. The dullest feel something which they may not always express or describe. It is the lifting of the burden of toil.

Repetition _____

Transition _____

Replacement _____

Parallelism _____

7. The classic definition of culture, framed by Sir Edward Tylor (1871, vol. 1, p. 1), reads, "Culture . . . is that complex whole which includes knowledge, belief, art, morals, law, custom and any other capabilities and habits acquired by man as a member of society." Stated more simply, culture is everything which is socially learned and shared by the members of a society. The individual receives culture as part of his social heritage, and, in turn, he may reshape the culture and introduce changes which then become a part of the heritage of succeeding generations.

Repetition _____

Transition _____

Replacement _____

Parallelism _____

8. A sociologist as an individual may properly make value judgments, support causes, and join reform movements, like any other citizen. As a scientist, he may not be able to prove whether television violence is harmful to children, and therefore will make no public recommendations; but as a parent he makes a decision according to his beliefs and values. As a scientist, he may not be able to say whether gambling should be forbidden or whether contraceptives should be distributed to unmarried coeds; but as a citizen he is free to express his opinions and support his own value judgments.

Repetition _____

Transition _____

Replacement _____

Parallelism _____

    9. Established businesses will have to adjust. All institutions set up to help full time wives will have to adjust. If they do, it will be acceptable for both women and men to set their own priorities, to make their own decisions about family-time and career-time, and to decide who will keep the home fires burning while another minds the store.

Repetition _____

Transition _____

Replacement _____

Parallelsim _____

## WRITING COHERENT PARAGRAPHS

    Paragraphs present one main idea, usually expressed in a topic sentence and supported by sentences that provide specific information. In order to make the relationships between the topic sentence and the supporting sentences clear, and to emphasize the connections among the supporting sentences themselves, a writer tries to achieve *coherence* in paragraphs. He or she does this with a number of devices: repetition of a word or phrase, use of transitional words, replacement of nouns with pronouns, and use of parallel sentence structure. All these devices can add coherence to a paragraph. Repetition emphasizes important ideas; transitional words bridge the gap from one idea to another; replacement of nouns with pronouns links one sentence with another grammatically; parallel sentence structure is another kind of repetition, only in this case form rather than words are repeated.

    If your paragraphs have a good topic sentence to limit your approach to your subject, and if you can arrange the supporting details into one of the patterns described in the previous chapter, you are ready to work on coherence. Adding coherence to a paragraph that already has organization and development is a kind of fine tuning or polishing. As you gain experience writing paragraphs, you will be able to build certain elements of coherence into your rough draft, and then you will have less work to do in revision.

# Paragraph Coherence

Examine the following paragraph. It has a clear topic sentence stated in the beginning of the paragraph. It has relevant details arranged in a comparison and contrast pattern. However, it needs work to make it more coherent.

<u>Language is the most important human ability and distinguishes humans from other animals.</u> Animals are the same as people in many ways. In some areas of activity, animals are better than humans. The jaguar can run faster. For strength, look at the great apes. Birds fly in the sky while we can only walk on the ground. People can talk. Animals only howl, or chatter, or wave at each other. Some scientists believe that some animals, like dolphins, have a language. No animal, no matter what these scientists say, has ever written a book. Humans do speak. People write words that last through many lifetimes. Language skill separates humans from animals. Because of language, humans can form governments. Morality and theology and art are possible. That is because this skill is the tool for all these important human activities.

This paragraph does have a topic sentence supported by specific information in a comparison and contrast arrangement. But it does not read smoothly. It seems to be a number of separate pieces that do not quite fit together. It can be improved by applying one of the four techniques described below.

## Repetition of Key Words or Phrases

The purpose of repetition is to keep the reader's attention on the important ideas in a paragraph. Too much repetition can be boring and ineffective. But a careful selection of key words or phrases to be emphasized through repetition will strengthen the paragraph and give it a certain amount of coherence.

In picking which words to repeat, keep in mind the important points that should be stressed. Since this paragraph concerns language ability, humans, and their ability to talk, these words should be repeated where possible:

<u>Language</u> is the most important human <u>ability</u>. Animals have many of the same <u>abilities</u>. In some areas of activity, animals are more <u>able</u> than <u>humans</u>. The jaguar can run faster. For strength, look at the great apes. Birds fly in the sky while we can only walk on the ground. We can <u>talk</u>. Animals <u>talk</u> by howling, or chattering, or waving at each other. Some scientists believe that some animals, like <u>dolphins</u>, can

"talk." No dolphin, no matter what these scientists say, has ever written a book. Humans not only talk. Humans write words that last through many lifetimes. Language ability separates people from animals. Because of language ability, humans can form governments. Morality and theology and art are possible. That is because this ability is the tool for all these important human activities.

Repeating "language," "ability," "talk," and "humans" instead of other similar words provides a level of coherence. "Dolphin" is used in two consecutive sentences, for emphasis. The paragraph is now more coherent, but the other techniques can still be used in further revisions.

## Transitional Words or Phrases

Sentences contain idea relationships that are complete in and of themselves. Since a paragraph is a series of sentences, each one of which contains its own idea relationship, it is useful to tie these sentences together. Transitional words or phrases link one sentence to another and show how one sentence relates to the others in a paragraph:

Language is the most important human ability and distinguishes humans from animals. Animals, though, have many of the same abilities. Moreover, in some areas of activity, animals are more able than humans. For example, jaguars can run faster. In addition, for strength, look at the great apes. Finally, birds fly in the sky while we can only walk on the ground. However, we can talk. Animals, on the other hand, talk by howling, or chattering, or waving at each other. Even though some scientists believe that some animals like dolphins "talk," no dolphin has ever written a book. Humans not only talk. Humans also write words that last through many lifetimes. Therefore, language ability separates people from animals. Because of language ability, humans can form governments. Further, morality and theology and art are possible. That is because this ability is the tool for all these important human activities.

Several different kinds of transitional words or phrases help to make this paragraph cohere. Words and phrases like "moreover," "in addition," "also," and "further" indicate that the sentence of which they are a part will provide additional information. Others like "though," "however," "on the other hand" show a change in direction in the sentence in which they occur. In other words, they signal information which will differ in some respect from that which went before. "Finally" shows the end of a list of details, and "therefore" introduces a conclusion that follows from the details already presented. All these words or phrases tie the sentences in the paragraph together and show relationships among them more clearly.

## Replacement of Nouns with Pronouns

Pronouns replace, or stand in the place of, nouns. That is the grammatical function of pronouns. In order for a pronoun to replace a noun, it must clearly refer back to that noun. Often in writing, we want to avoid using the same noun over and over again because we want to avoid tiresome repetition as opposed to repetition for emphasis. In such instances, we have two choices: (1) find another noun; or (2) replace the first noun with a pronoun. Both choices are useful. Finding similar nouns provides welcome variety. Replacing nouns with pronouns adds desirable coherence.

Replacing nouns with pronouns adds to coherence in two ways. Since usually only one pronoun can replace a noun, the same pronoun will be repeated, and repetition is a source of coherence. Less obviously, and perhaps more important, replacing nouns with pronouns will sometimes demand that you restructure your sentences in a certain way to make the noun-pronoun relationship clear. Examine our paragraph with some nouns replaced by pronouns.

> Language is the most important human ability and distinguishes humans from other animals. Animals, though, have many of the same abilities. Moreover, in some areas of activity, they are more able than humans. For example, jaguars can run faster. In addition, for strength, look at the great apes. Finally, birds fly in the sky while people can only walk on the ground. However, we can talk. They, on the other hand, talk by howling, or chattering, or waving at each other. Even though some scientists believe that dolphins "talk," no dolphin has ever written a book. Humans not only talk. We also write words that last through many lifetimes. Therefore, language ability separates us from animals. Because of our language ability, we can form governments. Further, we can think about morality and theology and art. That is because this ability is our tool for all these important human activities.

The first two "theys" refer to animals and tie together the details in the first half of the paragraph which list the things animals do better than humans. In the second half, "we," "us," and "our," all refer to humans and provide coherence for the details that describe human language ability. The sentence concerning morality, theology, and art was restructured to add another opportunity for pronoun repetition. By changing the subject from "morality, theology, and art" to "we," that sentence is made to follow more smoothly.

## Parallel Sentence Structure

Parallel sentence structure refers to sentences constructed in similar grammatical forms. For example, parallel sentence structure can involve a series of equation sentences, or action sentences, or action with verb sentences. Sometimes only one part of a sentence form is repeated. At other times, two or more elements of one sentence have the same form. In all these instances, the parallel structures are a kind of repetition and therefore add coherence:

> Language is the most important human ability, and distinguishes humans from other animals. Animals, though, have many of the same abilities. Moreover, in some areas of ability, they are more able than humans. For example, some, like jaguars, can run faster. In addition, others, like great apes, can lift heavier objects. Finally, still others, like birds, can fly in the sky while people can only walk on the ground. However, we can talk. They, on the other hand, talk by howling or chattering or waving at each other. Even though some scientists believe that dolphins "talk," no dolphin has ever written a book. Humans not only talk. We also write words that last through many lifetimes. Therefore, language ability separates us from animals. Because of our language ability, we can form governments. Further, we can discover moral issues, we can develop theologies, and we can create art. We can do all these things because language is our tool for these important human activities.

Parallel structure adds coherence at two key places in this revision: in the series of details that describe what animals can do better than humans, and in the list of human accomplishments that are possible because of language ability. These sentences are parallel to each other within each group. In the first group, the parallel structures include the same kind of subject: "some like jaguars," "others like great apes," and "still others like birds." Each of these subjects is followed by an action verb: "can run," "can lift," "can fly." The second group includes three sentences built around the subject "we," and followed by "can" and then a verb plus object structure: "can form governments," "can discover moral issues," "can develop theologies," "can create art." The last sentence sums up the paragraph and repeats this grammatical form, "We can do all."

This revised paragraph is now much more coherent than it was in the original form. The devices of repetition of key words and phrases, use of

Paragraph Coherence  217

transition words or phrases, replacement of a noun with a pronoun, and the use of parallel structure have all contributed to a smoother flow of ideas that also shows relationships clearly.

WRITING EXERCISE

I.  A. Revise the following by looking for key words or phrases to repeat. The topic sentence usually includes such words and phrases. In your revision, see if you can substitute a word (or a different form of a word) or a phrase from the topic sentence for the underlined words and phrases in the paragraph.

Television commercials appeal to male fantasies of success and glamour. A handsome man stands before a huge house and shows us a particular automobile. The <u>idea</u> (_____) is that if you buy this car, everything else comes along with it. In another <u>television advertisement</u> (_____) a <u>rich</u> (_____) man in an executive office tells us we should investigate a certain company for investment, and then he steps into his chauffeur-driven limousine. We can all share the <u>dream</u> (_____) of making the right financial moves as he does. Finally, there is the one that <u>calls on</u> (_____) the male dream of machismo. A famous ex-football player splashes on a certain cologne, and all day beautiful women pop into his life. It seems that to fulfill our <u>wishes</u> (_____) all we have to do is make the right investments, drive the right car, and wear the right cologne. The only trouble with this combined <u>idea</u> (_____) is that we can't be sure which to do first. The people in these commercials all seem to be <u>rich and attractive</u> (_____) to begin with.

B. What is the topic sentence of this paragraph?
   _____

C. Draw a triangle over the paragraph to indicate placement of the topic sentence.

D. What arrangement of detail does it follow?
   _____

II. A. Revise the following paragraph by inserting transition words or phrases in the blanks.

Hair styles create different images. _____, long, free-flowing hair suggests a natural look. _____, this style says we should just let our hair grow the way it wants to, and that the person who adopts this style wants to be free to be himself or herself. Hair styled in curls by a permanent _____ projects an image of self-consciousness. _____ the hair is no longer natural, it says that the person who wears it this way wants to be noticed for his or her hair. _____, hair which is cut very short seems to indicate a kind of simplicity. Short hair _____ says that the wearer can't be bothered with taking care of several pounds of hair, or in making it grow in a way it doesn't want to.

    B.  What is the topic sentence of this paragraph?

    C.  Draw a diagram over the paragraph to indicate the placement of the topic sentence.

    D.  What is the arrangement of details in this paragraph?

III.  A.  Revise the following paragraph by replacing the underlined nouns with pronouns. Write the pronouns in the parentheses.

    A parent who overhears a teenager on the phone might think the conversation was being conducted in a foreign language. The adult (_____) might be mystified by the slang words like "gross" which pepper the conversation and make it incomprehensible to mature ears. The older person (_____) might well think the teenagers are either silly or even rebellious for using a vocabulary that only they understand: that same parent, though, will visit a doctor or a lawyer and listen to these professionals speak in terms that are equally incomprehensible. It is likely that "conjunctivitis" or "fiduciary" will make no more sense to the person (_____) than did "gross" overheard in the teenager's conversation. Both teenagers and professionals have their own special languages, although the professional's language is accepted while the teenager's is not.

    B.  What is the topic sentence of this paragraph?

    C.  Draw a triangle over the paragraph to indicate the placement of the topic sentence.

    D.  What is the arrangement of details in this paragraph?

IV.  A.  The following paragraph has several blanks. Fill in these blanks so that the completed sentences will have parallel structure.

Paragraph Coherence

_____ pay attention in class instead of _____. _____ find a quiet place to study instead of _____. _____ try to remember facts from my books instead of _____. This program of self-discipline will definitely improve my grades next semester. I may not be able to _____, _____, _____, as much as I would like, but these things can wait. When the semester is over, I will be able to _____, rather than _____, when I see _____ where I used to see _____ on my grade report, and _____ on the faces of my teachers instead of _____.

    B.  What is the topic sentence of this paragraph?

        _____

    C.  Draw a triangle over the paragraph to indicate placement of the topic sentence.

    D.  What is the arrangement of details in this paragraph?

        _____

# 12

# The Essay

PREVIEW

Expository writing presents information and/or takes a position on an issue. Such writing is usually organized into paragraphs which then can be joined together to form an essay. An *essay,* then, is expository writing organized into a clear pattern of related paragraphs.

A paragraph is a group of sentences that develops, explains, and illustrates one general idea. In much the same way, an essay organizes paragraphs into a larger whole. The principles of organization for paragraphs and essays are the same: both present a package of information and/or opinions in which specific details form the basis of a broader idea.

Paragraphs present this broader, or main, idea as a topic sentence. Essays present a general idea expressed in a thesis statement. A thesis statement for essays identifies the limits of the subject to be discussed. It also suggests an organizational pattern for the essay by pointing toward the kind of development that will best explain the general idea of the thesis statement.

Because essays have an organizational pattern, they can be *outlined.* As a reader, you can outline an essay as an aid to comprehension and recall. As a writer, you can use an outline to plan the approach to the subject. In both situations, you should be familiar with the three-section structure of most essays: (1) an introductory paragraph that includes the thesis statement; (2) the development section of several paragraphs that relate to and explain the thesis statement; and (3) a concluding paragraph that restates the thesis.

**Key Terms**

**Expository writing.** Presentation of information and/or opinion on a subject.
**Essay.** Expository writing organized into related paragraphs.
**Outline.** A visual representation and summary of the main points of an essay.
**Major headings.** The most important sections of an essay, as indicated by the outline.
**Subheadings.** More specific points of an essay, as indicated by the outline.
**Introduction.** Beginning of an essay; includes the thesis statement.
**Development.** Body of an essay; contains paragraphs that explain the thesis statement.
**Conclusion.** End of an essay; restates the idea contained in the thesis statement.

The format, or organization, of the essay and the paragraph are similar. Both develop one main idea, but they differ in length and complexity. A paragraph consists of specific sentences that develop the main idea while an essay involves a group of organized paragraphs that serve the same purpose. Just as the specific sentences of a paragraph explain and refine the main idea, the paragraphs of an essay develop its main idea, but in a more complicated and extensive way. Since an essay is longer and broader in scope, it almost always has a conclusion. A paragraph may or may not contain a concluding statement.

## READING ESSAYS

Because of these similarities, reading an essay requires some of the same skills used to read paragraphs. The reader must be able to discover the general idea as well as the specific information that is used to develop the essay. A similar process of discovery helps the reader understand paragraphs.

**Organization of the Essay**

Because of its length, an essay should be approached first from an overall point of view; that is, the reader should look at its organization. The typical essay is usually organized in the following manner:

```
Introductory paragraph
Development paragraphs
Concluding paragraph
```

The introductory paragraph indicates the scope and purpose of the essay, presented in the form of a *thesis statement*. The thesis statement is a general statement of the main idea that controls or shapes the essay's development. Like the main idea or topic sentence of a paragraph, it guides the reading of the rest of the essay and it may appear at the beginning, middle, or end of the introductory paragraph. The development paragraphs that follow contain a stated or implied main idea in the form of a topic sentence. These main idea sentences are each a part of the thesis statement. Each development paragraph includes specific information that explains and refines its topic sentence and therefore directly relates to the thesis statement or general idea of the entire essay. The concluding paragraph reinforces the thesis statement by restating it. In some instances the concluding paragraph will summarize, evaluate, criticize, offer an opinion, or make a prediction based on the information presented in the development paragraphs.

The following example contains each of the parts the reader can expect to find in a well-written essay:

### Lost Friendship

One of life's pleasures is friendship. And one of life's sorrows is the loss of such a relationship. There are three common causes for lost friendships: betrayal, boredom, and distance.

Betrayal can take several forms. Lying, one form of betrayal, causes friendship to crumble because it diminishes the trust and confidence upon which friendship is based. A more dramatic form of betrayal is stealing from, or cheating, a friend. The real hurt in such cases is not the loss of material goods, but the deception or violation of trust.

Just as betrayal can destroy friendship, so too can boredom. One can grow bored with a friend when common interests are no longer shared. Or boredom might trouble a friendship when attitudes or values held by one party or the other change. In addition, over a period of time simple routine can lead to a loss of enthusiasm for the relationship.

A third cause of the loss of friendship is distance. Unlike betrayal or boredom, the creation of distance between friends is often unavoidable since external factors such as a change in job or school might cause one friend to relocate. Although some friendships can survive for long periods of time when the friends are physically separated, distance usually prevails and ends the relationship.

Betrayal, boredom, and distance all can break down a friendship. While it is not possible to prevent these things from happening, being aware of such possibilities may soften the reaction you have if they do occur.

The three questions to find the main idea, discussed in Chapter 9, may be used to determine the thesis statement of an essay as well as the topic sentences of individual paragraphs. In the essay above, the thesis statement, "There are three common causes for lost friendship: betrayal, boredom, and distance" is the general or controlling idea of the development paragraphs. The concluding paragraph contains a restatement of the thesis, as well as another related sentence, and ends the essay in a well-organized manner.

## Outlining the Essay

There will be times when you will want or need to outline an essay you read, particularly if the essay is long or complicated in organization. An outline provides the reader with a means of placing the essential parts of what is read into a framework. The three main parts of an essay— beginning or introductory paragraph, middle or development paragraphs, and end or concluding paragraph—can be represented with Roman numerals in an outline. Remember that each development paragraph is listed separately. An outline that includes the major parts of the friendship essay would look like this:

   I. Three causes for lost friendship are betrayal, boredom and distance.
  II. Betrayal can take several forms.
 III. Just as betrayal can result in lost friendship, so too can boredom.
  IV. A third cause for loss of friendship is distance.
   V. Betrayal, boredom, and distance are all causes for lost friendship.

The major parts of the essay—the thesis statement, topic sentences, and restated thesis statement—become the major headings of the outline. It is a good idea to write these headings in complete sentences so that when you refer to the outline at a later time, you can easily recall the ideas stressed in the essay.

You can further divide each of your major headings into subheadings that represent the details included in the development paragraphs. Subheadings can be indicated with capital letters:

   I. Three causes for lost friendship are betrayal, boredom, and distance.
  II. Betrayal can take several forms.
      A. Lying
      B. Stealing
      C. Cheating
 III. Just as betrayal can result in lost friendship, so too can boredom.
      A. Common interests no longer shared
      B. Change in attitudes or values
      C. Problem of routine

IV. A third cause for loss of friendship is distance.
   A. Move away
   B. Change in job, school, or neighborhood
   C. Difficulty of coping with separation
V. Betrayal, boredom, and distance are all causes for lost friendship.

This outline provides the reader with a fuller representation of the information supplied in the essay. The subheadings fill in the details. Distinguishing between the major headings and the subheadings emphasizes the difference in importance between and among ideas.

**Developing the Essay**

Writers use the same methods to develop ideas in an essay as they do in developing ideas in a paragraph. In addition to determining the structure of the essay and indicating it in an outline, the reader should also recognize the method of development. Recognizing the method of development helps the reader understand the writer's approach and judge whether or not the essay achieves its purpose. Here again is the essay on friendship:

### Lost Friendship

One of life's pleasures is friendship. And one of life's sorrows is the loss of such a relationship. There are three common causes for lost friendships: betrayal, boredom, and distance.

Betrayal can take several forms. Lying, one form of betrayal, causes friendship to crumble because it diminishes the trust and confidence upon which friendship is based. A more dramatic form of betrayal is stealing from, or cheating, a friend. The real hurt in such cases is not the loss of material goods, but the deception or violation of trust.

Just as betrayal can destroy friendship, so, too, can boredom. One can grow bored with a friend when common interests are no longer shared. Or boredom might trouble a friendship when attitudes or values held by one party or the other change. In addition, over a period of time simple routine can lead to a loss of enthusiasm for the relationship.

A third cause of the loss of friendship is distance. Unlike betrayal or boredom, the creation of distance between friends is often unavoidable since external factors such as a change in job or school might cause one friend to relocate. Although some friendships can survive for long periods of time when the friends are physically separated, distance usually prevails and ends the relationship.

Betrayal, boredom, and distance all can break down a friendship. While it is not possible to prevent these things from happening, being aware of such possibilities may soften the reaction you have if they do occur.

Notice that the thesis statement suggests the method of development: "There are three common causes for lost friendships: betrayal, boredom, and distance." The word "causes" establishes a cause-effect development for the essay, and each of the three causes is the topic for a development paragraph. The causes lead to the effect—namely, "lost friendships."

Process, definition, classification, and examples are some other methods of development. The following clues can help you recognize which method will be used in a particular essay:

*Process:* The thesis statement suggests a step-by-step approach to getting something done. Such steps are discussed in the development paragraphs of the essay.

*Definition:* The thesis statement defines something or someone. Aspects of that definition are discussed in the development paragraphs of the essay.

*Classification:* The thesis statement places an idea, event, or object into categories. These categories are discussed in the development paragraphs of the essay.

*Examples:* The thesis statement states that someone or something illustrates a quality, attitude, belief, accomplishment, and so on. These examples are presented in the development paragraphs of the essay.

*Comparison and contrast:* The thesis statement declares that there are similarities and/or differences between someone or something and someone else or something else. The development paragraphs list the points of similarity and/or difference.

The more skilled you become in recognizing the method of development of an essay, the better able you will be to read essays with understanding and to recall their main points.

## READING EXERCISE

Read the following essays. Each is followed by an outline that includes major headings and subheadings. The outlines are incomplete. See if you can supply the missing information from your reading and indicate the method of development used in each.

A. Essay

### Achieving Financial Security

In this age of inflation and increased costs for goods and services, financial security is a common concern. Although it is more difficult now than before, financial security can be achieved by managing your money carefully.

The first step is initiating an income. You can do this by working for others, or by working for yourself. In either case you earn money in the form of a salary or profits with which you pay your expenses. Or, if you are very lucky and have some money on hand, you can let your money work for you. Interest earned on savings or dividends earned from investments are both types of income.

The second step is to plan and control your budget. Make an inventory of your expenses in order to decide what must be spent. Stick to the budget you have drawn up and avoid extravagance as much as possible.

The third and final step to achieving financial security is to keep more than you spend. To reach this goal it may be necessary for you to increase your income. You might have to take a second job and/or make investments or increase savings. You might also have to pay cash to avoid high interest payments on installment loans.

If carefully followed, these three steps can help you become financially secure. Inflationary times may make it hard to take each step, but success is possible with persistence and discipline.

B. Outline
  I. Three steps can help you achieve financial security.
  II. Initiate an income
     A. Work for others
     B. _____
     C. Let your money work for you
  III.
     A. Inventory of expenses
     B. Stick to budget
     C. Avoid extravagance
  IV. Keep more than you spend.
     A. _____
     B. Pay cash to avoid high interest payments.
  V. If carefully followed, these three steps can help you become financially secure.
C. Method of development _____

A. Essay

### Who Is a Successful Person?

Some seemingly successful people commit suicide while others who appear to be content with themselves never achieve the outward signs of success. However, a truly successful person displays both an inner and an outer quality of success.

The inner attribute of the successful person takes several forms. Such a person exhibits an air of self-esteem. This self-respect causes the individual to feel a sense of self-worth, a good feeling about himself/herself. This good feeling produces a self-confidence that is quickly observed by those who come in contact with the successful person.

The outer quality or symbol of success can also take various forms: money, or position, or material possessions or recognition. Very often, the successful person's position provides him/her with the money to buy material possessions. That position may also contribute to the recognition that the successful person receives from others.

Inner and outer qualities define the successful person.

B. Outline

    I. _____
   II. The inner quality or attribute of the successful person takes several forms.

      A. _____
      B. _____

  III. _____
      A. Money
      B. Position
      C. Material possessions
      D. Recognition
  IV. Inner and outer qualities define the successful person.

C. Method of development _____

A. Essay

## Hanging Out

"Hanging out" is a common practice among teenagers. As a kind of socializing, teenagers "hang out" in different ways in different places.

Hanging out city-style involves establishing a territory or "turf" which is usually within walking distance of home or school. This territory can be a local corner, street or meeting place like a candy store, or gymnasium. Who hangs out where and with whom is usually determined by where the teenager lives. Often the neighborhood, nationality, race, and cultural background of the teenager determines his/her peer group.

Suburban-style hanging out doesn't center on turf in the way city-style hanging out does. Instead, the suburban teenager finds his/her peer group through affiliations with larger groups: school, clubs, and organizations provide a broader choice of associates. Peer groups are based more on common interests and less on neighborhood, nationality, race, and cultural background.

Hanging out in rural areas involves an even broader style than suburban hanging out, but is somewhat similar. Transportation from place to place is a necessity. Like the suburban teenager, the rural teenager must rely on affiliations with larger groups to provide a peer group. Organizations like 4-H Clubs, Girl Scouts, Boy Scouts, and churches and schools are groups rural teenagers join to hang out.

Whether city-, suburban-, or rural-style, hanging out is a common practice among teenagers. It enables socialization to take place outside the home. Teenagers need to be with their peers so that interaction, necessary for growth and adjustment, can take place. Without such contact, social adjustment may be inhibited or severely affected.

B. Outline
   I. The common practice of hanging out can be done in different ways in different places.
   II. City-style hanging out
      A. _____
      B. _____
   III. _____
      A. No territory or turf
      B. Finds peer group through affiliations with larger groups
   IV. Rural-style hanging out
      A. Broader but somewhat similar to suburban style
      B. _____
      C. _____
   V. _____

C. Method of development _____

A. Essay

### Becoming a Physician

Becoming a physician is a magnificent achievement. There are few accomplishments that can surpass it. It is a goal that many have but few realize.

The intense preparation and study necessary to become a physician exemplifies the depth of that achievement. Seven years of formal study at college and medical school and from one to three years at the hospital in training is grueling and expensive. Difficult courses and fierce competition make the experience almost intolerable at times.

However, the benefit of such an education to humankind cannot be measured. Doctors save lives with their ability to mend the human body. Because of their knowledge and capable judgments, they reduce the suffering people experience. They restore health that might otherwise be lost.

Finally, they enjoy prestige and power. Physicians are perhaps the most respected professionals in our country. As a consequence, they earn very high incomes and enjoy a kind of influence reserved for the very important. Despite the fact that many people resent the superior position enjoyed by physicians in our society, they are to be admired.

Intense preparation, the benefit to others they provide, and the prestige and power they experience are examples of their accomplishment. Becoming a doctor is a splendid achievement.

B. Outline
  I. Becoming a physician is a magnificent achievement.
  II. _____
    A. _____
    B. _____
    C. _____
  III. _____
    A. _____
    B. _____
    C. _____
  IV. _____
    A. _____
    B. _____
    C. _____
  V. Becoming a doctor is a splendid achievement.
C. Method of development _____

# WRITING ESSAYS

An expository essay attempts to inform or persuade by presenting an organized series of paragraphs. Like an individual paragraph, an essay develops one main idea. Although this development is more complicated and extensive because of the larger scope of the essay, the principles of organization and details supporting a general idea are the same as they are for paragraphs.

The typical essay has the following structure:

> Introductory paragraph
> Development paragraphs
> Concluding paragraph

The introduction announces the general idea the essay will develop. The development paragraphs provide material that explains and refines the general idea. And the conclusion restates the general idea in light of the supporting details. Of course, this structure can be modified to suit individual styles, but it is the basic form for essays.

## Thesis Statement

A thesis statement for an essay is similar to a main idea sentence for a paragraph. Both serve as guides for you as the writer. They express the general idea that defines your approach to the topic. Both are often stated in the actual paragraph or essay. In paragraphs such a statement of the writer's controlling idea is called a topic sentence, and as you have seen, topic sentences can occur in different places in paragraphs. In essays, the statement of the writer's thesis generally occurs in the introductory paragraph and then is repeated in the conclusion.

The steps for formulating a thesis statement are like those used to find a main idea sentence for a paragraph. You should first determine what you know about the topic, and then decide what general statement you want to make in the essay. The difference between a main idea sentence and a thesis statement is the narrowness of focus provided by each: a main idea sentence focuses your approach to the topic sharply so that one paragraph can develop your idea; a thesis statement, on the other hand, gives you a broader focus so you can develop your ideas in several paragraphs. Experience will teach you how to compose a thesis statement that will serve as a good controlling idea for an essay. The examples in the following section can provide a guide to begin giving you that experience.

## Composing the Thesis Statement

Suppose your topic is tourism. This topic can be approached in several different ways. You could write about your experiences as a tourist. Or perhaps you live in an area where tourism is important to the local economy. Let us assume you want to work on tourism's influence on the local economy. You could see both advantages and disadvantages:

|          Advantages           |          Disadvantages            |
|-------------------------------|-----------------------------------|
| Tourists spend money.         | Tourist business inflates prices for local residents. |
| Tourist industry provides jobs. | Local economy becomes subject to external pressures—boom or bust cycles. |

These observations could shape your approach to the topic and help you formulate an effective thesis statement. The advantages of tourism center on the money spent in the local area. Since this money stimulates the local economy and provides jobs, it is definitely a positive effect. On the other hand, tourism also frequently drives up prices because tourists need, and will pay high prices for, essential goods and services. Also, once an economy is tied to tourism, it runs the risk of being threatened by external conditions, such as a gasoline shortage or prolonged bad weather. Such an economy is therefore somewhat unstable. These ideas could lead to the following thesis statements:

I. Tourism in Hollow Hills is both helpful and harmful to the local economy.

II. A. The advantages of tourism to the local economy in Hollow Hills outweigh the disadvantages.

II. B. The disadvantages to the local economy in Hollow Hills outweigh the advantages.

All three of these thesis statements could organize your essay. The first is objective in that it does not take sides on the issue. The other two are argumentative, since each declares that one side or the other is correct in discussing the impact of tourism.

The job of a thesis statement is to set the limits for, and the direction of, your essay. If it is formulated well, it will naturally lead to a good structure for you to use in developing your ideas. For example, the three statements above lead to a comparison-contrast organization for your essay. Since each thesis statement includes both advantages and disadvantages, your essay will have to compare and/or contrast these factors. The structure of essays developed from these thesis statements would include the following elements:

Introduction
Body
  Advantages
  Disadvantages
Conclusion

The differences among these three essays would come from the emphasis as determined by the thesis statements. The objective thesis statement would shape an essay in which advantages and disadvantages would be presented equally. The two argumentative statements, on the other hand, would direct you to emphasize either the advantages or the disadvantages, since you would be attempting to support one side or the other.

If the argumentative thesis statements were formulated differently, with an emphasis on only the advantages or the disadvantages, the resulting essays would take different forms:

>Tourism is necessary to the economy of Hollow Hills.
>
>Tourism is detrimental to the economy of Hollow Hills.

Each of these thesis statements would focus on either the advantages or the disadvantages of tourism, but not on both. Papers written from these thesis statements would include the following elements:

>Introduction                Introduction
>Body—advantages             Body—disadvantages
>Conclusion                  Conclusion

Thus, the thesis statement narrows the approach to a topic and also helps shape and organize the details that develop the idea it expresses.

## Outlining

A thesis statement provides the direction for your essay. It is an important step toward ensuring good organization. The next step is construction of an outline. An outline serves as the framework within which to present details that support the thesis statement.

An outline is best constructed by working from the whole down to the parts of your essay. In that way, you can maintain control and be certain that each section of your essay relates directly to your thesis. Begin by writing your thesis. Then, underneath it, set up a blank outline:

>*Thesis:* Tourism in Hollow Hills is both helpful and harmful to the local economy.
>
>I. Introduction
>II.
>III.
>IV.
>V. Conclusion

Since essays nearly always begin with an introductory paragraph and end with a concluding paragraph, your outline should indicate those sections. The development, or body, of your essay can contain two, three, or more paragraphs. Your blank outline should give you room to decide how many sections you want to develop your ideas.

Each of the Roman numerals in the development section represents one major heading. As you fill in your outline, be careful to keep your major headings of equal importance. Often, your thesis statement will contain key words or phrases that define your approach to the topic. Your major headings, then, should relate directly to, or even be a restatement of, these key words or phrases:

*Thesis:* Tourism in Hollow Hills is both *helpful* and *harmful* to the local economy.
*Key words:* helpful, harmful

    I. Introduction
   II. Advantages of tourism
      (restatement of "helpful")
  III. Disadvantages of tourism
      (restatement of "harmful")
  IV. Conclusion

Next, each of your major headings can be divided into subheadings by referring to your original list of ideas:

    I. Introduction
   II. Advantages of tourism
      A. Tourists spend money.
      B. Tourist industry creates jobs.
  III. Disadvantages of tourism
      A. Tourism inflates prices.
      B. Economy based on tourism is unstable.
  IV. Conclusion

This outline organizes an approach to the topic. If it were used as the basis for an essay, it would ensure that the overall organization of the essay is sound.

A diagram that matches key words in the thesis statement and the outline can show how the outline ties ideas together:

*Thesis:* Tourism in Hollow Hills is both helpful and harmful...
*Key words:* helpful    harmful

   II. Advantages
      A. Tourists spend money.
      B. Tourist industry provides jobs.
  III. Disadvantages
      A. Inflated prices.
      B. Boom-bust economy.

Different kinds of thesis statements will produce different outlines, and these outlines in turn will provide various structures for the development of ideas. But in every case, the thesis statement's key words or phrases should be tied directly to the outline headings.

## Outlines and Development

The methods of developing ideas in an essay are the same as those used in organizing details in a paragraph. The model essay on tourism illustrates comparison and contrast development. Other types of development can be outlined as follows:

### Cause and Effect

*Thesis:* Effect X was caused by A, B, and C.
    I. Introduction
    II. Cause A
    III. Cause B
    IV. Cause C
    V. Conclusion

### Process

*Thesis:* Goal Y can be achieved through three steps.
    I. Introduction
    II. Step 1
    III. Step 2
    IV. Step 3
    V. Conclusion

### Definition

*Thesis:* Item Z can be defined according to two qualities.
    I. Introduction
    II. Quality 1
    III. Quality 2
    IV. Conclusion

### Classification

*Thesis:* That experience can be understood in terms of the length of time it takes to happen.
    I. Introduction
    II. Short time
    III. Medium time
    IV. Long time
    V. Conclusion

### Examples

*Thesis:* X is a magnificent achievement.
    I. Introduction
    II. Example 1
    III. Example 2
    IV. Example 3
    V. Conclusion

After you have shaped an outline so that the key words in your thesis statement are tied directly to the headings in the outline, one last step can be taken. Each of the subheadings can be formulated as main idea sentences so that when you write your essay, you will know exactly what each paragraph will say.

*Thesis:* Tourism in Hollow Hills is both helpful and harmful to the local economy.

*Key words:* helpful, harmful
  I. Introduction
  II. Advantages
     A. One advantage is that the money spent by tourists feeds the local economy.
     B. Another advantage is that the tourist industry provides jobs for local residents.
  III. Disadvantages
     A. A disadvantage is that the local merchants raise prices to an inflated level.
     B. Another disadvantage is that the local economy becomes dependent on external factors like weather and availability of gasoline.
  IV. Conclusion

Each of these main idea sentences can then help you compose paragraphs according to any of the methods of paragraph patterning and development discussed earlier (Chapters 9 and 10).

## WRITING EXERCISE

I. Develop your own thesis statements for the following:

A. Friendship

   Thesis statement _____

   _____

B. Financial security

   Thesis statement _____

   _____

C. Neighborhoods

   Thesis statement _____

   _____

D. Peer pressures

   Thesis statement _____

   _____

E. Career choices

   Thesis statement _____

   _____

II. Develop outlines for each of the thesis statements above. Begin by filling in the major headings.

A. Friendship

Thesis statement _____

_____

Key words _____

I. Introduction

II.

III.

IV.

V. Conclusion

B. Financial security

Thesis statement _____

_____

Key words _____

I. Introduction

II.

III.

IV.


V. Conclusion

C. Neighborhoods

Thesis statement _____

_____

Key words _____
I. Introduction


II.


III.


IV.


V. Conclusion

D. Peer pressures

Thesis statement _____

_____

Key words _____
I. Introduction


II.

III.


IV.


V. Conclusion

E. Career choices

Thesis statement _____

_____

Key words _____

I. Introduction


II.


III.


IV.


V. Conclusion

III. Fill in subheadings for one of the outlines in Exercise II.

Topic _____

Thesis statement _____

_____

I. Introduction

II. A.

B.

C.

III. A.

B.

C.

IV. A.

B.

C.

V. Conclusion

IV. Write the essay outlined above in Exercise III. Underline the thesis statement as it appears in the introduction and the conclusion.

# Appendix A
## Study Skills

PREVIEW

Students are expected to read textbooks, take notes, and take tests in school. The purpose of this appendix is to provide methods, suggestions, and procedures for accomplishing these tasks systematically.

**Key Terms**

> **SQ3R method of textbook reading.** A well-known method consisting of five steps—survey, question, read, recite, and review—for reading and studying textbook chapters or sections.
> **Speedwriting.** A fast system for taking notes during a classroom lecture; requires the user to eliminate vowels and use only consonants.
> **Objective tests.** Tests that have multiple-choice, fill-in, true-false and matching questions.
> **Essay tests.** Tests that require answers in composition form.
> **Directional vocabulary.** Words in essay questions that tell the student how the essay should be developed. Words like "compare," "enumerate," "criticize," "summarize," are examples of directional vocabulary.

Teachers expect students to be able to do three things: read textbooks, take notes, and take tests. Nearly every course involves these three study skills. The purpose of this appendix is to provide useful suggestions and strategies for each of these tasks.

# A METHOD FOR READING AND STUDYING TEXTBOOKS

A well-known method for reading and studying textbook material is called the *Survey Q3R method* or simply *SQ3R*.* It is designed to help students understand and retain textbook material by using a system or series of steps to guide them as they read and study. There are five steps to be followed: *survey, question, read, recite, review.*

### Step 1. Survey

This first step involves obtaining an overview of the chapter or section to be read. To do this, follow this guide:

- Read the title or heading of the chapter or section.
- Read the introductory sentence(s) or paragraph(s) that explain the scope and objective of the chapter.
- Read each of the subtitles or subheadings throughout the chapter or section.
- Take notice of any illustrations like maps, charts, tables, graphs, time lines, and so on that are part of the chapter or section.
- Read the summary that highlights the main points of the chapter or section.
- Skim the chapter or section for unfamiliar vocabulary or review the vocabulary list if one is provided.

The survey step gives the student a good idea of what the assignment is about. While it is not part of the careful reading the student will begin doing in step 2, it does allow time to "get ready to read and study."

### Step 2. Question

Textbooks are organized so that a large body of information is broken down into smaller units, each with its own title or heading. They are called *subtitles* or *subheadings* because they come under the broader chapter or section title or heading. These subtitles, when turned into questions, provide a purpose for reading: to answer specific questions about what is read. To accomplish this step,

- Locate the first subtitle or subheading.
- Turn that subtitle or subheading into a question using any one of these question words: "what," "where," "how," "why," "was," "did," "is," "who," "when." The word you choose should create a question, not change the intended meaning of the subtitle or subheading.
- Write the question down and leave enough space to write an answer.

*Developed by Francis P. Robinson and modified to include additional suggestions.

## Step 3. Read

Now read the information below the subtitle or subheading. As you read,

- Underline those words, phrases or sentences that you think answer the question.
- Make notes in the margin in your own words to clarify or explain the reading further.
- Make a note of examples or details that may be useful in answering the question.
- Stop reading when you reach the next subtitle or subheading.

## Step 4. Recite/Write

Now that you have read this first section, see if you can

- Close the book and answer the question you created from the subtitle.
- Use your own words to do so.
- Write down an answer that you think answers the question.

Repeat steps 2, 3, and 4 for each subtitle following the first.

## Step 5. Review

Now that your reading is complete, reexamine your notes. You should check to see that

- You have answered each question you created from the subtitles.
- Your responses should directly answer each question.
- Your answers should include those details and/or examples needed to enhance your understanding of what has been read.

Reviewing these notes just after reading and over a period of time should help you retain what has been read.

There are several advantages in using the SQ3R method. First, you approach the task of textbook reading with a system or strategy that makes it possible to begin the task with confidence. Second, SQ3R helps concentration. Each step requires doing something: create a question, read to answer the question, review to check answers to the questions created. Third, the method can help you focus on those parts of the reading that caused difficulty. If a question could not be answered or the answer was not understood, you can identify the difficulty and get help. Fourth, the SQ3R helps you anticipate the questions that could possibly be part of an exam based on the assignment. Answering subtitle questions gives you practice in answering questions about the material. And finally, the technique helps you prepare study notes in question and answer form for purposes of review.

## A METHOD FOR TAKING NOTES

Along with the notes taken when reading assigned textbook material, the notes taken in class usually constitute a student's resources for preparing for exams or, more generally, for understanding the body of information in a course. Therefore, acquiring a method for taking good notes in class is a necessity. The following suggestions will help you formulate such a method:

1. Use 8½ × 11 notebook paper. Title it with class, date, or whatever information is needed to distinguish the notes you take from others for another course or class.
2. Write your notes so that you leave space in the left margin. This space can be used to jot questions, write in key words, or add information at a later time.
3. Listen carefully. As you listen, write down main ideas. Teachers usually give cues when they state main ideas. Voice inflection, a slowing of pace, and repetition of key words, phrases, or sentences let you know what is important and what is not.
4. Details and examples are important. Make a note of them. If a new main idea is being presented and you are still jotting notes about a detail, skip several lines and go on to the next main point. You can get the detail you missed later and it will be that much easier because you did get the main idea related to it.
5. Try to write your notes legibly to avoid the frustration of not being able to read what you've written. Teachers talk faster than you can take notes. If you find yourself forced to scribble, then use a simple method of speedwriting: leave out all vowels except those that begin or end a word, or those that are needed to distinguish one word from another. For example: legal = lgl; democracy = dmcrcy; sentences = sntncs; avoid frustration, use speedwriting = avd frstrtn, use spdwrtng.
6. Rewrite your notes. If you use speedwriting, you will need to rewrite your notes for more fluent reading as you study. Rewriting your notes has several advantages. First, it gives you an opportunity to reorganize notes that were not well organized when you took them. Second, it reinforces the thoughts and ideas communicated in class and helps you to remember them. Third, rewriting may point up errors or confusions you have about what was said. If you do not rewrite, you may not discover these errors or confusions until time to prepare for the exam. Rewriting should be done before the next class so that questions you may have are cleared up before it's too late.

7. It is not necessary to put notes in outline form, but for some students outlining helps. Outlining makes it easier to locate and distinguish main points from details and examples. If you do decide to use an outline, use it when you rewrite your notes so that you may take full advantage of the outline's organization.
8. Keep your notes simple. Aside from complex concepts or abstractions you must learn, and therefore write in complicated sentences, keep the language of your notes simple so that you can understand and/or memorize information easily.

Notetaking requires practice. These eight suggestions should make your notetaking easier and more effective.

## PREPARING FOR AND TAKING TESTS

Preparing for exams requires intellectual, psychological, and physical readiness. Although the greater part of this section deals with intellectual preparation, some suggestions about psychological and physical preparation are appropriate.

Taking tests causes anxiety and stress in many people. Tests are used in many areas of our society, and they create competition, which can result in stress. Studies show that clear thinking cannot take place during periods of high anxiety. Therefore, your first step in preparing to take a test is to relax. Realize that your worry will change nothing; it will only prevent you from performing well. See the test as a useful means by which you can measure how much you have learned. Allow yourself sufficient time to study for the test. Do not try to cram or be a hero by staying up all night studying. Physical fatigue affects your mental ability, so get plenty of rest. Most of all, believe in yourself. Know that you can pass the test because you will be prepared for it.

### Objective Tests

Objective tests are those that require the student to answer multiple-choice, fill-in, true-false, and matching questions. Questions on objective tests usually have only one correct answer and are easily scored. These tests are called "objective" because no bias or personal prejudice on the scorer's part can affect the grade. Everyone has an equal chance to pass or fail an objective test.

To prepare for the objective test, these procedures should be followed:

1. Study everything. Since questions can be asked about any part of the subject, you should be prepared with knowledge about important topics as well as details and examples.
2. Use everything at your disposal to get information about the types of questions the teacher may use in the test. Class notes, quizzes, students who have already taken the course, and the teacher may provide you information of this kind.
3. Review your class notes and textbook notes carefully. Make certain that they are up to date and completed.

When taking the objective test, these procedures should be followed:

1. Read all the directions for all parts of the test carefully. Students very often lose credit because they fail to read and follow directions. Make sure you understand what to do before you start.
2. Check the point values for each part of the test. Then do the parts of the test according to the amount of credit given. Do those parts given the most credit first and those with the least credit last. In this way you will complete the most valuable part of the test even if time runs out.
3. Divide the remaining time into three segments. Do this so you can answer questions of varying difficulty during these segments.
4. Answer easy questions first. These are questions whose answers you know right away, automatically. Answering these first builds confidence and helps you avoid losing points. It also gives you more time to deal with questions that are not so easily answered.
5. Next answer more difficult questions. As you go through the test again, do those questions that require some brief thought to answer. Answering these questions and those that are easiest for you ensure getting the most credit on the test.
6. Answer the most difficult questions last. Take time to rephrase them if necessary and to think through each possible answer. Notice the use of absolute and conditional words and choose an answer that uses conditional words like "may," "might," "usually," "generally," "often." These words increase your chances of answering correctly. If no penalty is given for wrong answers, answer all these questions. You may be lucky and get some right.
7. Use any remaining time to review your paper. Be sure you have followed directions and answered all questions, but be careful *not* to change answers unless you are positive they are wrong.

## Essay Tests

Essay tests require the student to write compositions in response to questions. Even though the student must be careful to keep track of time, a primary disadvantage when taking essay tests, such tests do have several advantages.

When preparing for the test, the student enjoys the following advantages:

1. Overall preparation may be done in advance. Class and textbook notes can be reviewed and a list of topics can be developed. Unlike the objective test, the essay test consists of a limited number of questions. The carefully prepared student will develop questions from the list of topics before the test.
2. Since definitions and key terms are often the basis of essay tests, the student can study these before the test. Even if certain terms are not part of the questions, they can be incorporated into the answers given for other questions.
3. For each of the questions you have developed for the topics covered in class and in the textbook, you can prepare an outline. This procedure provides further practice for answering essay type questions.
4. For a few of your prepared questions, write out the answers in essay form. Then read your answers to eliminate unnecessary words or ideas and to check for clarity and logic.

Even though essay tests require lengthy responses in the form of compositions, preparing for them properly gives the student a measure of control over the grade he or she receives. To take the essay test, follow these procedures:

1. Allot enough time to do each essay thoroughly. Make your time allotments according to the point values for each question. If all the questions are given equal credit, spend equal time on each. Be careful not to run out of time.
2. Underline directional vocabulary in each question. Directional vocabulary includes words that tell the student how the essay should be developed. The following words are those most frequently used. Memorize their meanings and be careful to develop your essay in keeping with what such vocabulary directs you to do.

| | |
|---|---|
| **Compare** | Emphasize the similarities and differences between and among things. |
| **Contrast** | Emphasize the differences between and among things. |
| **Criticize** | Express your opinion as to the truth, faults, or merits of an issue. |
| **Define** | Give the meaning of a word or concept; place in the class or category that sets it apart from other things. |
| **Describe** | Recount; relate in sequence or story form; give an account of; tell about. |
| **Diagram** | Provide a drawing, chart, or plan of. |
| **Discuss** | Examine, analyze carefully; talk over; consider from various points of view. |
| **Enumerate** | List, number, name. |
| **Evaluate** | Give the good and bad points; give an opinion regarding the value of; cite advantages and disadvantages. |

| | |
|---|---|
| **Explain** | Make clear, spell out, interpret, tell. |
| **Illustrate** | Use a concrete example like a picture, diagram, chart, or figure to clarify an idea or issue, or use specific references to printed material for the same purpose. |
| **Justify** | Give reasons or evidence to support your position, conclusions, or decisions. |
| **Summarize** | Give main points in concise form. |
| **Trace** | Follow the course, trail, or development of. |

3. Outline or make note of all the ideas you want to include in each essay before you write it. Do all your outlines first. Sometimes additional ideas will come to you as you outline another answer. You have time to add these ideas to the outline before you begin writing.

4. Write your answers. Make sure that you get right to the heart of the questions in your opening sentences. Including key words from the questions in these sentences means you will not stray from the question. Write clearly and logically. Use transitions like "however," "therefore," "moreover," "in addition," and other coherence devices to create a unified composition. Try to avoid crossing out and other sloppy corrections; they create a less than favorable impression in the mind of the scorer.

5. Review your answers. Before you hand in your paper, check to see that you have answered the number of questions required, that you have answered each question completely, and that you have answered the question that was asked. Check your grammar, spelling, and punctuation before turning in your paper.

The study skills discussed here are those that will be required of you for nearly every course you take. Take time to study the suggestions and procedures offered. Using these skills effectively will give you better grades and increased academic success.

# Appendix B
# Punctuation and Usage

PREVIEW

Effective writing depends upon clear thinking, precise choice of words, appropriate and varied sentence structure, and the organization of ideas into well-developed paragraphs. These elements are the basis of good writing. However, punctuation and usage are also important. Without them, clear writing would be impossible.

*Punctuation* is the system of symbols that has developed over the centuries to help indicate the relationship of one part of a sentence to another, and to separate individual sentences from each other.

*Usage* is the application of a standard of grammatical correctness to the language. The natural structure of the language permits different ways of shaping words into sentences. Usage establishes certain choices as more acceptable than others. Within these acceptable choices, correctness can be further divided into formal and informal levels. The most important areas of concern for usage questions include subject-verb agreement, pronoun reference and agreement, and modifiers.

Adding the refinements of accurate punctuation and informed usage choices to your writing will improve your ability to communicate on paper. Sensitivity to these qualities in the material you read will also aid your comprehension of others' writing.

**Key terms**

    **Punctuation.**   A system of symbols that indicates the relationship of sentence parts.
    **Usage.**   Choices of acceptable grammatical options.

# PUNCTUATION

In English, puncutation marks occur at the end of a sentence, or at various places within a sentence. They include the following:

| | |
|---|---|
| period | . |
| question mark | ? |
| exclamation point | ! |
| comma | , |
| semi-colon | ; |
| colon | : |
| parentheses | ( ) |
| brackets | [ ] |
| dash | — |
| apostrophe | ' |
| quotation marks | " " |

These punctuation marks serve two purposes: they indicate grammatical structure, and they help avoid confusion. Knowing them and how they are used will enable you to read more efficiently and to understand an author's message more easily. Careful and correct use of these marks will clarify your own writing and assist your reader in understanding your ideas.

## End Punctuation Marks

The period [.], question mark [?], and exclamation point [!] are all found at the ends of sentences. They indicate that the sentence is finished, and they also tell the reader whether the sentence makes a statement, asks a question, or carries special importance.

Sentences that make statements end with periods:

> Today is Tuesday.
> According to the laws of inertia things in motion tend to stay in motion.
> One person's garbage is another person's treasure.

Sentences that ask questions end with a question mark:

> What day is it?
> Who is it?
> Is that true?

Sentences that carry special emphasis end with exclamation points:

> I don't believe a word of it!
> That was a fantastic show!
> Leave that alone!

Periods are also used with shortened spellings to indicate abbreviations of individual words:

| | |
|---|---|
| Master | Mr. |
| Wednesday | Wed. |
| New Mexico | N.M. |

## Internal Punctuation Marks

Commas (,), semi-colons (;), colons (:), parentheses (()), brackets ([]), and dashes (—) all occur within a sentence rather than at the end of it.

*Commas.* Commas *always* occur within a sentence. Commas are used for a number of reasons. They are used after an introductory word or phrase before the subject:

| Introductory Word(s) | Subject | Rest of Sentence |
|---|---|---|
| Then, | I | knew everything. |
| On the other hand, | they | were unsure. |

In a similar way, commas are placed after subordinate clauses that precede the main clause of a sentence:

| Subordinate Clause | Main Clause |
|---|---|
| If prices continue to rise, | a loaf of bread will soon cost a couple of dollars. |
| Whenever a new television series is introduced, | the network describes it as the most exciting new show ever. |

If the subordinate clause follows the main clause, there is generally no comma between the clauses: "A loaf of bread will soon cost a couple of dollars if prices continue to rise."

Commas are placed before a coordinating conjunction that separates two independent clauses:

| Independent Clause A | Conjunction | Independent Clause B |
|---|---|---|
| The wind howled, | and | the rain poured down. |
| Elected officials should be responsible, | for | their actions affect many people. |

A pair of commas is used to set off words or phrases that provide additional information in a sentence when this information is clearly useful but not necessary:

> If you drink too much coffee, *more than a couple of cups a day*, you may feel unusually tense or nervous.
> Good literature, *like good wine*, improves with age.

Similarly, a pair of commas can be used to set off transitional words or phrases:

> That book, *on the other hand*, is not worth the paper it is printed on.
> The hot weather, *moreover*, continued much longer than expected.

Commas are used to set off items in a list:

> Among my favorite things are *music, good food*, and *interesting people*.
> The movie will be shown at *8 p.m., 10 p.m.*, and *midnight*.

*Semi-colons.* Semi-colons separate two independent clauses when co-ordinating conjunctions are not used:

| Independent Clause A | Independent Clause B |
|---|---|
| The first attempt was difficult; | the second was almost impossible. |

Often, such sentences will have an adverb between the clauses, but these sentences still require a semi-colon:

| Independent Clause A | Independent Clause B |
|---|---|
| I tried many times; | *finally,* I succeeded. |
| We searched everywhere; | *however,* we could not find the missing book. |

Semi-colons are also used to separate complicated items in a series:

> I looked for a job on Monday, when the agencies were jammed; on Tuesday, when fewer jobseekers were present; and on every other day of the week until only the most persistent job hunters were still trying on Friday.

*Dashes and Parentheses.* Both dashes and parentheses are used in pairs, and both separate information that is additional or explanatory from the rest of a sentence. Commas are also sometimes used for this purpose, but the information they separate is more immediately relevant to the sentence than that which is set off by dashes and parentheses:

| Comma | We left on Saturday, the first available day, so that we would have the whole weekend for the trip. |
|---|---|
| Dashes and Parentheses | We left on Saturday—it was late September—so that we would have the whole weekend for the trip. |
| | We left on Saturday (it was late September), so that we would have the whole weekend for the trip. |

Dashes and parentheses are just about interchangeable: where you can use one, usually you can use the other. The visual difference between the two can provide a basis for choice. Dashes make the material they enclose seem more separate from the surrounding sentence, while parentheses seem to indicate that the material they include is more a part of the surrounding context.

One other point of difference can be noted. A single dash can set off information at the end of a sentence:

> We looked in every room—except where the child was hiding.

Parentheses are preferred to set off dates and numbers:

We ordered thirty (30) new machines.

The article appeared in the August (1980) issue of *Field and Stream*.

*Colons.* Colons introduce additional information in the form of a list or a series, or in an independent clause that explains another clause:

> I decided I would need to buy the following things for my trip to Florida: new luggage, two bathing suits, and lots of sun-tan lotion.
>
> There was nothing more I could say: the time for apologies was over.

Colons are also used between hours and minutes, after the salutation in letters, and after the names of characters in scripts:

| | |
|---|---|
| Hours and minutes | 8:20 P.M. |
| | 3:34 A.M. |
| Salutation | Dear Ms. Burner: |
| Script | JOHN: What can you mean by that? |
| | JOE: Nothing, nothing at all. |
| | JOHN: It sure didn't sound like nothing. |

*Quotation Marks.* These marks are put around a word or words to show that the indicated material deserves special attention. Usually, quotation marks tell the reader that the material is being repeated from an oral or written source:

| | |
|---|---|
| Oral: | He said, "It's never too late to learn something new." |
| Written: | In his article, Professor Jones notes, "Educators, at all levels, must place renewed emphasis on basic communication skills." |

Notice that a comma usually precedes the quoted material.

Sometimes, you will want to indicate that somebody quoted a third party. For such a situation, you use single quotation marks within the usual double quotation marks.

> She said, "I heard Jane yell out 'Later' to Roger as he walked away."

## Quotation Marks and Other Punctuation Marks

Most often, as in the examples above, the quoted material will have a period before the closing quotation marks:

> The jury said, "The verdict is guilty."

This period punctuates the sentence as well as the quoted material. Other end punctuation marks can be used the same way:

> The judge exclaimed, "You have been found guilty!"
> The prisoner said in disbelief, "Guilty?"

Less frequently, you will want to show that the sentence in which a quotation occurs is itself a question. In such cases, the question mark comes *after* the second quotation mark:

> Do you think he could have said "Never"?

When the attribution—that is, the subject and verb which identify the speaker—comes in the middle of a quotation, commas separate the quoted material from the attribution:

> "Close the door," he said, "before all the heat escapes from the room."

# CAPITALIZATION

Letters can be upper case (capital letters), or lower case. Capital letters, when they are used, are always at the beginning of a word:

> Maple Avenue
> December
> ABC Building Company

Most often capital letters indicate proper nouns—the names of particular persons, places, or things:

> Maple Avenue
> December
> Joanna Jones
> Mars
> Rangers

When these words do not apply to a particular person, place, or thing, the nouns begin with lower case rather than capital letter:

> I walked past the maple tree on the side of Maple Avenue.

The following types of proper nouns are usually capitalized:

| | |
|---|---|
| Names of individuals | John Smith |
| Names of peoples | Iroquois, German, Hispanic |
| Names of places | Paraguay, Mississippi River, New York City, Africa |

Titles of office are capitalized when they are followed by the name of a particular person:

> President Kennedy
> Pope John
> Queen Elizabeth

They are, however, lower case when no particular person is indicated:

> The president of the club resigned.

Here are some other words that are usually capitalized:

| | |
|---|---|
| Sections of the Bible | Genesis |
| | Revelation |
| Holidays | Fourth of July |
| | Labor Day |
| Days and months | Saturday |
| | April |
| Historical or literary periods | Middle Ages |
| | Romanticism |
| Planets and constellations | Jupiter |
| | Little Dipper |
| Geographical areas | Middle East |
| | the Orient |

## SUBJECT-VERB AGREEMENT

Subjects and verbs should agree—that is, be the same—in *number* and *person*. English has two numbers: singular and plural. It has three persons: first, second, third. If a subject is singular, its verb should be singular; if a subject is plural, its verb should be plural:

> *Singular:* The show opens tonight.
> *Plural:* Two shows open tomorrow.

Notice that verbs show singular number by adding an "s" in the present tense:

| | |
|---|---|
| singular (third person present) | opens |
| plural (all persons) | open |

Nouns show plural number by adding an "s":

| | |
|---|---|
| singular | show |
| plural | shows |

Subjects and verbs should also agree in person as well as in number. The three persons indicate the speaker, the person spoken to, and the person spoken about:

| | | |
|---|---|---|
| First person singular | I | the speaker |
| First person plural | we | |
| Second person singular | you | person spoken to |
| Second person plural | you | |
| Third person singular | he, she, it | person spoken about |
| Third person plural | they | |

Only the personal pronouns included in the list above have forms for these categories; other pronouns and nouns indicate number but not person. Also, only the common verb "to be" changes form for different persons; other verbs change form only in the third person singular:

| Personal pronouns with "be": | **Singular** | **Plural** |
|---|---|---|
| First person | I am | we are |
| Second person | you are | you are |
| Third person | he, she, it is | they are |

| Personal pronouns with "walk": | **Singular** | **Plural** |
|---|---|---|
| First person | I walk | we walk |
| Second person | you walk | you walk |
| Third person | he, she, it walks | they walk |

## PROBLEM AREAS

Although subject-verb agreement is usually a simple matter, some situations can be confusing.

**Compound Subjects**

A compound subject includes two subjects combined by a connective word. Since two subjects are involved, compound subjects are regularly followed by plural verbs:

| **Subject** | **Verb** | **Rest of Sentence** |
|---|---|---|
| John and Jim | *are* | friends. |
| Eating and drinking | *are* | habit forming. |

Sometimes compound subjects are joined by conjunctions that separate the subjects into different categories. Correlative conjunctions ("either/or" "neither/nor") are often used for this purpose:

| | | |
|---|---|---|
| John or Jim | *is* | right. |

In these situations, the compound subject is broken into distinct units by the conjunction "or." Because only one verb follows the compound subject, the rule is to have it agree with the subject closest to it. This rule is most meaningful when the two subjects are of different number or person:

| Subject | Verb | |
|---|---|---|
| John or his friends | *are* | right. |
| Either his friends or John | *is* | right. |
| Either Jane or I | *am* | right. |
| Either I or Jane | *is* | right. |

**Modified Subjects**

Many sentences have subjects that are modified by an adjective, a phrase, or even a clause. Subjects modified by adjectives pose few problems.

John is hungry.
Big John is hungry.
Big, bad John is hungry.

But when a subject is modified by a group of words that contains another word which looks like a subject, the agreement of the verb can be a little more difficult to determine:

John, of all of his friends, is likely to succeed.

In such constructions, the object of the explanatory phrase is sometimes mistaken for the true subject because it is closer to the verb. These "false subjects" usually come at the end of prepositional phrases. Notice that in such sentences, the true subject will still form a sentence if the prepositional phrase is removed, but the phrase will not form a sentence if the true subject is removed:

John, of all his friends, is likely to succeed.
John is likely to succeed.
Of all his friends is likely to succeed.

In the following sentences, the verb agrees with the true subject:

Jill along with Jack *was* bruised after falling down the hill.
The dog, together with its puppies, *was* lost in the snow.

The same reasoning explains agreement with subjects modified by other kinds of phrases and clauses:

I, faced with monumental obstacles, *am* unsure how to continue.

James, who lost all his money, *faces* another day with hope.

Of all the men in the room he, whom I had not seen for years, *was* the one who rose to greet me.

## Collective Nouns and Indefinite Pronouns

A *collective* noun is one that has a singular form, but refers to more than one person or thing. Common collective nouns include the following:

| | |
|---|---|
| jury | committee |
| family | team |
| band | audience |
| class | flock |
| group | |

Each of these words describes a collection of individual persons, animals, or things that functions as a unit. A basketball team, for example, consists of five individual players who work together to win a game. Because the meaning of the word emphasizes the unit, such words are generally understood as taking a singular verb.

The team *is* doing well this year.

The jury *has* reached a verdict.

The group *was* late arriving to class.

Before the curtain rose, the audience *was* silent.

Since a collective noun describes a group, it is also possible that you would want to talk about more than one such unit. In such a case, you would follow the usual rule for plurals:

The team*s are* evenly matched.

Three separate group*s were* working on the problem.

Indefinite pronouns are like collective nouns. Here are some examples:

| | |
|---|---|
| anyone | everybody |
| anybody | none |
| someone | nothing |
| everyone | everything |
| each | |

Some of these pronouns clearly refer to one person ("anyone," "anybody," "someone") and pose no agreement problems. The verbs following these pronouns should always be singular. Others, however, like "everyone," "everybody," "everything," equally clearly refer to several people or things. Nonetheless, these pronouns are treated like collective nouns in that they are followed by *singular* verbs:

Everyone *was* ready for the test.
Everybody *is* welcome to come to the party.
Everything I owned *is* gone foreover.

A few of these pronouns can refer to one or to several people or things. Most common among these is "none." In the most formal situations, "none" is followed by a singular verb:

After the guest finished eating the dessert, none *was* left.

Sometimes, however, the pull of meaning is strong, and in more informal circumstances, a plural verb follows the pronoun:

None of the top 40 hits *were* played by the university radio station.

## Nouns with Plural Forms

Nouns regularly form plurals by adding an "s." Generally, a noun in the plural form demands a plural verb:

Dogs *are* popular pets.
The flowers *were* beautiful.

Certain nouns, however, have a plural form but a strong singular meaning. These nouns too are followed by plural verbs:

These trousers *are* torn.
My glasses *are* broken.

A few nouns in plural form have developed singular meaning strong enough to demand a singular verb:

The news *is* a nightly horrow show.
Economics *is* a meticulous discipline.

Other nouns in plural form are sometimes seen as plural, sometimes as singular:

| | |
|---|---|
| Singular | Measles *are* awful. |
| Plural | Measles *is* a horrible affliction. |
| Singular | Athletics *is* on the decline. |
| Plural | Athletics *are* very important in an educational program. |

In these cases, the choice between singular and plural involves a decision about emphasis. A singular verb underscores the collective aspect of the noun; a plural verb intensifies the idea of the individual parts that make up the group.

## Subject-Verb Reversal

A verb always agrees with its subject even when the normal subject-verb word order is reversed:

| | |
|---|---|
| Normal | Depression comes after many sorrows. |
| Reversed | After many sorrows comes depression. |

In the reversed sentence, the temptation might be to have "come" agree with "sorrows": "After many sorrows come depression." However, such a choice would be wrong, since "depression," and not "sorrows," is the subject. Always be sure to locate the subject of the sentence before choosing a number for the verb.

## Subject and Subjective Complement

When a subject is followed by a subjective complement of a different number, the verb agrees with the subject:

| Subject | Verb | Subjective Complement |
|---|---|---|
| Eggs | are | my favorite food. |
| A tree | is | different things to different people. |

The rule in these cases is clear enough, even though the correct sentence might sound awkward. In fact, the incorrect sentence will sound at least as awkward, if not more so. One solution would be to rewrite the information to avoid the problem: "Trees mean different things to different people."

## Expletive Constructions

Expletives occupy the place of a subject in a sentence, and the true subject then follows the verb. The most common expletive pattern begins with "there":

| Expletive | Verb | Subject | |
|---|---|---|---|
| There | is | a hole | in this shoe. |

Removing the expletive and placing the subject in its usual position shows why the verb should agree with the subject: "A hole is in this shoe."

In formal usage, the subject always agees with the verb in an expletive sentence. In more casual circumstances, a singular verb is sometimes found where a plural would be more formally correct:

| | |
|---|---|
| Informal | There *is* John, Jane, and Reginald. |
| Formal | There *are* John, Jane, and Reginald. |

## Subject-Verb Person Agreement

The person of a verb generally does not pose problems, but in sentences containing "be" and a compound subject of different persons, a choice has to be made:

Either you or I *am* to blame.
Either I or you *are* to blame.

The rule here is the same as that which governs agreement of number with compound subjects: the verb agrees in person with the subject closest to it.

## Relative Pronouns as Subjects

Relative pronouns ("who," "which," "that") are often subjects of clauses. Although these pronouns do not change to indicate number, the verbs they govern do. Relative pronouns have *antecedents*—that is, nouns or noun equivalents to which they refer: "He is the man *who* is the winner of the contest." Relative pronouns take the number of their antecedents; therefore, the verb they govern also takes the number of the antecedent. In the example above, "man" is singular, as is the verb "is" governed by the relative pronoun "who."

In some sentences, though, the antecedent is not as clearly established. The most common difficulty is encountered in sentences such as the following: "This is one of the books *which are* on my list to read." The rule is that pronouns agree with their antecedents (the nouns to which they refer) in person and number. In the sample sentence, the relative pronoun "which" refers to "books" and is therefore plural in number. "One" can also be considered the antecedent in such sentences, and then the verb following the relative pronoun is in the singular: "This is one of the books *which is* on my list to read."

Reversing the sentence, though, clearly indicates that the antecedent is usually the noun in the prepositional phrase: "Of the books which are on my list to read, this *is* one." This reversal separates the pronoun "one" from the noun "books," with which it can be confused, and demonstrates that the noun is the antecedent of the relative pronoun "which." Since the noun is plural, the verb governed by the relative pronoun should also be plural.

# PRONOUN REFERENCE

Most pronouns take the place of nouns; they are almost meaningless by themselves. A noun such as "dog" defines a particular class of domestic animals. But a pronoun such as "he" only identifies some masculine being, human or animal. Other pronouns, such as "it," "they," or "which," communicate even less meaning by themselves than does "he."

For pronouns to communicate clearly, they must refer to the noun they replace. They then communicate the same concept as does that noun. Pronouns should agree in number and person with the nouns they replace. Problems in pronoun usage usually arise because of reference and agreement.

**Faulty Pronoun Reference**

The noun to which a pronoun refers is called the *antecedent* of the pronoun. If a pronoun has no antecedent, the pronoun cannot communicate clearly: "She sang as I had never heard *it* sung before." In this sentence, "it" has no antecedent; the appropriate correction would be to add the missing antecedent: "She sang the *song* as I had never heard *it* sung before."

A common reference problem involves the relative pronouns "who," "which," and "that": "He finished early, *which* is exactly what he had intended." Here, "which" has no clear antecedent; rather, it seems to refer to the entire preceding clause. The sentence could be improved by rewriting it to eliminate the vague pronoun reference: "As he had intended, he finished early." Sometimes, the antecedent of a relative pronoun is unclear: "Our vacation ended well after its bad beginning *which* we had hoped for." Again, recasting the sentence takes care of the problem: "As we had hoped, our vacation ended well after its bad beginning."

A slightly different kind of problem is illustrated in the following sentence: "She and her mother often fought, but she always thought she was to blame." The problem here is too many "shes," so that it is unclear whether the pronouns refer to the mother or the daughter. A revision would eliminate the problem by repeating the noun: "She and her mother often fought, but she always thought her mother was to blame."

**Antecedent Agreement Problems**

Subject-verb agreement of relative pronouns was a problem discussed above; a different kind of agreement problem sometimes occurs in sentences such as the following: "He knew the boss liked *a hard worker* because *they* seemed to get promoted." In this sentence, the singular antecedent—"a hard worker"—is incorrectly followed by a plural pronoun—"they." The simplest solution in this case would be to make the antecedent plural: "He knew the boss liked *hard workers* because *they* seemed to get promoted."

Collective nouns and indefinite pronouns as antecedents also cause some difficulty. Collective nouns are singular in form but plural in meaning. This difference between form and meaning causes confusion when a pronoun replaces the noun: "The jury has reached *its/their* decision." The rule in these cases is clear. The verb governed by the collective noun is singular: "The jury *has.*" Similarly, the pronoun that replaces the collective noun should be singular:

> The jury has reached *its* decision.
> The committee is trying to find *its* direction.
> The team was happy with *its* victory.

> Certain indefinite pronouns also are treated like collective nouns:

> Everyone *is* ready to do *his* job.
> I will talk with anyone who *is* ready to do *his* work.

In these sentences, both the verbs and the pronouns which have indefinite pronouns as antecedents are in the singular.

The rule that demands a singular pronoun in the cases mentioned above has also prescribed a masculine pronoun. Of course, a feminine pronoun would make just as much sense, and be equally inaccurate. The compromise position is to use both gender pronouns, as has been the practice in this book: "Everyone is ready to do *his* or *her* job."

## SENTENCE ERRORS

Sentence errors can be divided into three categories: *fragments, comma splices,* and *run-ons.* Some of these problems are caused by faulty punctuation; others result from structural weaknesses.

### Fragments

Sentence fragments are words or phrases punctuated as sentences—that is, beginning with a capital letter and ending with a period. But these fragments do not contain an *independent* subject-verb relationship, and they therefore should be included in another sentence or rewritten so that they do make an independent subject-verb statement.

Some fragments are phrases:

> I love the morning sun. *Especially on a cold winter day.*

Such fragments are most easily corrected by attaching them to the sentence to which they naturally belong:

I love the morning sun, especially on a cold winter day.

Some fragments are clauses:

I bought the new amplifier. *Which I had wanted for a long time.*

The traffic on the expressway was stalled. *Because a truck had broken down in the right-hand lane.*

These clause fragments, like phrase fragments, can be attached to another sentence:

I bought the new amplifier which I had wanted for a long time.

The traffic on the expressway was stalled because a truck had broken down in the right-hand lane.

Another method of correction is to remove the introductory word and have the clause stand as its own sentence:

I bought the new amplifier. I had wanted it for a long time.

The traffic on the expressway was stalled. A truck had broken down in the right-hand lane.

This correction works because a clause contains a subject-verb relationship. The introductory words "which," "because," and others like "who," "that," "since," make the clauses subordinate and therefore dependent upon being attached to a main clause in a complex sentence. Complex sentences are generally more interesting stylistically than a series of very short and simple sentences so that usually a correction of a fragment which produces a complex sentence is desirable.

## Comma Splice

A comma splice combines two independent clauses: "The newspaper was difficult to read, it was soggy from the rain." A comma splice is a sentence error because two independent clauses require either a stronger mark of punctuation and/or a conjunction to combine them into one sentence:

| | |
|---|---|
| Semi-colon | The newspaper was soggy from the rain; it was difficult to read. |
| Coordinate conjunction | The newspaper was soggy from the rain, and it was difficult to read. |
| Subordinate conjunction | The newspaper was difficult to read because it was soggy from the rain. |
| Conjunctive adverb | The newspaper was soggy from the rain; therefore, it was difficult to read. |

Frequently comma splice problems arise in sentences containing conjunctive adverbs such as "however," "therefore," "moreover," and "consequently." These words are not true conjunctions, and when they are used to combine clauses, they must be punctuated with semi-colons as in the example above.

**Run-on Sentences**

A run-on sentence is similar to a sentence with a comma splice, except that it does not have the comma: "The newspaper was difficult to read it was soggy from the rain." The solutions for run-ons are the same as those for comma splices. The two clauses must be combined with a conjunction, and/or an appropriate punctuation mark.

**Check List for Sentence Errors**

1. Be sure every group of words that is punctuated as a sentence contains at least one subject-verb relationship.
2. Be careful to connect clauses beginning with "who," "which," "that," "because," "since," and so on to a main clause.
3. Combine independent clauses into one sentence with a conjunction or a semi-colon, or make them separate sentences.

# MODIFIERS

Modifiers are words or phrases that limit and refine the meanings of other words, phrases, or clauses. There are two broad categories of modifiers: (1) adjectives that modify nouns; (2) adverbs that modify verbs, adjectives, other adverbs, or clauses.

**Adjectives**

Adjectives are words or phrases that modify nouns. They occur either right before or right after the noun they modify, or they are separated from the noun by a linking verb:

| | |
|---|---|
| Before | *Big, tall* John entered the room. |
| After | John, *big* and *tall*, entered the room. |
| Linking verb | John was *big* and *tall*. |

## Adverbs

Adverbs are words or phrases that modify verbs, adjectives, other adverbs, or clauses. They can occur in a variety of positions:

| | |
|---|---|
| Verb | Susan spoke *softly* to her brother. |
| | Susan *softly* spoke to her brother. |
| | Susan spoke to her brother *softly*. |
| | *Softly*, Susan spoke to her brother. |
| Adjective | An *extremely* dedicated person is needed for this job. |
| | The night, *quite* black, descended on the town. |
| Adverb | After the accident, he was *barely* alive. |
| | Susan spoke *very* softly to her brother. |
| | He wrote *extremely* quickly. |
| Clause | *Generally*, dogs make good pets. |
| | *Usually*, hard work leads to success. |

## Problem Areas

Modifier problems arise because of position in the sentence, lack of a clear relationship between modifier and word or words being modified, and comparison of modifiers.

*Squinting Modifier.* This is a modifier, usually an adverb, which is so positioned in the sentence that it can modify what comes before or after it. The result is ambiguity and confusion:

| | |
|---|---|
| Unclear | He was sure *on Monday* they would have a chance to talk things out. |
| Clear | He was sure they would have a chance to talk things out *on Monday*. |

*Misplaced Modifier.* Some common adverb modifiers, such as "only," "just," and "nearly," can occupy a variety of positions within a sentence. In each position, though, the meaning of the sentence changes because a different part is modified by the adverb:

*Just* Mary finished her work on time.
Mary *just* finished her work on time.
Mary finished her work *just* on time.

Care must be exercised in placing these adverbs so that they modify what you want them to, and so that the sentence says what you intend it to.

*Dangling Modifiers.* A modifier must have something to modify. When it does not, it will appear to modify whatever comes next in the sentence:

| | |
|---|---|
| Dangling | *Climbing fast*, the mountain was soon behind him. |
| Revised | *Climbing fast*, he soon put the mountain behind him. |
| Dangling | *Rowing hard*, the boat swept over the waves. |
| Revised | *Rowing hard*, Jane swept the boat over the waves. |
| | Jane, *rowing hard*, swept the boat over the waves. |

*Comparison of Modifiers.* Adjectives and adverbs can be compared by adding "er" and "est," or by using "more" and "most." The choice between these two forms is usually based on the number of syllables in the modifier word. Longer words generally take the "more/most" comparative forms:

| **Adjective** | | **Adverb** | |
|---|---|---|---|
| big | difficult | fast | efficiently |
| bigger | more difficult | faster | more efficiently |
| biggest | most difficult | fastest | most efficiently |

Two common adjectives are compared by changing the words themselves:

| | |
|---|---|
| good | bad |
| better | worse |
| best | worst |

Only one of these comparative forms should be used:

| | |
|---|---|
| Error | She was the *most* happi*est* person in the family when she heard the good news. |
| Correct | She was the happi*est* person in the family when she heard the good news. |

*Adverb-Adjective Confusion.* Adverbs and adjectives have clearly defined modifier functions. However, in certain situations these functions are sometimes confused.

*Intensifier* adverbs are used to intensify the meaning of another modifier: "That steak was *extremely* tough." Using adjectives for this purpose, though, is a common mistake: "Cowboy Rex sells *real* good fast food" should be "Cowboy Rex sells *really* good fast food."

Verbs should be modified by adverbs, and not by adjectives:

| | |
|---|---|
| Error | He played the difficult piece *beautiful*. |
| Correct | He played the difficult piece *beautifully*. |

Adjectives, not adverbs, modify subjects of linking verb sentences:

|  | **Subject** | **Linking Verb** | **Modifier** |
|---|---|---|---|
| Error | She | felt | terribly. |
| Correct | She | felt | terrible. |

## PUNCTUATION AND USAGE EXERCISE

I. The following paragraph lacks both punctuation and appropriate capitalization. Rewrite the paragraph with proper punctuation and capitalization.

john was walking down elm street when he saw doctor wilkes the president of his college who stopped and asked him do you know what time it is my watch has stopped and i think i am late for a very important meeting john looked at his wrist for he had just bought a new digital watch 322 he said exactly thank you doctor wilkes exclaimed i am not as late as i thought moreover i may even have time for a cup of coffee would you care to join me although he was taken by surprise john said he would be glad to spend some time with president wilkes in fact he had a list of things he would like to discuss tuition costs outrageously expensive textbooks and inadequate heating in the classrooms and dorms john expected doctor wilkes to be taken aback the president though replied that these were all important issues and he would welcome the opportunity to discuss them with john.

II. Some of the following contain errors in subject-verb agreement and some are correct as they are. If the sentence is correct, put a C next to it. If it is not correct, rewrite it in the space provided.

1. Dogs and cats are said to be natural enemies.

2. Smoking, along with drinking, are not good for you.

3. Either rest or vitamins are better for you.

4. Hers, among all the entries in the contest, was the winner.

5. The jury were told to consider all the evidence.

6. The coach thought that the team, even with a tough schedule of opponents, was ready for the season.

Punctuation and Usage

7. Each of these apples look delicious.

8. None of the cake was left.

9. After the hot summer days comes the cold winter nights.

10. Good news, like dollar bills, are always welcome.

11. There are fire and smoke up ahead.

12. There is one thing I would like to know.

13. That song is one of a few which is surprisingly popular.

14. He is one of those people who have never won a prize.

15. Oranges is my favorite fruit.

III. Some of the following contain errors in pronoun usage and some are correct as they are. If the sentence is correct, put a C next to it. If it is not correct, rewrite it in the space provided.

1. As we had hoped, the weather, which had threatened rain, turned out to be fine.

2. We left early which had been our plan.

3. Everyone in the crowded room hoped they would be able to leave soon.

4. The team was proud of the way they had played.

5. The class was surprised to see their teacher so confused.

6. Anyone who is finished can close his or her book and leave.

7. The judge told the jury that its decision should be made solely on the basis of the evidence.

8. Our new car did not get good gas mileage which was very disappointing to us because the salesperson had said they would.

9. She hoped Stan and her father would get along well together but she knew how unpredictable he was.

10. The committee, after many weeks of work, finally finished its report.

IV. Some of the sentences below are correct and some are not. If the sentence is correct, put a C next to it. If it is not correct, rewrite it in the space provided.

1. Jean was really into jogging. Especially on warm spring mornings.

2. Because I was so late. We decided not to go shopping.

3. Shirley decided to go on a diet when she realized she would soon be going to the beach.

Punctuation and Usage

4. Sam liked to stay up late watching television when his last final was over he watched three reruns and one old movie.

5. I'm sure you'll like the book; everyone who has read it has been impressed.

6. The kids were excited about moving to a new neighborhood. Although they would be leaving many good friends behind.

7. *Hamlet* is truly a great play, moreover, it has a new message for each new generation.

8. Jason always rushed his work consequently he made a lot of mistakes.

9. The car seemed to be running badly even though it had just been tuned up.

10. George was sure his idea would work though he did not know whether it would be accepted, he felt he had to try.

V. Some of the sentences below contain modifier errors and some are correct. If the sentence is correct, put a C next to it. If it is not correct, rewrite it in the space provided.

1. We were only sure that John would do it.

2. Only Henry managed to finish the test.

3. He was convinced immediately that his day would come.

4. Last year, the store did well.

5. Studying as hard as possible, the book still didn't make sense to her.

6. Working at his own pace, Jason soon finished waxing the car.

7. That was the most difficult problem I have ever solved.

8. Young George was the least smartest student in the class.

9. The centerfielder made the most extraordinary catch I have ever seen.

10. That's a real good amplifier.

11. That old car still runs good.

12. That's a truly fine piece of work.

13. He found himself in an extremely intolerable position.

14. Don't you think that that picture looks well over there?

# Index

## A

Abbreviations:
  given in dictionaries, 31
  period used for, 250
Absolute language, 76, 77–78, 85–87, 89
Abstract words, 60, 67–68
Accuracy (factual), 85–86
Action sentence, 99, 100, 103–4, 110–11
Action with object sentence, 99, 100, 104–6, 111–12
Additional (explanatory) material of a sentence, punctuation of, 251, 252, 253
Adjectives, 265
  comparison of, 267
  confused with adverbs, 267–68
Adverbs, 266
  comparison of, 267
  confused with adjectives, 267–68
  conjunctive, 264–65
  intensifier, 267
Agreement:
  noun-pronoun, 262–63
  subject-verb, 255–60, 263
  subject-verb-person, 261
Analogy method of paragraph development, 173, 174, 177–78, 191–92
Antecedent of a pronoun, 262–63
Antonyms, 32, 43
  as context clue, 46–47
Apostrophe, 250
Attitude, emotional, shown by connotative words, 59–60, 62–64, 68–70

Author's purpose, 2, 19–21
  as determining paragraph patterns, 153–55
  recognizing, 19

## B

Balance of a paragraph, 152, 158
Bandwagon approach to persuasion, 11
Bible sections, capitalization of, 255
Brackets, 250

## C

Capitalization, 254–55
Card file, for learning new words, 28–30
Card stacking technique of persuasion, 11
Cause and effect method of paragraph development, 173, 174, 180–81, 195–97, 225, 234
Cause and effect relationships:
  incorrect, 91–92
  sentence devices to show, 120
Clarity of a paragraph, 152, 153, 154, 157
Classification, as a method of paragraph development, 173, 174, 179–80, 194–95, 225, 234
Clauses, 116, 121
  independent, 119, 128–29, 251, 252
  main, 251

  to modify subject, 257–58
  punctuation between, 251
  subordinate, 119, 128–29, 251
Clues, 28, 43, 46–48
Coherence of a paragraph, 204–17
  methods of, 204–5
Collective nouns, agreement with, 258, 262–63
Colon, 250, 253
Combined method of paragraph development, 181–82, 197
Comma(s), 250, 251, 252, 253, 254
Comma splice, 264–65
Communication:
  types of (listening, reading, etc.), 23–24
  units of (word, sentences, etc.), 44
  verbal and nonverbal, 84–85
Comparison (grammatical), of modifiers, 267
Comparison and contrast method of paragraph development, 173, 174, 175–76, 188–89, 225, 234
Complement, subjective, 260
Complex sentence, 116, 118–19, 121, 128–29
Compound sentence, 116, 117–18, 126–28
Compound subject, agreement with, 256–57
Concept context, 44, 53–54
Concluding paragraph of essay, 221, 222–24, 230
Conclusion, logical. *See also* Inference
  from deductive reasoning, 15–17
  from inductive reasoning, 14–15, 16–17

273

Conditional language, 76, 78–79, 85–87, 89
Conjunction:
  coordinating, 116, 117–18, 126–28
  correlative, 117, 118, 256–57
  to create compound subjects, 256–57
  subordinating, 117, 118–19, 128
Conjunctive adverbs, 264–65
Connotation, 59–60, 62–64, 66, 68–70
  determined by purpose, 62, 64, 69–70
Constellations, capitalization of, 255
Context, 24, 43
  clues from, 28, 43, 46–48
  dictionary to show, 45
  to distinguish meaning of words, 43–54, 59–60, 67–68
  types of, 44
  in vocabulary building, 28
Coordinating conjunction, 116, 117–18, 126–28
Correlative conjunction, 117, 118, 256–57
Correspondence, punctuation of, 253

## D

Dangling modifier, 266–67
Dash, 250, 251
Dates, punctuation of, 252–53
Days, capitalization of, 255
Deductive reasoning, 1, 15–17
  vs. inductive reasoning, 16–17
Definition (dictionary), 31, 43
Definition clue, 47
Definition method of paragraph development, 173, 174, 178–79, 192–94, 225, 234
Denotation, 59–62, 66–68
  determined by purpose, 62, 66, 69–70
Derivation of words, 31
Descriptive context, 44, 54
Details, in writing, 8–9
  arrangement of, 167–69
  in comparison/contrast, 189
  supporting topic sentence, 173, 174, 185–86, 212–13
Developing paragraphs of an essay, 221, 222–24, 230
Development:
  of an essay, 224–25, 229–35
  of a paragraph, 173–97, 225, 234
Dictionaries:
  layout and use of, 31–32, 87–88
  for meaning of words, 45, 87–88
  in vocabulary building, 30–32
Dilemma type of complex sentence, 121
Directional vocabulary, 241, 247–48
Direct statement, 138–39

## E

Either-or reasoning, 90–91
Emotional attitude, shown by connotative words, 59–60, 62–64, 68–70
Emphasis, 8
  exclamation point used for, 250
  in a paragraph, 152, 154
  simple sentences for, 127–28
End punctuation, 250
Entry (in dictionary), 31
Equation sentence, 99, 100, 102–3, 109–10
Errors, sentence, types of, 263–65
Essay(s), 220–35
  development of, 224–25, 229–35
  organization of, 221–24
  outlining of, 220, 223–24, 232–35
  paragraphs in, 220, 221–24, 230
Essay tests, 241, 246–47
Example (stylistic technique), 44
Example clue, 47–48
Examples, use of, as method of paragraph development, 173, 174–75, 186–88, 225, 234
Exclamation point, 250, 254
Expository writing, 220, 221
Explanatory material of a sentence, punctuation of, 251, 252
Expletive construction, 260

## F

Fact, 1, 76
  vs. opinion, 2–5
  probability of, 2–4
  stated in absolute language, 86, 89
First person, 255–56
Fragments, sentence, 263–64

## G

Generalization, faulty, 89–90
General statement, 136
General-to-specific reasoning, and vice versa, 14–17
Geographical areas, capitalization of, 255
Glittering generalities, 11
Grammatical forms of words (parts of speech), 31, 51–52

## H

Headings, major and sub-, 221
Historical periods, capitalization of, 255
Holidays, capitalization of, 255

## I

Ideas, of equal and unequal importance, how to relate, in sentences, 117–19, 126–29
Identification clause of a complex sentence, 120–21
Illustration (stylistic device), 44
Illustration clue, 47–48
Implied meaning, 6–7
Indefinite pronoun, agreement with, 258–59, 262–63
Independent clause(s), 119
  in complex sentences, 128–29
  punctuation between, 251, 252
Indirect statement, 140–41
Inductive reasoning, 1, 14–15
  and deductive reasoning, 16–17
Inference, 1, 5–9
  compared to implication, 6, 8, 9
Intensifier adverbs, 267
Internal punctuation marks, 251–54
Introductory paragraph of an essay, 221, 222–24, 230
Introductory words and phrases, comma after, 251
Items in a list, punctuation between, 251, 252

## J

Jargon context, 44, 52–53
Just-plain-folks approach to persuasion, 11

## L

Language:
  absolute and conditional, 76, 77–78, 85–87, 89
  denotative and connotative, 59–71
  persuasive, 1, 10–12, 90–91
Letter(s), capital and lower case, 254
Letters (correspondence), punctuation of, 253
Linking verb, 102, 110, 267–68
List, punctuation of items in, 251, 252, 253
Listening, in communication, 23
Listening vocabulary, 24
Literary periods, capitalization of, 255
Logic. *See also* Reasoning
  errors in, 89–92
  in sentences, 80–81, 89–92

## M

Main clause, comma to set off, 251
Main idea, 135–48. *See also* Thesis statement; Topic sentence
  expressed in a topic sentence, 136, 145

# Index

how to determine, 136–41
implied, 140
Major headings, 221
Making sense, 76–92
Methods of paragraph development, 173–97
Modification of subject, and agreement, 257–58
Modifiers:
 adjectives and adverbs, 265–66
 clauses, 257–58
 comparative forms of, 267
 dangling, 266–67
 problems with, 266–68
 specific and general, 36–37
 squinting (misplaced), 266
Months, capitalization of, 255

## N

Name calling, 11
Names, capitalization of, 254
Negative connotation, 60, 62–64
Neutral connotation, 60
*Non sequitur*, 92
Nonverbal communication, 84–85
Note taking, 241, 244–45
Nouns:
 agreement of, with pronoun, 262–63
 agreement of, with verb, 255–61, 263
 collective, 258
 plural forms, 259
 pronoun to replace, 207–8, 215–16, 261–63
 specific and general, 35–36
Number (grammatical), and agreement, 255
Number expressions, punctuation of, 252–53

## O

Object, of a sentence, 104
Objective test, 241, 245–46
Opinion, 1, 76
 vs. fact, 2–5
 judging the reasonableness of, 4–5
 stating, with conditional language, 86–87, 89
Organization of an essay, 221–24
Outlining an essay, 220, 221, 223–24, 232–35

## P

Paragraph(s), 135–48, 152–69
 arrangement of, in an essay, 220, 221–24, 230

coherence in, 204–17
details in, 167–69, 173, 174, 185–86, 212–13
development of, 173–97, 225, 234
main idea of, 135–48
patterns and types of, 152–58
topic sentence of, 135–48, 173, 174, 185–86
Parallel structure, 204, 208, 216–17
Parentheses, 250, 251–52
Parts of speech, 31, 51–52
Period, 250, 254
Periods, historical and literary, capitalization of, 255
Person (1st, 2nd, 3rd), agreement of, 255–56
Persuasive language, 1, 10–12
 detecting, 10
 logic errors in, 90–91
 techniques of, 11–12
Phrase, 117, 121, 129–31
 to modify subject, 257
Placement:
 of modifiers in sentence, 266–67
 of topic sentence in a paragraph, 135, 147–48, 152–58
Planets, capitalization of, 255
Plural-form nouns, 259
Plural number, 255
Positive connotation, 60, 62–64
Prefix, 24
 and vocabulary building, 25–26
Process method of paragraph development, 173, 174, 176–177, 190–91, 225, 234
Pronoun(s):
 agreement of, 258–59, 262–63
 antecedent of, 262–63
 faulty reference of, 261–63
 indefinite, 258–59
 relative, and agreement, 261
 to replace nouns, 207–8, 215–16, 261–63
Pronunciation, shown in dictionary, 31
Proof of facts, 2–4
Propaganda, 11–12
Proper nouns, capitalization of, 254
Punctuation, 250–54
 for effective writing, 249
 end punctuation, 250
 internal punctuation, 251–54
 list of types of, 250
Purpose, author's, 2, 19–21

## Q

Question mark, 250, 254
Question sentence, 250
Question stage of SQ3R, 242
Quotation marks, 250, 253–54
Quoted material, punctuation of, 253–54

## R

Reading:
 as a form of communication, 23
 SQ3R method, 241, 242–44
 in vocabulary building, 27–28
 types of, 28
Reading between the lines, 6–7
Reading stage of SQ3R, 243
Reading vocabulary, 24
Reasoning. *See also* Logic
 deductive, 1, 15–17
 inductive, 1, 14–15, 16–17
Recite/write stage of SQ3R, 243
Recreational reading, 28
Reference, faulty, of pronoun, 261–63
Relative pronoun, antecedent of, 261
Repetition of words, for coherence, 204, 205–6, 213–14
Replacing noun with pronoun, 207–8, 215–16
Reversal of subject and verb, 260
Review stage of SQ3R, 243
Robinson, Francis P., 242
Root, 24
 and vocabulary building, 25
Run-on sentence, 265

## S

Scripts of plays, punctuation of, 253
Second person, 255–56
Semicolon, 250, 252
Sense, making, 76–92
Sentence(s). *See also* Statements
 absolute and conditional, 77–79, 85–87, 89
 compound and complex, 116–19, 126–29
 errors in, 263–64
 fragments, 263–264
 logic in, and meaning of, 80–81, 89–92
 making sense with, 76–92
 punctuation of, 250–54
 relationship of ideas in, 117–21
 run-on, 265
 simple, 99–112, 116
 subject and verb in, 100–101
 types, forms, and constructions of, 99–112, 116–19
Sentence combining, 117, 121–23, 129–31
Simple sentence, 99–112, 116
Singular number, 255
Speaking, as a form of communication, 1, 23
Speaking vocabulary, 24
 contrasted to written vocabulary, 33
Specific definition in dictionary, 31
Specific statement, 136
Speech, parts of, 31, 51–52

Speedwriting, 241, 244
Squinting modifier, 266
SQ3R method, 241, 242–44
Statement(s). *See also* Sentences
   direct and indirect, 138–41
   of fact or opinion, 76–77
   general and specific, 136
   period used for, 250
Study reading, 28
Study skills, 241–248
Subheadings, 221
Subject (of a sentence), 99, 100, 109
   agreement of, with verb, 255–61, 263
   compound, 256–57
   modified by phrase or clause, 257–58
   relative pronoun as, 261
   reversal of, with verb, 260
Subjective complement, 260
Subject matter, influencing method of
   development, 173, 174
Subordinate clause, 119, 128–29
   comma used after, 251
Subordinating conjunction, 117, 118–19, 128
Suffix, 24
   in vocabulary building, 25–26
Surrounding words, and context, 52
Survey stage of SQ3R, 242
Survival reading, 28
Synonyms, 32, 43
   as context clue, 46

## T

Tension in a paragraph, 152, 153–54, 156
Testimonials, 11
Tests:
   essay and objective, 241, 245–48
   preparing for, 245–48

Textbooks, how to read, 241, 242–44
Thesaurus, 32, 88–89
Thesis statement, 220, 230–32
Thinking skills, 1–21
   in daily life, 1–2
Thinking skills checklist, 21–22
Third person, 255–56
Three questions
   to determine main idea, 136–38
   to formulate topic sentence, 145–47
Time (expressions of), punctuation of, 253
Time (grammatical), in a complex sentence, 119–20
Titles, capitalized, 255
Topic sentence, 135–48, 152–58
   composing, 166–67
   details to support, 167–69, 173, 174, 185–86, 212–13
   direct and indirect, 138–41
   as main idea, 135–48, 185
   placement of, 135, 136–38, 147–48, 152–58, 185
   and thesis statement, compared, 230
Total vocabulary, 24
Transitional words in a paragraph, 204, 206–7, 214–15
   comma to set off, 251

## U

Usage:
   correct grammar, 249, 258–68
   correct vocabulary, 32

## V

Verb(s), 99
   agreement of, with subject, 255–61, 263

forms of (conjugation), 256, 261
   linking, 102
   reversal of, with subject, 260
   in sentences, 99, 100, 109
   specific and general, 34–35
Verbal communication, 84–85
Verification of facts, 2–4
Vocabulary, *See also* Words
   building, 23–37, 44
   contribution of, to a sentence, 77, 79–80, 87–89
   directional, 241, 247–48
   types of, 24

## W

Wide reading, 27–28
Word(s). *See also* Vocabulary
   absolute and conditional, 78, 79
   abstract, 60, 67–68
   capitalized, 254–55
   choice of, 8, 87–89
   context of, to show meaning, 43–54, 59–60, 67–68
   denotation and connotation of, 59–70
   dictionaries to show usage of, 30–32
   learning new words, 23–37, 44
   specific (exact) vs. general, 33–37
Word economy, 121–23, 129–31
Writing:
   author's purpose in, 2, 19–21
   of essays, 229–35
   as a form of communication, 23
   importance of punctuation and usage in, 249
   of paragraphs, 165–69, 185–97, 212–17
   of sentences, 109–12, 126–31, 145–48
Writing vocabulary, 24
   improving, 33–37

## Acknowledgments, *continued*

PAGE 64: From *I Have a Dream* by Martin Luther King, Jr. Copyright © 1963 by Martin Luther King, Jr. Reprinted by permission of Joan Daves.

PAGES 64, 181–82: From *PREP: For Better Reading* by W. Royce Adams. Copyright © 1980 by Holt, Rinehart and Winston. Reprinted by permission of Holt, Rinehart and Winston.

PAGE 65: From *Are You Listening?* by Ralph G. Nichols and Leonard A. Stevens. Copyright © 1957, McGraw-Hill Book Company. Used with the permission of McGraw-Hill Book Company.

PAGE 65: Marilyn Manley, *Interpretation of Literary Materials*, 1974. Reprinted by permission of Cambridge Book Company.

PAGE 65: Jonathan H. Turner, *Studying the Human System*. Copyright © 1978 by Goodyear Publishing Company.

PAGES 66, 181: From *Certain People: America's Black Elite* by Stephen Birmingham. Copyright © 1977 by Stephen Birmingham. By permission of Little, Brown and Company.

PAGES 81, 83, 108, 177: Doris Wilcox Gilbert, *Breaking the Reading Barrier*, © 1959. Reprinted by permission of Prentice-Hall, Inc., Englewood Cliffs, New Jersey.

PAGE 107: Reprinted from *Reading for Concepts*, Book H, by William Liddle, copyright 1977, with permission of Webster/McGraw-Hill.

PAGE 107: From Book A of *Read Better—Learn More* by Theodore Clymer and others © copyright 1972 by Ginn and Company (Xerox Corporation). Used with permission.

PAGE 107: *The Changing World: North and South America*, "Riche Island" General Learning Corporation, 1970.

PAGE 108: William Ince and Roger Goodman, *How to Prepare for the Reading Skills Test, 1978*. From New High School Equivalency Examination. © Trafalgar House Publishing, Inc.

PAGE 108: "Cataclysm in a Corn Patch," Broadcast #2655, University of California Radio Service, 20 October 1946.

PAGE 138: "The War of the Noses" by Francesca Stanfill. © 1980 by The New York Times Company. Reprinted by permission.

PAGE 140: From Jessica Mitford, *The American Way of Death*, © 1963 by Simon & Schuster, Inc. Used with permission of the publisher.

PAGES 140–41: Reprinted by permission of Elsevier/Nelson Books from the book, *The World I Live In*. Copyright © 1935 by Helen Keller.

PAGE 141: "Winning the Fight Against Crib Death," by Jane M. Grogan and Marilyn Goldstein. Reprinted by permission of Newsday.

PAGE 142: "A Glass with a Racy Past" by Terry Robards, © 1980 by The New York Times Company. Reprinted by permission.

PAGE 143: John Hope Franklin, *From Slavery to Freedom: A History of Negro Americans*, 3rd edition. Copyright © 1967, Alfred A. Knopf, Inc. Reprinted by permission.

PAGES 143–44, 211: From *Sociology*, 2nd ed. by Paul Horton and Chester Hunt. Copyright © 1968, McGraw-Hill Book Company. Used with the permission of McGraw-Hill Book Company.

PAGE 144: Specified brief excerpt from "Here Is New York," p. 123 in *Essays of E. B. White*. Copyright 1949 by E. B. White. Reprinted by permission of Harper & Row, Publishers, Inc.

PAGE 153: Gerry Parker, "The Other Woman in Evita." *Sunday Newsday*, 20 July 1980.

PAGES 155, 162: Walter Pauk, *Six-Way Paragraphs*. Providence, R.I.: Jamestown Publishers, 1974. Reprinted with permission.

PAGES 157, 180–81, 182, 184, 185: Laraine E. Fleming: *Reading for Results*. Copyright © 1978 Houghton Mifflin Company. Used by permission.

PAGE 158: Alton Slagle, *Newsday Sunday Magazine*, Travel Section, 20 July 1980.

PAGE 159: D. X. Fenton, "The Weekly Gardener," *Sunday Newsday*, 20 July 1980.

PAGES 159, 161–62: Gilmore/Sack/Yourman, *88 Passages to Develop Reading Comprehension*, (Reader) January, 1972.

PAGE 160: *Of Human Bondage*, W. Somerset Maugham.

PAGE 163: Unsigned Editorial: HELP THE NEEDIEST FIRST! Copyright 1964 Christian Century Foundation. Reprinted by permission from the May 27, 1964 issue of *The Christian Century*.

PAGE 164: "New Frontiers in Conception" by Anne Taylor Fleming. © 1980 by The New York Times Company. Reprinted by permission.

PAGE 164: From "Tall Tales from Nature," Broadcast #3047, University of California Radio Service, 17 February 1952.

PAGE 165: Gilmore/Sack/Yourman, *100 Passages* (Reader), p. 6, 1965.

PAGE 174: *Black Enterprise Magazine*. Copyright 1980 The Earl G. Graves Publishing Co., Inc., 295 Madison Avenue, New York, NY 10017. All rights reserved.

PAGE 175: Eugene Schoenfeld, *Jealousy: Taming the Green Eyed Monster*, Holt, Rinehart and Winston, Inc., 1979.

PAGE 176: (1) Norman Lewis, *Reading, Spelling, Vocabulary & Pronunciation*, Book 1, p. 105, published by Amsco School Publications, Inc. © 1967, 1982. (2) Norman Lewis, *Reading, Spelling, Vocabulary & Pronunciation*, Book 3, p. 93, published by Amsco School Publications, Inc. © 1967.

PAGES 177–78: Marvin Karlins and Lewis M. Andrews, *Biofeedback: Turning on the Power of Your Mind*, Harper & Row, Publishers, Inc., 1972.

PAGE 178: "The Economy as Titanic" by Lester C. Thurow. © 1980 by The New York Times Company. Reprinted by permission.

PAGES 183: From *Break-Through: From Reading to Writing* by John W. Presley and William Dodd. Copyright © 1980 by Holt, Rinehart and Winston. Reprinted by permission of Holt, Rinehart and Winston.

PAGE 183: Louis Eisman and Charles Tranzer, *Biology and Human Progress*, 4th ed., © 1972 (Englewood Cliffs, N.J.: Prentice-Hall, Inc.). Used by permission.

PAGES 183–84: From *The Indian Heritage of America* by Alvin M. Josephy, Jr. Copyright © 1968 by Alvin M. Josephy, Jr. Reprinted by permission of Bantam Books, Inc.

PAGE 205: Todd and Curti, *Rise of the American Nation*, 1968, Vol. II, Harcourt Brace Jovanovich, Inc.

PAGE 206: Claude Brown, *Manchild in the Promised Land* (New York: Macmillan, 1965).

PAGE 206: From R. K. Carr, et al., *American Democracy in Theory and Practice: Essentials of National, State, and Local Government* (New York: Holt, Rinehart and Winston, 1958).

PAGE 206: From *Black Folktales* by Julius Lester, New York: E. P. Dutton & Co., Inc.

## Acknowledgments, continued

PAGE 207: Sylvia Resnick, "Noise: It Can Kill You," Coronet 1976. Reprinted by permission of the author.
PAGE 207: Stephen C. Lewis and Edward Erickson, Jr., *Focus on the Written Word* (Washington: Edutex International, Inc., 1975).
PAGE 207: *Barchester Towers*, Anthony Trollope.
PAGES 207–208: *The Vital Arts: Reading and Writing* by Dorothy Rubin. (Copright © 1979 by Dorothy Rubin.)
PAGE 209: *Kidnapped*, Robert Louis Stevenson.
PAGE 209: "A Time Dilemma in Adoption," *Newsday*, 21 September 1980.
PAGE 209: Mark Liff, "Get Off My Case Teach," New York *Daily News*, 21 September 1980.
PAGE 210: Gerri Hershey, "Still Smokin'," New York *Daily News*, 21 September 1980.
PAGE 210: *Tom Sawyer*, Mark Twain.
PAGE 211: *Sister Carrie*, Theodore Dreiser.